MORE TAXING
THAN TAXES?

MORE TAXING THAN TAXES?

The Taxlike Effects of Nontax Policies in LDCs

Edited by
Richard M. Bird

A Sequoia Seminar

ICS Press

Institute for Contemporary Studies
San Francisco, California

More Taxing Than Taxes?
Copyright © 1991 by the Sequoia Institute

Inquiries, book orders, and catalogue requests should be addressed to ICS Press, 243 Kearny Street, San Francisco, California 94108. (415) 981-5353.

This book is derived from the proceedings of one of the seminars in a series conducted by the Sequoia Institute. Both the seminar series and this publication were funded by the United States Agency for International Development.

PDC-0092-A-00-6050-00

U.S.A.I.D.

Library of Congress Cataloging-in-Publication Data

More taxing than taxes? : the taxlike effects of nontax policies in
   LDCs / edited by Richard M. Bird.
      p.   cm.
   Includes bibliographical references.
   ISBN 1-55815-089-7 : $29.95—ISBN 1-55815-088-9 (pbk.) : $12.95
   1. Tax incidence—Developing countries—Congresses. 2. Taxation—
Developing countries—Congresses. 3. Revenue—Developing
countries—Congresses.   I. Bird, Richard Miller, 1938–   .
II. Sequoia Institute.
HJ2323.D44M67   1991
336.2'009172'4—dc20   90-39909
                                                              CIP

Contents

Preface

In 1990 ICS Press was pleased to publish *World Tax Reform: Case Studies of Developed and Developing Countries*, edited by Michael J. Boskin and Charles E. McLure, Jr. In *More Taxing Than Taxes?* McLure joins three of the contributors to *World Tax Reform* and several others in asking whether nontax policies are not *More Taxing Than Taxes?* The evidence of this volume supports an answer of yes. And, as if adding insult to injury, it appears that the poorer a country's citizens are, the more likely and definite is this affirmation.

Together these two volumes provide a more comprehensive evaluation of tax *burdens*, resulting from both tax and nontax policies, than is available in *any* combination of other publications. ICS Press takes great pride in that accomplishment by these two books.

This is the fourth Sequoia Seminar publication from ICS Press. Forthcoming books in the series address topics that are of critical importance for the development of individuals and societies. The one thing they have in common is the uncommon: unique perspectives. An aim of Sequoia Institute in this series is to address issues that are as widely ignored in the literature, or as generally "hidden" from ready observation and measurement, as they are fundamentally important. An earlier volume, *Beyond the Informal Sector*, put a new cast on the "hidden," or underground, economies that one of its contributors, Hernando de Soto, has done more than perhaps anyone else to make visible. A book now in development—*If Texas Were Chile*—takes an uncommon and revealing look at the association between financial stability and the extent to which interstate (or international) capital flows are allowed to occur. Other volumes will examine African finance, the prospects for development *with* democracy, and capital markets in development.

But the topics of Sequoia Seminar publications are misleading, just as some of the most easily acquired observations of the world and its development are. Consequently, what the readers of these volumes get is rarely what they see—typically they get far more. This outcome is what ICS Press bet on when making its bid to publish the series. There is considerable satisfaction in enabling readers to share in our pleasure.

Robert B. Hawkins, Jr.
President and CEO
Institute for Contemporary Studies

San Francisco, California
December 1990

Foreword

This is the fourth publication resulting from an ongoing series of seminars introduced by Sequoia Institute in 1987. Consistent with its theme—Including the Excluded: Extending the Benefits of Development—the series has two primary objectives:

(a) to shed new light on critical issues of Third World development and its assistance

(b) to serve as a catalyst for a new generation of thinkers and ideas that will accelerate the inclusion of *all* people in the process of individual and societal development

Assumed, and hence neither stated by (b) nor thought to qualify as (a)'s "new light," is that the development of collectivities ("societal" is shorthand) is itself accelerated by hastening the inclusion of *all* individuals in the *process* of development. Attempts to broaden the distribution of *products* of development (at whatever stage) to the neglect of the processes (and human opportunities) that enable them appear to incur dire consequences, most evident today in the communist world and its remnants. As the preceding book in the series concluded, "It seems apparent that a shorter path must be broader; that the path to realizing human potentials will be made less treacherous and distant by its broadening. Conversely, exclusion of those who wish to make the journey portends a destination never reached."

In contrast with most readers' ready acceptance of the foregoing, few who complete the present volume are likely ever again to think of taxes and citizens' burdens as they previously had. This book clearly sheds new light on the taxing consequences of both tax and nontax policies. And fulfillment of the other principal objective of the series is manifested by its origins within one section of one paper prepared for the series' initial seminar volume. There Charles E. McLure, Jr., observed:

> Many nontax policies followed by developing countries have effects on income distribution and allocative efficiency quite similar to those of taxes. Yet these effects are seldom considered in studies of taxation and its impact on the economy. The most obvious of these, the pricing policy of public enterprises, is worth considering in some detail [omitted here because of its incorporation within Malcolm Gillis' paper in the present volume]. But taxlike consequences of the pricing policies of state enterprises are virtually never considered in incidence analysis.
>
> It should be stressed that public enterprise pricing is only the tip of the quasi-tax iceberg. Other important examples include credit policies that effectively tax savers and subsidize borrowers, minimum wages that tax employers and subsidize workers, price controls that tax producers and subsidize consumers, unnecessary regulations that tax production and provide employment for participants in the regulatory process, etc. . . . any analysis of tax policy which omits the effects of these quasi taxes is incomplete and may be misleading. In particular, conventional figures on tax collections as a percentage of GDP substantially understate the true impact of taxes and quasi taxes on income distribution and allocative efficiency (pp. 29–30 of "Fiscal Policy and Equity in Developing Countries," in Elliot Berg, ed., *Policy Reform and Equity: Extending the Benefits of Development*).

That was the catalyst, this book its effect.

This series, sponsored principally by the Agency for International Development (A.I.D.) is an outgrowth of the agency's policy endeavors during the past several years. Support for these seminars continues a commitment by the agency to encourage the reexamination of established precepts and practices pursuant to the formulation of more effective development policies. In accordance with this objective, the series strives to enlarge the supply of talent and ideas dedicated to development issues. One component of this effort, of course, is the publication and dissemination of each seminar's proceedings. Another is to bring together, within each seminar, several promising scholars who are relatively new to the international development field, by virtue of their youth or the concentration of their previous scholarship on other subject matter, for interacting with established development scholars and practitioners.

The support and cooperation of numerous A.I.D. officials has been instrumental to the success of the seminar series. The sadness of Administrator Alan Woods's death while in office is intermingled with gladness that the value of his support for this series survives. When the series was embryonic, Assistant Administrator Richard E. Bissell was there supporting our vision of what the child might become. Within the Bureau for Program and Policy Coordination, the A.I.D. technical office most responsible for this endeavor, Neal S. Zank warrants particular mention for his provision of both encouragement and valuable technical assistance to the series from its inception. The series has been sustained and expanded by the current administration of the agency, most notably administrator Ronald W. Roskins and assistant administrator Reginald J. Brown, and by the contributions of Fred J. Kirschstein, the agency's current project officer for the series.

The authors represented in this book join me in expressing appreciation to ICS Press and Janet Mowery, Trudy Kaplan, and Roger Magyar, in particular, for their unstinting editorial efforts in bringing this manuscript to press. I especially appreciate the bet on this series placed by the president of ICS, Robert B. Hawkins, Jr.; he was as a patient, nurturing parent to the series, before seeing the offspring.

Neither the Agency for International Development nor Sequoia Institute necessarily shares the opinions expressed in any of the series volumes. Nonetheless, the diversity of ideas and evidence found in their pages is expected to stimulate the formulation of better ideas and practices than would otherwise occur—and the peaceful burial of others.

One idea and practice whose burial should be facilitated by the present volume is that of conceiving taxes as being "too low" because the revenues that a government receives from *explicit* taxes (income, sales, property, capital gains, value added, et al.) are lower relative to its gross domestic product than those of other countries. The greater the magnitude of a country's *implicit* taxes, the more are efforts to increase explicit tax revenues of its government(s) tantamount to adding insult to injury. Conversely, this volume raises a positive corollary of such pain—that governments *might increase by decrease*—effecting increased revenues (even with no changes in explicit tax policies) by decreasing the (taxlike) burdens on citizens of nontax, non-revenue-generating, policies.

Should explicit taxes have their rates raised, their points of incidence lowered, their implementation more extensively and rigorously applied? This volume demonstrates that any answer to these questions is unsatisfactory in the absence of answering another: whether and to what extent nontax policies are *More Taxing Than Taxes?*

Jerry Jenkins
Series Director/Editor

December 1990

MORE TAXING
THAN TAXES?

1   *Richard M. Bird*

More Taxing Than Taxes?:
An Introduction

The subject of this volume may at first glance seem strange. What are these peculiar things variously labeled "implicit taxes," "quasi taxes," "hidden taxes," "tacit taxes," or "shadow taxes" and their counterparts on the expenditure (subsidy) side? The reference to obscurity in most of these terms is not the only parallel to the "underground," "hidden," "black," "shadow," or "informal" economy that has attracted so much attention in the past decade. Most of us were probably peripherally aware that such a thing as the hidden economy existed before the recent explosion of literature brought it forcibly to our attention. Seldom, however, did we adequately appreciate the size, ubiquity, and implications of the phenomenon, particularly in the developing economies. Much the same is true of the hidden taxes that are the subject of this volume. In some sense most of us already know that such things exist, but few, if any, of us have a very clear idea of either their potential magnitude or their implications for public finance and development policy.

Although the four principal papers included in this volume by no means exhaust the territory that might be included under the general heading of implicit taxation, in total they provide an excellent starting place for the important task of identifying and quantifying the "hidden costs" not just of taxes and expenditures in developing countries but of a whole host of nonbudgetary instruments of government policy in all countries. Indeed, this volume may launch a major industry of sorting out exactly what is meant by implicit taxes and subsidies, figuring out how important such things are in different contexts, and deciding what should be done with this new knowledge. Should this book fall short of that, it is hoped that another or others will succeed in its stead, for the need to address the subject will only grow by its neglect.

This brief introduction first defines—albeit roughly—the basic concept of implicit taxation and then surveys briefly the surprisingly few previous references to this important notion to be found in the literature on development finance. The chapter concludes with a brief overview of the book.

While by no means comprehensive, even the brief survey of the literature contained in the present chapter illustrates two important points. First, like Moliere's Monsieur Jourdain, who found to his surprise that he had been talking prose all his life, many development economists have been talking about implicit taxation all along without realizing it, although few have as yet taken this idea very far. Second, as this book illustrates, a much wider variety of concepts may usefully be lumped together under the heading of implicit taxation than seems generally to be realized. Moreover, for some purposes it seems essential to consider this phenomenon as a whole rather than, as has been the virtually invariable practice, only this or that component part, such as the "inflation tax" or the "taxlike" effects of quantitative trade restrictions.

Indeed, the references to the tax and taxlike aspects of nontax policies found scattered throughout the literature bear some resemblance to the story of the blind experts describing an elephant. Some said it was long and flexible, like a snake; others said it was round and rough, like a tree; still others said it was large and flat, like a wall. None of them realized they were all describing different aspects of the same creature. This book is a first attempt to look at the elephant as a whole. The description of the beast it offers may still be crude, but at least it should make it clear that we are dealing with a single live, and growing, creature.

Glimpses of the Elephant

Perhaps the clearest and most comprehensive examination of the phenomenon of implicit taxation in the literature may be found in a 1985 article by the late Alan Prest. Addressing the quasi taxes of Britain, Prest's careful definition of implicit taxation is worth quoting at length:

> By analogy with an explicit tax, an implicit tax must have the general economic characteristics of compulsory deprivation [of private sector purchasing power]; but without there being any flow of funds . . . from the private to the public coffers. . . . With an implicit tax, Group A may find its purchasing power reduced whilst Group B's increases; but such a transfer takes place by means other than through the government's formal tax-collection and expenditure-disbursement machinery [though due in some fairly direct way to government action].[1]

In other words, an implicit tax, like an explicit tax, makes those who pay it worse off, and, again as in the case of taxes, the proceeds are often transferred in such a way as to make someone else better off. The only difference is that there is no budgetary evidence of the transaction: no legislature passes a tax act; no tax collector calls at your house; no taxpayer has any occasion to complain about the inequitable and inefficient nature of the tax system to which he or she is subjected—indeed, most do not even know they have been taxed. Nonetheless, the deed is done: you are poorer—and, in all likelihood, someone else is richer—as a result of government action. If something sounds like a tax and acts like a tax, it seems only logical that it should be considered equivalent to a tax. Thus it is only reasonable to subject these quasi taxes to the same kind of critical analysis with respect to equity and efficiency as attends considerations of formal, explicit taxes.

Among the implicit taxes Prest identified in Britain were tariffs and import controls, the cross-subsidization of some groups at the expense of others through the pricing policies of public enterprise, the losses imposed by inflation on holders of money, rent and other price controls, building restrictions, land use controls, minimum wage laws, entry controls on particular occupations, output controls (for example on fisheries), controls on consumption (for example of drugs), and many other kinds of government regulation. In all these cases, he argued, "implicit taxes can perform the traditional functions of explicit taxes with respect to resource allocation, income and wealth distribution and stabilisation"[2]—although it is generally both conceptually and practically difficult to quantify these effects.

The parallel to the better-known concept of implicit expenditures—so-called tax expenditures—arising from special provisions in the tax law and brought to public notice largely through the work of Stanley Surrey is clear.[3] As in the case of tax expenditures, the economic consequences of implicit taxes tend to be much less transparent, and hence much less discussed, than those of explicit budgetary transactions. Nonetheless, again as in the case of tax expenditures, the scope and scale of implicit taxation are such that these taxes must clearly be taken into account whenever possible. Although there is no presumption that implicit and explicit taxes are necessarily correlated—indeed, they may often be substitutes— "ignoring implicit taxation may easily invalidate comparisons of tax/ GNP ratios for the same country at different times or for different countries at the same time."[4]

Once the phenomenon of implicit taxation is identified and recognized as important, what should be done about it? The approach favored by Prest was to attempt to compile an official supplementary budget statement of implicit taxation similar to the "tax expenditure budgets" now found in the United States and a number of other countries.[5] Such an enterprise does not appear to have been attempted anywhere, however, perhaps because of the obvious lack of incentive for any government to make clear to its people how much they are being taxed. All that are available at present appear to be such partial calculations as estimates of the size of the "inflation tax" in this country or an occasional call for a "regulatory budget" in that. Nonetheless, despite the paucity of concrete evidence, there is good reason for thinking that implicit taxation is as pervasive and important a phenomenon in every country as Prest suggested it was in Britain. Furthermore, there is additional reason (much of it afforded by the papers in this volume) for thinking that the issue may be of particular importance in developing countries, where such additional resource-affecting interventionist policies as industrial licensing, price controls, obstacles to capital movements, and foreign exchange rationing are common.

In a paper at an earlier Sequoia seminar that was the proximate mover for the present seminar, Charles McLure noted that conventional tax studies invariably understate the real burden of taxation because they omit both the excess burden of explicit taxes—a factor that studies in developed countries have shown to be important (and which is emphasized and further developed in the paper by Dan Usher in the present volume)—and the entire burden of such taxlike policies as inflation, overvalued exchange rates, credit controls, minimum wages, price controls, trade taxes, public enterprise prices, and regulations.[6] The similarity of McLure's words to the earlier (and quite independent) arguments of Prest with respect to Britain is hardly coincidental. Most countries have similar policies, and nowhere have the implications of such implicit taxes or their obvious parallels to explicit taxes been carefully examined.

A recent *World Development Report* on the role of the public sector in development, for example, though recognizing the close analogy between quantitative restrictions and price controls and taxes, focused almost exclusively on the budgetary trail left by formal taxes and expenditures, apart from a brief mention of the inflation tax and a useful chapter on public enterprises.[7] An earlier

World Development Report had been somewhat more ambitious, attempting to quantify the high degree of price distortion arising from government policies in many developing countries and associating such distortions inversely with economic growth.[8] The only equally ambitious attempt to put a figure on the impact of "nontax taxes" as a whole appears to be a paper on India by Mohammed and Whalley, which estimates that the "rents" generated by distortionary government policies, particularly controls on goods and financial markets, might be as high as 45 percent of gross national product.[9]

As a rule, however, the pattern in the development literature appears to be at best a passing mention of the phenomenon of implicit taxation, with emphasis more on the passing than on the mention. The massive Newbery-Stern treatise on optimal taxation and developing countries, for example, explicitly recognizes at various points the ambiguity of using the tax-to-income ratio as a measure of fiscal impact, the concept of a "shadow tax" (the discrepancy between market and shadow prices), and the wedge introduced between the statutory and the real tax system by evasion—but it does nothing with any of these ideas.[10] Other recent works have touched on different aspects of the elephant: for instance, Clive Gray has set out clearly the relevant issues with respect to public enterprise pricing;[11] Maxwell Fry has done the same with respect to some aspects of financial regulation;[12] and Anne Krueger and colleagues have performed a similar service for trade policy.[13]

Unfortunately, the only study that seems to have attempted to stand back and look at the beast as a whole was never published. After summarizing a wide variety of partial studies of implicit taxes—the term they used—on labor, on capital, and on goods in different countries, Rabushka and Bartlett concluded their pioneering work in this field as follows:

> In conclusion, there are a whole range of governmental actions which can be categorized as implicit taxes, in that they increase the prices of goods, the cost of doing business, or lower the rate of return. While it is extremely difficult to calculate the precise level of such "taxes", they impact on incentives in the same way that explicit taxes do. Since such implicit [taxes] may be of significantly more

importance than explicit taxes in determining a developing country's growth prospects, further research in this area should be a high priority, in order to quantify and categorize such "taxes" and, hopefully, lead to their reform.[14]

The present book is, in a sense, both a first step in this direction and a further plea for more research on this important subject.

Outline of the Book

Against this background the aim of this book is twofold. First, the papers and discussion contained herein obviously contribute to closing the information gap with respect to the phenomenon of implicit taxation. Second, the book sets out an agenda for future research. As demonstrated here, people in developing countries are clearly "taxed" much .nore than we, or they, think. Until we understand more fully the scope and effects of such taxation, it seems unlikely that the most meaningful set of development policies for any particular country can be designed or implemented.

The full title of the pioneering paper by Prest cited earlier was "Implicit Taxes: Are We Taxed More Than We Think?" His answer for Britain was unequivocally yes. After reading the following papers, it is impossible to do other than agree with him with respect to most developing countries as well. As noted earlier, this book may launch an important new area of research: the identification and quantification of the hidden costs of not just explicit but implicit taxes and expenditures. At the very least, readers should come away with a much clearer idea of the importance of considering as carefully and explicitly as possible the effects of implicit as well as explicit taxes in developing, as in developed, countries. This book by no means covers the entire domain of implicit taxation. There is nothing here, for example, about either labor market interventions or price controls. Nonetheless, in total the papers and discussion in this volume undoubtedly provide a more comprehensive starting point for further inquiry into this subject than is to be found elsewhere in the literature.

To begin with, however, the first paper, by Dan Usher, delves not into hidden taxes as such but rather into the hidden costs of explicit taxes and expenditures—the excess burden of taxes and transfers, the extra excess burden arising from tax evasion, the potentially high and distorting administrative and compliance costs of many kinds of taxes, and the variety of "rent-seeking" activities to which taxes and transfers inevitably give rise. As Usher notes, the real economic cost of raising a dollar in taxation and transferring it to someone else (or even to the same person) may be as much as two or three times the recorded amount of the tax burden as usually measured. Usher's careful analysis serves to put us on notice that an additional dollar of public expenditure must be similarly "profit-able"—that is, produce two or three dollars of "excess benefits"—if expansion of the public sector is to make sense. Moreover, since almost every one of the "hidden" costs Usher identifies seems equally applicable—if even more difficult to discern and measure— with respect to implicit taxes, his paper also suggests that the dimensions of the implicit tax problem too are likely to be consid-erably greater than may at first be thought.

The second paper in the volume, by John Whalley, turns our attention both to distributional concerns and to the importance of the broader open economy context in determining the nature and size of the taxlike effects of trade policies. In passing, Whalley notes that financial policies constitute an important link between trade policy and the economy as a whole, either ameliorating or com-pounding the taxlike effects of a country's trade policies. The following paper, by Wayne Thirsk, therefore appropriately focuses on government intervention in the financial sector and the variety of quasi taxes to which such intervention gives rise.

Thirsk's paper and the ensuing discussion of its content also suggest that the taxlike effects of financial regulation may be more akin to those of explicit taxes in many developing countries than is indicated by Prest's assessment of the phenomenon in Britain. As previously quoted, Prest deemed implicit taxes (in contradistinction to explicit taxes) to entail neither (1) employment of "government's formal tax-collection and expenditure-disbursement machinery" nor (2) "flow of funds . . . from the private to the public coffers." In most countries these may be two ways of saying the same thing. But, as Thirsk's paper makes clear, only the first can be safely attributed to quasi taxes in many developing countries.

That implicit taxes can and frequently do effect a flow of funds from private to public coffers (or vice versa) is reinforced by the fourth and final paper prepared for this volume, wherein Malcolm Gillis surveys the many ways in which "tacit taxes" and "sub rosa subsidies" are implemented in many developing countries through state-owned enterprises. Perhaps the most transparent instances of such enterprises effecting revenue transfers from citizens to their governments are the various marketing boards for the purchase of agricultural products that have been established by numerous governments. In conjunction with below-market prices for agricultural products dictated by the same governments, farmers are paid less by the marketing boards than they would have otherwise received, the governments then export these "on the cheap" purchases at world market prices and pocket the difference. Tax*like*?

A successor volume, fully recognizing these things that we *do* know *and* further reducing our ignorance about the less transparent, might be entitled *The Taxing Effects of Tax and Nontax Policies*. For now, we must guess too much because we know too little. An awareness of parts of the elephant, however, is preferable to none at all. And, at a minimum, the combination of parts provided by this book poses a fundamental question: midst such ignorance, might we be of greater service by questioning more and intervening less?

Dan Usher

The Hidden Costs
of Public Expenditure

The full cost of any good, service, or transfer provided by the public sector is the sum of the *resource cost* and of other costs that, collectively and for the want of a better term, may be called *hidden costs*. Resource cost is the minimum purchase price of what the public sector provides. The resource cost of a road is payment for gravel, use of machines, labor, and so on. The resource cost of a transfer, such as unemployment insurance or the old-age pension, is necessarily zero because no resources are used up when A pays a dollar to B. The hidden costs of public expenditures include the following:

- *overhead cost* of tax collection and provision of services

- *deadweight loss* in the tax-induced shift of resources from more-taxed to less-taxed activities

- *concealment cost* incurred by the putative taxpayer in tax evasion and tax avoidance

- *intimidation cost* of the criminal justice system in constraining officials to behave honestly and citizens to respect the law in their dealings with the government
- *magnification of deadweight loss in transfer programs*
- *waste of resources in seeking eligibility for transfers* as people alter their behavior in light of the prospect of entitlement to public largess
- *rent seeking*, which is a special case of the cost above
- *public sector inefficiency*
- *corruption*, which is the public sector counterpart of ordinary crime

To say that public expenditures are costly, or more costly than one might at first suppose, is not to say that public expenditures are unwarranted. Any civilized and prosperous society requires a large public sector. The objects of government expenditure include the three items on Adam Smith's classic list—(1) "the duty of protecting society from the violence and invasion of other societies"; (2) "the duty of protecting, as far as is possible, every member of society from the injustice and oppression of every other member of it, or the duty of establishing an exact administration of justice"; and (3) "the duty of erecting and maintaining certain public works and public institutions which it can never be for the interest of any individual, or small number of individuals to maintain"—together with a number of items that have become essential aspects of governments since Adam Smith's day.[1] Smith's third item can be generalized to the provision of "public goods." In addition, any modern government must deal with externalities—especially the protection of the environment and the control of potentially dangerous "medicines." Citizens in a democracy demand a certain amount of redistribution and some public provision of services as insurance against the most devastating effects of poverty.

Nor should it be supposed that actual markets are in any sense ideal for the production and distribution of goods. Actual markets never work as well as the markets described in models of perfect competition. The local grocery store has a bit of monopoly power. Efforts by workers and by firms to prevent accidents on the job are likely to be inadequate. Externalities crop up everywhere because everybody is affected to some extent by the activity of his neighbors. Advertising is often harmful on balance. Much of the activity of the businessman is predatory. Vast resources are wasted in bargaining. Speculation makes little else but millionaires. Large firms exercise dangerous monopoly power and influence over the state. There is no corner of the private sector that an omniscient, omnipotent, and benevolent dictator could not improve to some extent.

Of course, actual governments are not omniscient, omnipotent, or entirely benevolent. There is uncertainty about the consequences of public sector decisions. Some market failures cannot be corrected without creating worse and more costly failures in their place. Policies that might be on balance advantageous when administered by a government of saints might not be advantageous when administered by the fallible, partly honorable people that we are. Ideally, public sector decision making is a weighing of all costs and all benefits of projects or programs in this imperfect world. Over the past fifty years the public sector has grown significantly in virtually every country. Nothing in this paper can be interpreted as implying that such growth was entirely unwarranted. But hidden costs tend to rise significantly with the size of the public sector. The larger the public sector, the greater the need to scrutinize every activity of government to ensure that it is still worthwhile when all costs— resource costs and hidden costs together—are taken into account.

This paper, which is about the costs of public expenditure, begins with a brief look at benefits to emphasize that talk of costs is all but meaningless except in a context where costs and benefits are compared. The question at issue is always what the government should do and what it should desist from doing. Decisions about entire projects or programs require comparison of total cost and total benefit. Decisions about how much of any particular good or service to provide in the public sector require comparison of marginal cost and marginal benefit. The emphasis in this paper is on marginal comparisons.

A decision is to be made, for instance, about the provision of guns to the army. Each gun costs one dollar from the manufacturer, no matter how many guns are purchased. The government, as the disinterested servant of its citizens, chooses a number of guns in accordance with citizens' preferences for protection as well as for the ordinary goods and services that must be forgone when guns are bought instead. People's desire for protection is reflected in a community demand curve in which the marginal valuation of protection declines with the number of guns bought.[2]

The question to which this paper is addressed is, What is the critical marginal valuation of guns—or, for that matter, any item of public expenditure—above which it is appropriate for the government to undertake the expenditure and below which it is not? In particular, if a gun costs a dollar, would the appropriate rule be for the government to buy that gun if and only if the value to the community of the protection afforded by one extra gun is a dollar or more? The answer to that question depends on how the word "cost" is understood. It is no, if cost is understood to be the dollar of payment to the manufacturer for the purchase of a gun. It is yes, by definition, if cost is understood to include (in addition to the purchase price) a number of "hidden costs" that are not typically included in the assessment of cost by accountants but are burdensome to citizens nonetheless. If each dollar of direct expenditure entails two dollars of extra cost, then the government should purchase guns—or anything else—only up to the point where the benefits derived from the guns are worth at least three dollars, one dollar of direct cost and two dollars of extra cost. To recognize extra costs that have not been recognized before is, of course, to introduce a stricter standard for public expenditure. Less expenditure can pass a three-for-one test than a one-for-one test.

Any assessment of the costs and benefits of public sector activity requires a criterion or objective. The establishment of such a criterion does not commit one to a Hegelian view of the state as an entity with a higher objective than that of its citizens. The criterion may be the citizens' objective for the state rather than the state's objective for itself. But there must be a criterion somewhere if policy is to be counted as effective or otherwise. Cost must be a source of harm. One cannot speak of harm without at the same time implying that some social objective is unattained or attained to a lesser degree than might otherwise be the case. Assessment of the benefit side of public expenditure would need to take account of the post-tax and post-transfer distribution of income among citizens as well as of the magnitude of national income, for the benefits of transfer programs can be evaluated in no other way. Since my purpose in this paper is to enumerate hidden costs and provide examples of how they arise, I can get by with a cruder working criterion, which is the simple maximization of national income as a whole. "Costs" for this purpose are reductions in total real national income.

The Costs of Public Expenditures

Resource cost. By "resource cost" I mean the minimal cost of public activity to the government, abstracting from the effects of dishonesty or want of incentive on the part of public officials and ignoring costs associated with the private sector response to taxation, public services, and transfers. The resource cost of running a hospital is what must be paid to doctors, nurses, janitors, sellers of medical equipment, the electricity company, and so on to keep the hospital running. Resource cost would include all purchases of goods and services, regardless of whether these are acquired by contract (as when the government hires a lawyer) or by employment (as when an engineer becomes part of the civil service) and regardless of whether goods are bought (as when the army purchases a tank) or made (as when a prototype of a new product is constructed in the National Research Council).

Overhead cost. The term "overhead cost" may be more or less extensive in its coverage. It may be restricted to the fixed cost of the entire public sector, such as Parliament and the Ministry of National Revenue, but it could be broadened to cover the otherwise

unallocatable costs in planning for and establishing specific programs. Overhead costs vary considerably. The old-age pension is
relatively inexpensive to administer, for it is obvious who is old and
who is not. The subsidization of investment in select firms is more
expensive because it is by no means obvious who the appropriate
recipients of such programs should be. The provision of welfare to
the poor is also expensive because a staff of highly paid profes-
sionals is required to determine eligibility and to watch for
cheaters.[3]

Deadweight loss in taxation. Deadweight loss is best analyzed in
stages, beginning with a simple example and proceeding to the
analysis of the entire tax system.[4] Consider a carpenter whose house
requires plumbing and a plumber whose house requires carpentry.
Both parties can do both jobs, but each is naturally best at his own
trade. The carpenter could do the job of plumbing in 10 hours, but
the plumber can do it in 6 hours. Similarly, the plumber could do the
job of carpentry in 10 hours, but the carpenter can do it in 6 hours.
The two jobs may be allocated on a do-it-yourself basis, by barter, or
by purchase.

Obviously the efficient procedures are purchase and barter, for
these procedures require a total of twelve hours of work for the two
jobs together instead of the twenty hours that would be required if
each party did his own repairs. We rule out barter by supposing that
the parties are unaware of each other's requirements. That leaves a
choice between purchase and do-it-yourself. Suppose the wages of
carpenters and plumbers are both $20 per hour, so that the cost of
each job is $120. Suppose also that the rate of income tax is 50
percent. The tax has no effect on the time required to complete both
jobs on a do-it-yourself basis. But with a 50 percent tax each party
would need to work 12 hours to earn the $240 that is required to pay
for the carpentry or the plumbing out of after-tax earnings. It would,
therefore, be in each party's interest to do the job himself in 10
hours, even though he could hire somebody else to do it in 6 hours.

The effect of the tax in this instance is to induce each party to
waste 4 hours of labor, with a social value of $80. In total 8 hours or

$160 worth of output or leisure is lost, and not one penny of tax is collected on the transaction. This $160 is just as much a cost of the public service financed by the tax as another $160 that is actually paid for goods purchased by the government. This $160 is part of the *deadweight loss* or, as it is sometimes called, *excess burden* of the tax system. The full cost of public activities includes deadweight loss as well as overhead cost and the resource cost of that activity. This example is of a portion of the tax base that vanishes altogether in response to taxation. The example is easily generalized to the case where the tax base shrinks but does not vanish.

Imagine a society where the only public expenditure is on guns for the army and the only source of public revenue is the taxation of water from a public well. For convenience, suppose that the well provides an unlimited supply of water at no alternative cost to the taker. The demand curve, $x(t)$, for water from the well is as indicated in Figure 2.1. The curve shows the amounts of water, x, that each person would buy at alternative prices, when the tax on water, t, and the price of water are one and the same in this example because tax

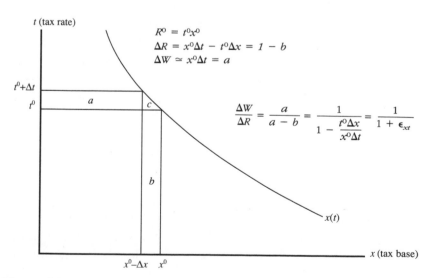

Figure 2.1.

is the only component of price. Since water is costless to produce, its price to the consumer is precisely the tax. The axes of the figure are labeled accordingly.

A hidden cost of taxation is a gap between the marginal social cost of taxation, called ΔW, and marginal revenue from taxation, called ΔR, where ΔW and ΔR are both associated with a small increase in the tax rate, Δt. There is no hidden cost if the ratio $\Delta W/\Delta R$ is just equal to 1. In that case guns costing one dollar from the manufacturer should be purchased up to the point where the value of the extra protection from an additional gun is just equal to one dollar. Otherwise, if $\Delta W/\Delta R$ is greater than 1, guns should be purchased up to the point where the marginal valuation of a gun costing one dollar is just equal to $\Delta W/\Delta R$. In the conditions described in Figure 2.1, the value of the ratio $\Delta W/\Delta R$ can be determined from the shape of the demand curve for water, which is the only taxed good. More generally, the value of the ratio $\Delta W/\Delta R$ can be determined from the elasticity of tax base to the tax rate.

Initially the tax rate is t^0, the tax base is x^0 (where $x^0 = x(t^0)$), and the tax revenue is $t^0 x^0$. To acquire the extra revenue for the purchase of additional guns, the tax rate must rise somewhat. Let the tax rate increase from t^0 to $t^0 + \Delta t$. The tax base shrinks from x^0 to $x^0 - \Delta x$, where, by definition, $\Delta x = x(t^0) - x(t^0 + \Delta t)$. Note that both Δt and Δx are defined to be positive numbers as long as the curve $x(t)$ is downward sloping. The revenue changes from $t^0 x(t^0)$ to $(t^0 + \Delta t)(x^0 - \Delta x)$, and the change in revenue, denoted by ΔR, becomes

$$\Delta R = x^0 \Delta t - t^0 \Delta x - \Delta t \Delta x$$
$$\simeq x^0 \Delta t - t^0 \Delta x \qquad (1)$$

where the term $\Delta t \Delta x$, represented by the triangular area c in the figure, may be ignored because, as the product of two small changes, it is itself small.

The central idea of deadweight loss is that the cost to the taxpayer of an increase in tax from t^0 to $t^0 + \Delta t$ is the extra amount he must pay for what he buys. The marginal cost of the increase in taxation is

$$\Delta W = x^0 \Delta t \qquad (2)$$

which is just equal to the area a in Figure 2.1. This ΔW is the amount that the taxpayer would be prepared to pay as a lump sum to escape the increase in the tax rate from t^0 to $t^0 + \Delta t$. It is essential to recognize in this context that ΔW is not the same as the change in the tax that he actually pays. The change in tax paid is ΔR, not ΔW, where $\Delta R = a - b$. The area b represents the tax he no longer pays as a consequence of the reduction in his purchase of the taxed good. The contraction of the tax base is of no net benefit to the taxpayer (even though it represents a net loss to the tax collector) because it is merely a shift of purchasing power between goods that are worth the same to the consumer at the margin. To be more exact, the gain to the consumer in the marginal switch from taxed to untaxed goods as the tax rises from t to $t + \Delta t$ is just the area c, which is small enough to be ignored in this calculation.

It follows immediately that the marginal cost of taxation to the taxpayer exceeds the revenue from the tax wherever the tax base shrinks in response to an increase in the tax rate. Specifically,

$$\Delta W = x^0 \Delta t > x^0 \Delta t - t^0 \Delta x = \Delta R \tag{3}$$

as long as $\Delta x > 0$. The difference between ΔW and ΔR is commonly referred to as marginal deadweight loss. The ratio $\Delta W / \Delta R$ is the marginal social cost per unit of additional public revenue. It follows immediately that

$$\frac{\Delta W}{\Delta R} = \frac{x^0 \Delta t}{x^0 \Delta t - t^0 \Delta x} = \frac{1}{1 - \dfrac{t^0 \Delta x}{x^0 \Delta t}} \equiv \frac{1}{1 + \epsilon_{xt}} \tag{4}$$

where ϵ_{xt} is the elasticity of the tax base with respect to the tax rate, which is the same as the elasticity of demand for water from the well in this example.[5] The ratio $\Delta W / \Delta R$ is equal to 1 when this elasticity is equal to 0. Otherwise it is greater than 1. If the value of the elasticity of demand for water from the well were -0.5, the value of $\Delta W / \Delta R$ would be 2, signifying that the government should buy guns up to the point where the public's marginal valuation of guns is twice the price from the manufacturer.

The example is easily generalized to the case where the taxed good is costly to produce. As shown in Appendix A (at the end of this chapter), equation 4 remains valid, although the elasticity of the tax base to the tax rate, ϵ_{xt}, is no longer equal to the elasticity of demand. It now depends on both the elasticity of demand for the taxed good and its elasticity of supply. Specifically,

$$\epsilon_{xt} = \frac{-t\epsilon^D \epsilon^S}{P^D \epsilon^D + P^S \epsilon^S} \tag{5}$$

where P^D, P^S and t are gross-of-tax price, net-of-tax price, and tax per unit, so that $P^D - P^S = t$, and where ϵ^D and ϵ^S are the *absolute values* of the elasticities of demand and supply of the taxed good.

It follows immediately from equation 5 that there is no marginal deadweight loss to taxation when the initial value of t is equal to zero. With no tax there can be no distortion in allocation of purchasing power between taxed and untaxed goods, the marginal valuation of each good is just equal to its cost of production, and a small shift in purchasing power between one and the other can do no harm. Only when the tax is significantly greater than zero does a shift in purchasing power from taxed to untaxed goods entail a loss of revenue to the government and a gap between ΔW and ΔR. A second implication of equation 5 is that there is no deadweight loss to taxation if either $\epsilon^S = 0$ or $\epsilon^D = 0$, for in each case the value represented by the area b in Figure 2.1 would be just equal to zero. The conditions $\epsilon^S = 0$ and $\epsilon^D = 0$ correspond to a situation in our carpenter and plumber example where their purchases of taxed goods are independent of the rate of tax because the carpenter and the plumber cannot do each other's jobs at all. It is easy enough, however, to pick plausible values of ϵ^S, ϵ^D, and t for which the ratio $\Delta W/\Delta R$ is very large. For example, the set $\epsilon^S = \frac{1}{2}$, $\epsilon^D = \frac{1}{2}$, and $t = P^S$ (which is equivalent to a sales tax of 50 percent of the retail price) yields a value of $\Delta W/\Delta R$ of 1.2; the set of $\epsilon^S = 1$, $\epsilon^D = 1$, and $t = P^S$ yields a value of $\Delta W/\Delta R$ of 1.5; and the set $\epsilon^S = 10$, $\epsilon^D = 2$, and $t = P^S$ yields a value of $\Delta W/\Delta R$ of 11, signifying that the full social cost of taxation would be eleven times the tax revenue.

Estimates of the ratio $\Delta W/\Delta R$ have varied considerably, but a number as high as 2 is not considered preposterously large.[6] If 2 were the correct number, it would signify that all public goods and public programs are really twice as expensive as they appear to be. Ignoring ordinary overhead cost, the payment by the government of a dollar for military equipment, for the transfer of income to the poor, or to subsidize investment would have an effect on the taxpayer that is equivalent to a lump-sum (and therefore nondistortionary) tax of two dollars. Arguments for public expenditure to defend ourselves, to provide infrastructure, to correct for market failure, or to provide transfers for worthy groups of people seem less compelling when the cost to the taxpayer is two dollars for each dollar of expenditure than when the cost is only one. To be sure, many activities of government are fully worth the price. If the protection of the ozone layer of the atmosphere requires large public expenditure, then that expenditure must be borne, regardless of whether a dollar of revenue costs the taxpayer one dollar or two.

This simple case has a fairly wide application. It covers economies where broad-based taxes are administratively difficult to collect and reliance must be placed on a few taxes on goods, such as those entering into foreign trade, for which transactions are easily identified. It covers the choice between purchasing on the market and do-it-yourself activities. Suitably modified, it covers the labor-leisure choice where labor produces taxed benefits while leisure produces untaxed benefits. It covers ordinary excise taxes levied on some goods but not on others, where there are no special reasons, other than those associated with the cost of tax collection, for singling out certain goods to be taxed and allowing other goods to escape tax.

Among the most important of the disparities in tax rates is the double taxation of saving in the income tax. If the price of apples is and will remain at 50 cents each and if the rate of interest, interpreted as a reflection of the marginal rate of substitution in production between present and future goods, is 5 percent a year, then the social cost, P^S, of providing one apple thirty years hence is 11.16 cents; $P^S = 50e^{-.05 \times 30} = 11.16$. When the rate of the income tax is 50 percent, a person who wishes to put aside enough money today to buy himself an apple thirty years hence has to invest considerably more than 11.16 cents. Ignoring transaction cost, a firm that can earn 5 percent on its capital is prepared to pay that rate on its loans, and the saver can expect to earn 5 percent on his money. But the annual interest on one's saving is counted as part of one's income and is subject to the income tax. Thus, if one can earn 5 percent before tax, he can earn only 2.5 percent after tax. The present value of 50 cents spent thirty years ahead, when the net rate of interest on saving is only 2.5 percent, is 23.62 cents; $P^D = 50e^{-.025 \times 30} = 23.62$. This is the sum one must put aside today to buy an apple then. When the interest rate is 5 percent and the rate of the income tax is 50 percent, the effect of the double taxation of saving on the prices today of apples delivered thirty years hence is to create a gap between the demand price of 23.62 cents and the supply price of only 11.16 cents, as though "future apples" were being taxed at a rate of 47 percent of the retail price.

The income tax is logically equivalent to a pair of excise taxes on consumption and saving where the tax on saving is approximately twice the tax on consumption. There is a bias against saving in the income tax that creates a disincentive to save and opens a wedge between ΔW and ΔR of the sort we have been discussing.

In fact, a not unreasonable choice of ϵ^S, ϵ^D, and t in equation 5 could produce a negative value of $\Delta W/\Delta R$, which, paradoxical as this may at first appear, has a simple economic interpretation. Consider the effects on ΔW and ΔR of a gradual increase in the tax rate. As is evident from Figure 2.1 the marginal cost of taxation to the taxpayer, ΔW, has to remain positive as long as the tax base has not shrunk away altogether. The marginal revenue, ΔR, which is equal to the difference $a - b$, becomes progressively smaller until it eventually turns negative. From here on there is everything to lose and nothing to gain from further increases in the tax rate, for a greater dead-weight loss and a smaller revenue would be generated. The value of $\Delta W/\Delta R$ becomes negative when this occurs.

The process by which $\Delta W/\Delta R$ first grows without limit and then turns negative is best illustrated by converting Figure 2.1 to a Laffer curve. Figure 2.2 is derived from Figure 2.1 by changing the units on the axes. The vertical axis shows the tax revenue xt (which was an area in Figure 2.1), the horizontal axis shows the tax rate t, and the curve is an ordinary Laffer curve with a maximal tax revenue at a tax rate t^*. By definition, the change in revenue resulting from a small increase in t is

$$\frac{dR}{dt} = x + t\frac{dx}{dt} = x(1 + \epsilon_{xt}) \tag{6}$$

where ϵ_{xt} is the elasticity of the tax base to the tax rate. The elasticity of the Laffer curve is

$$\frac{t}{R}\frac{dR}{dt} = 1 + \epsilon_{xt} \tag{7}$$

which is the inverse of the marginal social cost of tax revenue, $\Delta W/\Delta R$. The marginal social cost of tax revenue is positive and growing on the good (left) side of the Laffer curve. It rises to infinity at the top of the curve, signifying that a further increase in the rate

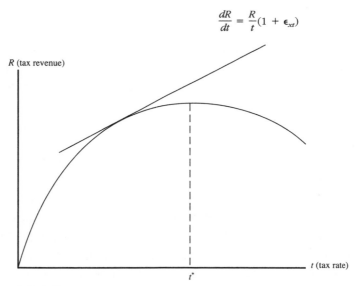

Figure 2.2. Laffer curve.

of tax has costs but no benefits. It is negative on the wrong side of the Laffer curve, signifying that a reduction in the rate of tax would have benefits but no costs.

This analysis of marginal deadweight loss per unit of tax revenue has to be qualified in one very important respect. Everything turns on the requirement that the area b in Figure 2.1 represent a deduction from tax revenue but not from the cost of taxation to the taxpayer. The requirement is expected to hold because the taxpayer has optimized his purchases before the increase in the tax rate, so that the value *to him* of a dollar's worth (at retail prices) of taxed goods is exactly equal to the amount of untaxed goods or do-it-yourself activity or leisure that he might have procured instead. The requirement fails to hold when the taxed good is the bearer of an externality.

Suppose all public revenue is raised by a tax on gasoline. The cost of production of gasoline is 50 cents per gallon, the tax is an additional 50 cents, and the retail price is therefore equal to one dollar per gallon. The externality associated with gasoline is that the fumes from the exhaust of automobiles pollute the atmosphere; the harm done by pollution, to all consumers together, is valued at 25 cents per gallon of gasoline. Consumers respond to taxation by adjusting their purchases so that the benefit from a gallon of gasoline is just equal to the benefit of a dollar's worth of other, untaxed goods. They do so despite the facts that gasoline costs only 50 cents to produce and that each gallon of gasoline does 25 cents' worth of harm to other people. Now consider a slight increase, Δt, in the rate of the tax, leading to a reduction in gasoline consumption of Δx. The net social loss from the reduction in gasoline consumption is no longer equal to $50\Delta x$ cents, which is the value of the area b in Figure 2.1. The net social loss is only $25\Delta x$ cents, which is the difference between the tax loss of $50\Delta x$ cents and the externality gain of $25\Delta x$ cents. The measure of $\Delta W/\Delta R$ in equation 4 would be a substantial overestimate in this case. By the same token, the measure of $\Delta W/\Delta R$ in equation 4 would be an underestimate if the taxed good were the bearer of a positive externality or if the untaxed good were the bearer of a negative externality, as would be the case if taxed work is conducive to good conduct and clean living while untaxed leisure is conducive to dissipation and crime.

The requirement also fails to hold when an increase in a tax on one good diverts the taxpayer's expenditure to another equally taxed good. In that case the value $t\Delta x$, or b, appears neither as a component of the cost to the taxpayer, ΔW, nor as a component of the change in revenue, ΔR. The reduction in revenue, $t\Delta x$, from one good is balanced by an equal increase in revenue from another. For equation 4 to be valid, the tax base, x, cannot be the quantity of one among a number of taxed goods. It must be the entire tax base, so that anything excluded from x is automatically untaxed. Ideally, when an actual tax base consists of several kinds of taxes, the rates of each kind of tax should be set so that $\Delta W/\Delta R$ is the same regardless of which tax is raised.

Finally, the balance between marginal cost and marginal benefit of any public expenditure is affected by the impact, if any, of the public expenditure on the activity of the taxpayer. If the public expenditure is for a city park and the effect of the park is to induce people to substitute in the use of their time from taxed labor to untaxed leisure, the resulting loss of tax revenue has to be counted as part of the hidden cost of the park. If the public expenditure is for a marina, however, and the effect of the marina is to induce people to work more and take less leisure in order to purchase expensive and highly taxed yachts, the resulting increase in tax revenue is a hidden benefit of the marina.

The situation is illustrated in Figure 2.3, which is a modification of Figure 2.1. The axes are the same, and the demand curve $x(t,G)$ in Figure 2.3 should be thought of as identical to the demand curve $x(t)$ in Figure 2.1. The term G refers to the quantity of whatever the government purchases with its tax revenue. The shift of the demand curve when that quantity increases from G to $G + \Delta G$ is the effect of the publicly supplied goods on the taxpayer's purchases of taxed goods. As the figure is drawn, the shift is to the right. Consequently, the area d, which is equal to $t^0(\partial x/\partial G)\Delta G$, is a hidden gain from

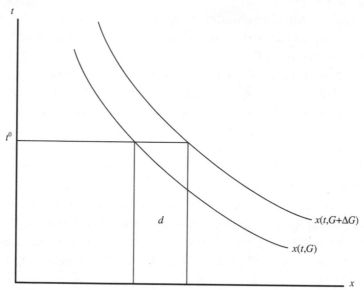

Figure 2.3.

public expenditure. Note, however, that one cannot say a priori whether the shift in the demand curve $x(t,G)$ is to the right or to the left. As drawn, the curve covers the example of the marina. The example of the park would correspond to a leftward shift in the curve.[7]

Equation 4 continues to be approximately valid when x is the entire tax base and t is the average rate of tax on that base. As a general rule, the elasticity of the tax base to the tax rate decreases as the tax base broadens, so that in the limit where taxation is levied as a fixed sum per head—which is equivalent to a tax on every commodity—the elasticity of base to rate falls to zero and the ratio $\Delta W/\Delta R$ approaches unity, indicating that there is no hidden cost to taxation (in the category of deadweight loss) at all. Similarly, if all revenue is levied by a proportional income tax and pretax income is entirely invariant with regard to the rate of tax, then the ratio $\Delta W/\Delta R$ is again equal to 1. The required invariance, however, is of income declared rather than income earned, a distinction that becomes important when taxation can be escaped to some extent by do-it-yourself activities or by outright tax evasion.[8]

The concealment of taxable income. The contraction of the tax base in response to an increase in the tax rate has so far been attributed to the tax-induced shift of purchasing power from more valuable taxed goods to less valuable untaxed goods.[9] A similar and additional contraction, with a similar impact on the ratio of marginal cost to taxpayers per unit of marginal tax revenue, occurs when an increase in the tax rate induces taxpayers to devote extra resources to tax avoidance. The general principle is that people devote resources to legal or illegal tax avoidance up to the point where the marginal cost of tax avoidance is just equal to the tax saved. Hence, when a tax is increased from t to $t + \Delta t$, it pays the taxpayer to devote a bit of extra resources to tax avoidance because the return to tax avoidance is greater by Δt than it was before. The magnitude of this effect depends on the cost of concealment of the tax base. Let this be $C(v)$, where v is the amount of the taxable base that is concealed from the tax collector or sheltered from taxation in some other way. The optimal v from the point of view of the taxpayer is defined by the condition $dC/dv = t$. As shown in Appendix B, the measure of $\Delta W/\Delta R$ in equation 4 remains valid in this case, but the elasticity of the tax base to the tax rate increases to account for the effect of concealment. Specifically,

$$\epsilon_{xt} = -\left\{ \epsilon^D \frac{y}{x} + \epsilon^C \frac{v}{x} \right\} \qquad (8)$$

in the special case where the elasticity of supply of the taxed goods is infinite. In this formula, y is the total consumption of the taxed good, x is the amount on which tax is paid, v is the amount concealed (so that $y = x + v$), ϵ^D is the absolute value of the elasticity of demand for the taxed good, and ϵ^C is the absolute value of the elasticity of the cost of concealment with respect to the amount of the potential base that is concealed. The marginal cost to the taxpayer associated with an increase in public revenue may be high either because ϵ^C is high or because ϵ^D is high. Anything that causes the tax base to contract as the tax rate increases drives up the marginal social cost of public revenue.

Legal tax avoidance and illegal tax evasion have been placed on exactly the same footing in equation 8 because they are, in essential respects, the same from the point of view of the amoral taxpayer. Each entails the nonpayment of tax at some cost—the use of resources to discover ways to make income tax exempt in one case and the use of resources to hide income, together with the risk of punishment, in the other. Each course of action proceeds up to the point where its marginal cost per dollar of tax saved is just equal to one. Each drives up the marginal cost of public funds by causing the tax base to shrink as the tax rate increases. The two are not the same from the point of view of the general public or the government because they involve different kinds and amounts of intimidation cost.

Intimidation cost. Virtually any task that the public sector is called on to perform involves the establishment of rules. Rules require enforcement. Enforcement entails costs that must be counted as part of the total cost of public programs. Among these costs are the citizens' time and money devoted to evading the rules without getting caught, the cost to the government of identifying infractions of the rules, and the cost to the government (and ultimately to the taxpayer) of punishing people identified as rule breakers. These last two items may together be identified as intimidation cost, the cost borne by the government in enforcing compliance with the rules. Intimidation cost becomes a hidden cost of public expenditure when an increase in the tax rate leads to an increase in the amount of tax evasion and a corresponding increase in the amount of public expenditure necessary to enforce compliance with the tax laws.

Marginal deadweight loss, marginal concealment cost, and marginal intimidation cost may be strictly additive as hidden costs of public expenditure, although there are circumstances where this is not quite so. These costs are strictly additive when tax evasion is costly but foolproof, as when tax evasion consists of working underground where productivity is low but the tax collector cannot find you. Suppose that 1,000 cameras are sold when the tax is $50 per camera and that, of these, 200 are sold on the black market where the tax is not paid. Suppose also that an increase in the tax to $51 per camera leads to a reduction in total sales to 995 cameras, of which 205 are now sold on the black market, so that tax is paid on only 790 instead of 800 cameras. Finally, suppose that the rise in the tax leads to an increase in enforcement cost from $3,000 to $3,100, to ensure that sales on the black market are not larger than has been assumed. These numbers must be the joint outcome of complex optimizations by tax evaders and tax collectors, the nature of which does not concern us here.

The marginal cost to the taxpayer of the increase in the tax, ΔW, is $800—the product of the original tax base of 800 cameras and the increase in the tax. The marginal revenue is only $290; it is the new revenue of $40,290 ($= 790 \times 51$) less the original revenue of $40,000 ($= 800 \times 50$). In addition, there is an extra cost to the government of $100 in monitoring tax collection, so that the net gain in revenue, ΔR, is reduced to $190. Thus the marginal social cost per dollar of net revenue, when all three of the hidden costs we have considered so far are taken into account, is

$$\frac{\Delta W}{\Delta R} = \frac{800}{190} = 4.21$$

If a new item of public expenditure has to be financed by an extra tax on cameras or if, as would be socially optimal, the value of $\Delta W/\Delta R$ is the same—and turns out to equal 4.21—for all sources of tax revenue, then that expenditure is only worthwhile if the benefits are just over 4.2 times the resource cost of the new item of public expenditure.

Concealment cost, borne by the tax evader, and intimidation cost, borne by the government, remain additive when tax evasion is not foolproof and punishment is by imprisonment. They cease to be additive when punishment consists of a fine, for in that case the private *cost* of paying the fine is matched by a public *benefit* from the receipt of the revenue from the fine. To the tax evader the source of evasion cost is irrelevant; it may be the reduction in productivity in working underground, the expected fine, or the uncertainty when evasion may or may not be detected. He evades up to the point where marginal cost equals the tax saved, regardless of how the cost is composed. To the government—that is, to the citizen in his capacity of beneficiary of publicly supplied goods—the fine is a benefit that must be set against other forms of intimidation cost, so that only the net cost matters. The $3,000 of intimidation cost in the example must be thought of as the difference between expenditure on police, prisons, revenue agents, and so on and the revenue from fines.

How transfers magnify deadweight loss. I have so far been reasoning as though all citizens are exactly alike, each having an equal share of all costs and all benefits of public activity.[10] The analysis carries over to the transfer of income from rich to poor, through the progressive income tax or the provision of welfare, but costs and benefits must be reassessed. Suppose, for convenience, that there are two distinct social classes, the prosperous and the unprosperous, denoted by the superscripts P and U. The prosperous are the net payers of the transfer, and the unprosperous are the net recipients. The critical statistic in this analysis is the ratio, Q, of the full cost to the payers of the transfer to the full benefit to the recipients, where full costs and benefits are defined to allow for hidden costs of taxation. The full cost of a transfer is the reduction, B^P, in the welfare of all net *payers*. The full benefit from a transfer is the increase, B^U, in the welfare of all net *recipients*. By definition, Q equals B^P/B^U. With no deadweight loss in taxation, the values of B^U and B^P must be the same, so that $Q = 1$. Otherwise the value of Q is necessarily greater than 1, signifying that the transfer itself is costly. A value of Q of, for instance, 4 signifies that it is necessary to impose costs on net payers that are the equivalent of a lump-sum tax of four dollars to convey benefits to net recipients that are the equivalent of a lump-sum subsidy of one dollar.

Three general types of transfers can be identified. In the first only the ultimate payers are taxed, and only the ultimate receivers are allowed to share in the transfer. This is approximated by welfare payments to the very poor where the payments are financed by an income tax with a high enough personal exemption that the very poor are exempt. In the second type of transfer both payers and receivers are taxed at the same rate, but only the net receivers are eligible for benefits. This is approximated by subsidies to farmers or for investment in selected industries. In the third type of transfer, which is the main concern in this section, both groups are gross recipients as well as taxpayers, but taxes are proportional to income while transfers are constant per head, so that the poor become net recipients and the rich net payers. The old-age pension is a transfer of this kind. The three variants of Q in equations 9, 10, and 12 below are derived in Appendix C.

In the first type of transfer, where the net beneficiary pays no tax and the net benefactor receives no transfer, the value of Q is simply the marginal cost of public revenue.

$$Q^1 = \Delta W/\Delta R \qquad (9)$$

with $\Delta W/\Delta R$ as defined in equation 4. The assumption behind this formula is that the benefactor incurs a deadweight loss when his tax is increased but the beneficiary receives his income as a lump sum. In the second type of transfer, where the revenue to finance the transfer is acquired by a general tax on beneficiary and benefactor alike, the deadweight loss is borne by both parties, and the value of Q is larger.

$$Q^2 = \frac{\Delta W}{\Delta R}\left(\frac{1}{1 - [(\Delta W/\Delta R) - 1](n^U y^U / n^P y^P)}\right) \qquad (10)$$

where n^U and y^U are the number and income per head of net recipients and n^P and y^P are the number and income per head of net payers. The value of Q^2 is necessarily equal to 1 when $\Delta W/\Delta R$ is equal to 1, and it is normally greater than $\Delta W/\Delta R$ when $\Delta W/\Delta R$ is greater than 1. Q^2 can turn negative, however—signifying that even net recipients, those for whom $\Delta T > \Delta R$, can lose on balance from redistribution—if $\Delta W/\Delta R$ is large or the total pretransfer income of recipients is large relative to the total income of the net payers, that is, if

$$[(n^U y^U)/(n^P y^P)] > 1/[(\Delta W/\Delta R) - 1] \tag{11}$$

The meaning of this inequality is that the transfer is on balance costly to net recipients as well as to net payers when the recipient's net income from the transfer is outweighed by the recipient's share of the resulting deadweight loss.

In the third type of transfer, where everybody pays tax in proportion to income and everybody receives the same transfer per head, the value of Q becomes

$$Q^3 = \frac{n^P((\Delta W/\Delta R)y^P - \bar{y})}{n^U(\bar{y} - (\Delta W/\Delta R)y^U)} \tag{12}$$

where $\bar{y}$ is the average income per head in the population as a whole. In this case the transfer can only be beneficial to the net recipients if $\Delta W/\Delta R < \bar{y}/y^U$, that is, if the marginal cost of public funds is less than the ratio of average income per head, $\bar{y}$, in the population as a whole to the average income per head of the net beneficiaries of the transfer, y^U. Otherwise the net beneficiaries' share of the transfer is less than their share of the burden of taxation, and the transfer is of no net benefit to anybody at all.

It may be useful to compare the costs of the three forms of transfer within the same numerical example. Suppose $\Delta W/\Delta R = 1.5$, $n^U = n^P$, $y^U = 1$, $y^P = 3$, and, accordingly, $\bar{y} = 2$. Then

$$Q^1 = 1.5$$
$$Q^2 = 1.5[1/(1 - (.5)(1/3))] = 1.8$$
$$Q^3 = [(1.5)(3) - 2]/[2 - (1.5)] = 5$$

Even a low marginal cost of public funds yields a high marginal cost of transfers when a great deal of money has to flow through the public sector to effect a small net transfer between one group and another.

The "obvious" moral to be drawn from the comparison of the costs of these three forms of transfer is that the first is the cheapest and therefore the best. The moral is that transfer programs should be targeted as closely as possible to the group or groups that are the intended beneficiaries; programs designed to better the condition of the poor should be means tested rather than universal. There is some force to this argument, but it is not decisive. On the other side are the moral argument that means-tested programs should be avoided because they are humiliating to the recipients and the economic argument that restricted transfers may give rise to private behavior that is similar in kind to and no less costly than the private response to taxation that is the source of ordinary deadweight loss.

Waste of resources in transfer seeking. The central proposition to emerge from this examination of tax evasion and tax avoidance is that private maneuvers to avoid taxes place a wedge between the marginal cost of tax to the taxpayer and the marginal revenue acquired. There is a comparable proposition about the expenditure side of the budget. A similar and additional wedge is created by private maneuvers in response to public provision of goods, transfers, or privileges. Suppose once again that society consists of two classes of people, the prosperous and the unprosperous. But nobody is born into a social class. Every person has the same prospects at birth, represented by a probability of becoming prosperous, π, which is a function of his effort, E, where effort may be thought of as working long hours, saving, diligence, or anything at all to improve one's chance of becoming prosperous. An effort function, $\pi(E)$, with an assumed diminishing marginal effectiveness of effort (that is, π' > 0 and $\pi'' < 0$) is illustrated in Figure 2.4, with π on the vertical axis and E on the horizontal axis.

Each person's utility depends on his consumption, C, which is a "good," and his effort, E, which is a "bad." The utility function is $u(C, E)$ with diminishing marginal utility of consumption and increasing marginal disutility of effort. Each prosperous person earns a gross income y^P, and each unprosperous person earns a

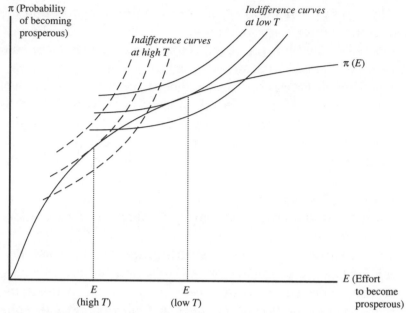

Figure 2.4. Optimal effort at alternative transfers to the unprosperous.

gross income y^U, where $y^U < y^P$. In the absence of transfers, consumption and gross income would be the same. In the presence of a transfer of T to each unprosperous person financed by a universal proportional income tax at a rate t, the consumption of the unprosperous, C^U, and the consumption of the prosperous, C^P, are

$$C^U = (1 - t)y^U + T \qquad (13)$$
$$C^P = (1 - t)y^P \qquad (14)$$

where T and t are connected by the budget constraint

$$(1 - \pi)T = t((1 - \pi)y^U + \pi y^P) \qquad (15)$$

From the original utility function connecting C and E can be derived an expected utility function representing each person's welfare as dependent on his probability of becoming prosperous, π, and his effort, E, with y^P, y^U, and T as parameters.[11] The associated indifference curves are commensurate with the effort function, $\pi(E)$, and may be illustrated, together with the effort function, in Figure 2.4. The shapes of these indifference curves, however, are not independent of the size of the transfer. In principle the transfer T could be set so large that a person no longer cares whether he becomes prosperous or not. Utility would then depend on E alone, and the indifference curves would be a set of vertical lines with utility increasing to the left. Lower the transfer and prosperity becomes desirable once again, causing the indifference curves connecting π and E to tilt clockwise. The smaller is T, the greater is the value to a person of a given increase in his probability of becoming prosperous, and the flatter his indifference curves must be.

Two sets of indifference curves—a relatively flat set corresponding to a low value of T and a relatively steep set corresponding to a high value of T—are combined with the effort function $\pi(E)$ in Figure 2.4 to illustrate how the optimal E is chosen and how this varies with the size of the transfer. At any given T, the person chooses E to place himself on the highest possible indifference curve consistent with the effort function. It is immediately evident from the figure that a person supplies a high level of effort when the transfer is small and a low level of effort when the transfer is large.[12]

This is a classic "moral hazard" problem. If people could form binding contracts for effort and redistribution of income, they would choose full insurance (a value of T high enough that $C^P = C^U$) and a value of E high enough to maximize utility in that case. When such contracts are not enforceable, the value of T must be very much lower to provide people with an incentive for effort. Any selective transfer creates an incentive for all potential recipients to make themselves eligible for the transfer by creating, or by not avoiding, the conditions in which the transfer is supplied. Actions to make oneself eligible for a transfer may bring about a reduction in the national income as a whole.

This general principle has many manifestations. Unemployment insurance reduces the incentive of those with jobs to keep them, of those currently unemployed to look for jobs, and of all workers to acquire assets to tide them over possible periods of unemployment.[13] The provision of welfare reduces one's incentive to avoid becoming poor. The provision of special benefits to unmarried mothers is often claimed to be a major cause of the recent increase in illegitimacy among the poor. Medicare reduces one's incentive to keep well and avoid accidents. Bailouts to firms that would otherwise fail reduce the firms' incentive to avoid actions that might lead to failure. Deposit insurance diminishes the bank's incentive to be prudent in its investments. Like the deadweight loss in taxation, these private incentives generated by public activity have to be counted as part of the cost of the activity, a cost that is worth bearing when the benefit is substantial but not otherwise.

Commodity effects. A second and complementary principle about the effect of public expenditure on private incentives is that small in-kind transfers have no effect on the market as a whole. Suppose it is determined that lettuce is particularly good for you and there is a public decision to induce people to consume more lettuce by providing each person with one free (that is, tax-financed) head of lettuce per month. The policy would have some effect if many people were accustomed to eating less than one head of lettuce per month. It would have no effect at all if everybody normally ate, for example, three heads of lettuce per month. Given one lettuce free, people would merely reduce their normal purchase and would consume the same amount as before. To influence lettuce consumption, the government would need to provide more than people normally consume or to subsidize *all* lettuce consumption.

The general principle that a small public provision of a good has no effect on the market equilibrium is illustrated in Figure 2.5. All three panels contain identical demand and supply curves. Price, P, is measured on the vertical axis, and quantity, Q, is measured on the horizontal axis; the supply curve is flat at a price P^s, and the market equilibrium quantity in the absence of public provision or subsidization of consumption is Q^0. Suppose the government mistakenly believes that it can induce people to consume more of the good by

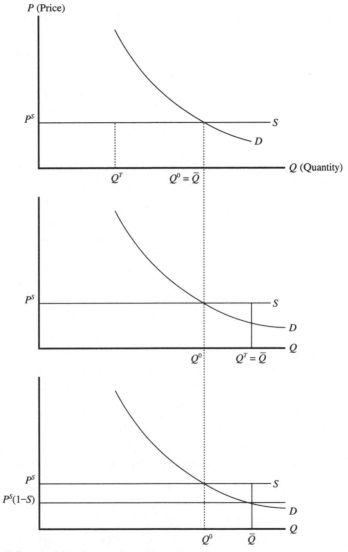

Figure 2.5. Possible effects of public provision on total consumption. Q^0 = quantity consumed with no public provision; Q^T = the amount of public provision; $\bar{Q}$ = quantity consumed with some public provision or subsidization.

providing an amount Q^T, where $Q^T < Q^0$. As illustrated in the top panel of Figure 2.5, the effect of the public provision of Q^T is to reduce private provision accordingly so that total provision—designated as $\overline{Q}$—remains unchanged at Q^0. The recipients of the public provision must gain at the expense of those who are taxed to pay for it, but the effect on the recipients' behavior is the same as if they had received a transfer of income of $\$P^SQ^T$. If everybody received a transfer of Q^T units financed by an increase in each person's tax of $\$P^SQ^T$, then everybody would become worse off to the extent of the deadweight loss from the tax.

Two ways for the government to influence total consumption are illustrated in the middle and bottom panels. The first, illustrated in the middle panel, is to provide more of the good than people would be prepared to buy for themselves at the going price. Here $Q^T > Q^0$. The effect of public provision in this case is to drive out all private provision. The public provision of Q^T has effected a net increase in consumption of $Q^T - Q^0$. Public policy is beneficial in this case if the social gain, however measured, from the extra provision of the good, $Q^T - Q^0$, exceeds the marginal excess burden of the tax required to finance the purchase of total consumption, Q^T.

The same extra provision, $Q^T - Q^0$, can be obtained at lower cost to the treasury by subsidization, as illustrated in the bottom panel. A subsidy of a portion, s, of the cost price reduces the market price from P^S to $P^S(1 - s)$ and increases the quantity demanded from Q^0 to $\overline{Q}$. In this case an increase in consumption of $\overline{Q} - Q^0$ has been bought with an expenditure of $sP^0\overline{Q}$ per person rather than an expenditure of $P^0\overline{Q}$. The saving is not just a reduction in the transfer from all taxpayers to consumers of the subsidized good; it is a saving of real resources that would otherwise be wasted in tax evasion or tax avoidance.

The general principle that one cannot affect a market by a partial subsidization has many applications. The improvement of the housing of the poor brought about by public housing is nowhere near commensurate with the amount of housing provided under the program and might in certain circumstances be altogether illusory. Public housing could actually worsen the accommodation of the poor if, for example, each poor family would have occupied 1,000 square feet in the absence of public housing and is offered 900 square feet at a low rent under the public housing program. Of course, even in this extreme case where public housing fails to improve accommodation, it must succeed as a vehicle for transferring purchasing power to the poor if the public housing is occupied at all. What is more likely, however, is that public housing offers most beneficiaries a better accommodation than they would otherwise rent, so that the situation is more like that depicted in the middle panel of the figure than like that depicted in the top panel.

The principle is also exemplified, with some complications, by the old-age pension.[14] Consider a bachelor whose sole motive for saving is to provide for his old age, who retires at age 65, and who, in the absence of a publicly funded old-age pension, would have accumulated $200,000 of capital at that time. If the public pension provides a stream of income with a present value at his 65th birthday of $100,000, it would be rational for that person to accumulate $100,000 less over the course of his working years, especially if he is taxed during those years to finance the old-age pensions of others. When the public pension is funded, the reduction of $100,000 in cumulative private saving is matched by an increase of $100,000 in cumulative public saving, and there is no net effect on total investment or capital formation, although the title to the capital has changed. When the public pension is unfunded and pay-as-you-go, there is no public saving to match the decline in private saving, and there must be a reduction in net capital formation. What appears to the recipient of the old-age pension as a substitution of public saving for private saving may constitute a reduction in saving for the economy as a whole, depending on how the public pension is financed.

It is essential to the argument that the recipient of the old-age pension be a bachelor. The polar opposite case is that of a family whose capital today has been accumulated over many generations and whose investment decisions take account of the interests of many generations to come. For such a family a pay-as-you-go old-age pension can have no effect whatsoever on consumption and saving today, because anticipated benefits from the old-age pension and anticipated taxes to finance those benefits just cancel out, leaving the present value of post-tax and post-transfer income as it would be without the old-age pension and without the taxes to finance it. A family's allocation of consumption over time is no more affected by the taxes and transfers associated with the old-age pension than a person's allocation of consumption over the months of a year is affected by the fact that the income tax is collected all at once in April. In both cases lending and borrowing are timed to effect the optimal stream of consumption within the given resource constraint.

Even for the bachelor there are important qualifications to the argument that the pension leads to a reduction in private saving, dollar for dollar. The income of the old is certainly augmented by the old-age pension if the amount of the pension exceeds what the person would have provided for himself in its absence. The case where the pension has no effect on the consumption of the old is covered by the top panel of Figure 2.5, where Q is reinterpreted as the annual consumption of the retired and P is the rate of substitution in use between consumption in one's working years and consumption in retirement. The case where the pension does affect the consumption of the old is covered by the second panel. A country's decision to establish an old-age pension is in part a manifestation of the political influence of the old, but it is also in part a judgment that there are enough people whose savings in the absence of a pension would be less than the pension—the circumstances shown in the second panel—to justify the social cost of the circulation of income through the tax and transfer system of the government.

Very much the same considerations apply to the firm-specific subsidization of investment. Public subsidization of investment may be general or firm-specific. Subsidization is general when, for example, all investment is made eligible for a tax credit. Subsidization is firm-specific when the government selects particular investments by particular firms, awards subsidies to these investments, and denies them to all others. Firm-specific subsidization may be undertaken by ad hoc decisions of the cabinet. It may also be arranged in programs designed to favor investments in specific areas of the country, industries, kinds of firms (such as firms owned by native people), or projects that are especially innovative and different from the normal run of business activity. Sometimes a project is considered for a subsidy only if it would not be otherwise commercially viable. Firm-specific subsidies are often alleged to create jobs, a claim that attributes the total employment associated with the subsidized project to the subsidy itself. Politicians running for office or public officials justifying their activities will proudly point to the many jobs "they" have created with the subsidies to investment that they grant.

Such claims may be justified. Although the social value of investment is usually reflected in private profitability, there are instances where this is not so, and there may be a case for subsidization when such instances are identified. Investments to create new products may generate social benefits that cannot be captured in the return to the entrepreneur. Even the grant of a patent may be insufficient to enable the innovator to cover the cost of investment, although the consumer surplus from the new product may be more than sufficient. Similarly, an investment in a depressed region may be privately unprofitable without a subsidy but socially advantageous if the investment provides work to those who would otherwise be on welfare because they have no alternative source of employment.

While it is true that firm-specific subsidization of investment may be socially advantageous in certain cases, it is highly unlikely that a program of firm-specific subsidization or ad hoc subsidization by politicians or bureaucrats will be socially advantageous on balance. A distinction must be drawn here between the benefit of the subsidy and the benefit of the subsidized investment. Obviously the investment itself must be beneficial on balance for the subsidization to be justified. That is a necessary but not sufficient condition for the subsidy to be socially advantageous. An additional but absolutely necessary requirement for the subsidy to be beneficial is that the investment would not be profitable otherwise. The reason why firm-specific subsidization is unlikely to be beneficial in practice is that it is difficult, bordering on impossible, for public officials to determine with any acceptable degree of certainty whether these two conditions obtain in any particular case.

Knowing that subsidies are available, firms have an incentive to claim that projects are unique when they are not or that projects would not be commercially viable without subsidization. Such claims are difficult to verify and even more difficult to refute by the public officials whose task it is to determine whether they are valid. Dishonesty is surely endemic in such an environment. More importantly, projects can be substitutable in many subtle ways. The introduction of a subsidized project in a region may drive up the wage of labor and thereby drive out an established firm that would otherwise have remained viable. Or the introduction of the subsidized project might forestall the development of another yet unrecognized project that would not require a subsidy at all. The subsidized project might use up local savings that would otherwise be channeled by the banks to other investment in the region. Firm-specific subsidization of investment might possibly increase the total investment in the favored categories, but there is no assurance that this will occur, and there is a virtual certainty that the increment to investment, if any, will be well short of the total value of subsidized investment. The jobs "created" may in reality be transferred from other projects or firms. Subsidized firms might bump unsubsidized firms, just as public provision bumps an equal amount of private provision in the circumstances of the top panel of Figure 2.5.

These difficulties with firm-specific investment subsidies are compounded by a problem of information. Public officials administering a program of firm-specific investment subsidies must either rely on judgment and intuition in deciding whether a project is appropriate for subsidization or fall back on simple general rules—such as to subsidize all investment within a region—that lead inevitably to the support of many projects that would go forward regardless. Furthermore, the same want of a precise criterion that makes the initial evaluation problematic removes all possibility of a proper ex post audit. It can, of course, be determined whether the subsidized investment actually takes place and whether the new project employs as many workers as was claimed in the initial application. What cannot be determined ex post is whether the subsidy was really necessary, whether the subsidized firm bumped some preexisting firm from the market or forestalled another investment that would have appeared if the subsidy had not been granted. The usual measure of "success" in this context—that the subsidized project is thriving—might equally well be treated as a measure of failure.

The absence of a solid criterion for evaluating firm-specific investment subsidies creates an opening for dishonesty in government. A perfectly administered subsidy program would convey no net advantage to the recipients, for the subsidies would be no larger than necessary to induce firms to engage in some socially advantageous but privately unprofitable behavior. But an imperfect program, such as any actual program must be, necessarily conveys large windfall gains to many if not all of the recipients, who, as owners of firms, are normally rich and who might be inclined to reward their benefactors. Malfeasance in the provision of firm-specific investment grants could, in principle, be constrained by allowing firms to sue for redress when injured as a result of improper actions by the granting agencies. This remedy is not feasible in practice because there is too broad a range within which it is not absolutely clear whether the granting agency is acting improperly.

The probable redundancy of a good portion of the firm-specific investment subsidies raises the possibility that a large program of subsidies may inhibit more investment than it promotes. The mechanism by which this perverse outcome may occur is this: Each dollar of investment generated by firm-specific investment subsidies requires an expenditure of x dollars. In a perfectly administered program, the value of x might be less than 1 because only part of the cost of the investment would be covered by the subsidy, but in any actual program x would almost certainly exceed 1 because many

subsidized projects would have gone forward regardless and because some subsidized projects bump established firms or other
unsubsidized projects. The x dollars must be financed through the
tax system, which entails some deadweight loss. The required
increase in tax revenue can only be obtained from a marginal
increase in tax rates, which could easily induce taxpayers to shift
purchasing power from saving to consumption because of the
double taxation of saving.

If y is the marginal reduction of private saving per dollar of tax
revenue raised, then a requirement to raise x dollars must reduce
private saving by xy. Total investment is increased or decreased by a
program of firm-specific investment subsidies according to whether
the value of xy is less than or greater than 1. One cannot say a priori
whether the primary effect of the subsidization of projects that
would not be viable in the absence of subsidies is outweighed by the
secondary effect of the churning of money through the tax system.
The balance could go either way.

**The relative efficiency of the public and the private sectors
of the economy.** It is often said that government is inefficient,
by which is meant that more man-hours are typically required to do
a given job in the public sector than in the private sector.[15] Among
the alleged reasons are that the public sector, by virtue of its
monopoly of the services it provides, is more likely to fall prey to
union restrictions and that civil servants, who have little fear of being
fired, have relatively little incentive to work hard. There is some
evidence that the government is less efficient than private firms at a
number of tasks, notably garbage collection, which is sometimes
performed by the government directly and sometimes performed by
the private sector under contract. Many, but not all the tasks of
government could be contracted out to the private sector. The
private sector is less likely to perform these tasks well when
privatization requires the establishment of a monopoly than when a
number of firms in competition can share in what were once
functions of government.

Rent seeking. The term "rent seeking" is usually employed in the context of quotas rather than of public expenditure, but the basic principle applies to both.[16] Whenever the government establishes a valuable prize, be it a patent for innovative research, entitlement to import a product protected by a quota, or an industrial subsidy granted on any principle whatsoever, an incentive is created for people and firms to employ resources in competing for the prize. In the context of public expenditure, rent seeking occurs when governments exercise discretion about who the recipient of a subsidy or a valuable contract will be.

A contract yielding $1 million of profit is awarded at random to a "suitable" firm, where suitability refers to the acquisition of a machine that costs $100,000 and has no use whatever apart from the contract. If only one firm buys the machine, that firm is sure to win the contract and to pocket the $1 million over and above the cost of the machine. Clearly, this windfall gain will be competed away. On the assumption that firms are risk neutral, a suitable machine will be purchased by eleven firms, of which one will, by chance, be awarded the contract. Of the $1.1 million spent by the eleven firms on the contract-specific machinery, all but $100,000 is wasted. What at first appears as a transfer from the government to one privileged or lucky firm turns out to be a social waste in circumstances where ex ante profits are normal. This example is generalized and its implications are qualified in Appendix D. The example would be essentially the same from the point of view of the rent-seeking firms if the $100,000 per firm were spent on lobbying or bribing public officials.

Rent seeking is a rather general term that may cover any of three kinds of activity: lobbying (which includes advertising), bribery, and what might be called positioning. Lobbying is almost always pure waste. The same is usually true of bribery, as is discussed below. By "positioning" I refer to a kind of behavior exemplified in the preceding paragraph: A quota or some other valuable privilege is allocated by the government to firms on the basis of a property or characteristic of the firms, and the choice among eligible firms is at random. The acquisition of the property becomes like the purchase of a lottery ticket. Firms position themselves for the prize by acquiring the property.

It should be recognized that rent seeking as positioning can be socially beneficial.[17] Research expenditure to procure a patent is the obvious example. Another example of useful rent-seeking expenditure is competition over design. Each of ten firms may be ex ante equally eligible for a contract, but they may propose designs for the project that are ex post different one from another and not equivalent in the assessment of the public officials who are awarding the contract. Rent seeking in this case is socially useful expenditure on design before it is known who the winner of the contract will be. The winner of the contract must be guaranteed an above-normal profit as an inducement to all eligible firms to risk the expenditure on design in circumstances where the expenditure of all but one contestant is wasted.

Corruption. Assessment of the cost of a program or project in the public sector must take account of the possibility that the administrators of the program or project will turn out to be corrupt, for perfect and constant honesty is not to be expected in this imperfect world.[18] Corruption may take many forms: kickbacks on government contracts, bribes to the police to overlook infractions of the law, selling of offices, selling of credentials, or demanding payment for licenses to which the applicants are entitled. Corruption may be more or less conspiratorial, ranging all the way from uncoordinated acts of impropriety by officials, through organized malfeasance by entire departments or branches of government, to government-wide predatory activity that is in the limit indistinguishable from despotism.

It is sometimes argued that corruption involves no social cost because it is a mere transfer of income from the private sector to public officials. This argument is generally false in my opinion, no less so for corruption than for theft, which is also a transfer from one person to another. The cost of corruption stems from the tenuousness of the connection between the private gain to the corrupt official and the social loss from his actions. Consider an amoral official who is weighing the pros and cons of a corrupt act—such as granting one firm a contract that should by rights go to another. He benefits from his misbehavior as long as it is undetected. He also runs some risk of detection and punishment. Like any potential criminal, he acts corruptly if his expected gain exceeds his expected loss.

Note particularly that the social cost of the corrupt act is no part of the official's calculation. The calculation is a weighing of *his* benefit if the corrupt act is undetected, the burden of punishment if the corrupt act is detected, and the risk of detection. The social cost of his action can be very much larger than his expected gain, but that is none of his concern, except insofar as the punishment and the probability of detection are connected to social cost. A reasonable government would try to choose punishment and probability of detection to be commensurate with the social cost—in this case as in the setting of punishments for ordinary crimes—but the attempt may not be entirely successful. In particular, if the amoral official is sure that a corrupt act will be undetected, he will commit the act regardless of how small the value of his personal benefit or of how large the social cost, as long as he has no more lucrative alternatives.

A privilege inappropriately granted to firm A yields a benefit of $10 to that firm at a cost of $2,000 to the general public. Firm A offers the official a bribe of $5. Obviously, the official rejects the bribe if there is a significant probability of detection and if the punishment is severe. He also rejects the bribe if those who are harmed in the transaction can come up with a larger competing bribe, as they could well afford to do, for they would willingly pay, say, $15 to avoid a $2,000 loss. Neither of these conditions need obtain. Firm A may be in a position to offer an undetectable bribe, while those harmed by the official's decision may be too dispersed to organize for the provision of a competing bribe or may be unable to make the bribe undetectable, since the subscription to finance a bribe might well come to the notice of the police. The undetectable bribe might take the form of an unspoken offer of employment at an unspecified time when the official retires from the public service.

The social cost of public sector malfeasance may take many

forms: the loss of potential benefit when a contract is granted to the less efficient firm, the reduction of use of a licensed service when the cost is driven up by bribes paid by practitioners, the harm to consumers of services when licenses are granted to unqualified practitioners, and the waste of resources in rent seeking when opportunities for rent-seeking behavior are deliberately created for the benefit of the dispensers of rent. This last point needs some elaboration.

As mentioned above, rent seeking may be lobbying, positioning, or bribery. Rent seeking becomes bribery when the steps firms must take to compete for rents are beneficial to the rent giver and illegal. It is irrelevant from the point of view of the rent seeker whether the appropriate steps are advertising or bribery. His only concern is to draw the best balance among the size of the prize, his total expenditure to increase his chance of getting it, and his probability of success.[19]

As long as there is some component of bribery in rent seeking, it may be in the interest of corrupt governments to create circumstances where privileges are to be dispensed. Suppose—for good reasons or for bad—an industry is to be protected and the government must choose whether to protect the industry by tariffs or by quotas distributed free of charge to certain privileged firms. Tariffs are preferable in most circumstances because they generate public revenue while "free" quotas do not. A totally predatory government would levy a tariff and use the proceeds to augment officials' wages. A corrupt government, which cannot use tariff revenue to augment officials' wages directly but is quite willing to increase officials' income if that can be accomplished secretly, might prefer quotas. The quotas would be awarded to privileged firms rather than auctioned off, on the understanding that the recipients of quotas are beholden to the officials who grant them. With a reasonable degree of collaboration among officials at different levels of the hierarchy, policy can be designed to create privileges for grateful firms within the private sector.

Our numerical example can easily be reformulated so that it

pertains to rent seeking in the subsidization of investment. Suppose that a $2,000 subsidy is certain to be dissipated in wasteful rent seeking but that the dispenser of the subsidy can expect to skim off $5 of benefit with no risk of detection. The subsidy generates a riskless gain to officials of $5 and a loss to the general public of $2,000 in the form of taxation to finance the subsidy or of loss of genuine public services that could have been financed instead. The operation is advantageous to officials when no alternative form of corruption is more profitable.

A more extended example illustrates the complex interaction between public and private benefits when officials are inclined to be corrupt. The government is deciding whether to license doctors in the circumstances represented by the demand and supply curves for medical services in Figure 2.6. The vertical axis shows the consumers' marginal valuation, P, of the services of one doctor for one year. The horizontal axis shows the number of doctors, n, practicing during the year. The demand curve shows the marginal valuation of the annual services of a doctor as a function of the number of doctors. The supply curve is assumed to be flat; its height, P^s, is the alternative cost of a doctor—the sum of the amount he could earn in another profession and his annualized training cost. To speak of the demand for and supply of doctors in this way is to ignore that the decision to become a doctor is made, once and for all, at the beginning of a person's working life. The simplification is harmless and convenient in the context of the analysis of corruption.

The justification for the public licensing of doctors may be to take advantage of economies of scale in identifying professional qualifications. Assume the following:

a. Nobody employs a doctor unless he is known to be qualified.

b. Individual patients can determine whether doctors are qualified at a cost, to all patients together, of m per doctor, so that the supply curve of qualified doctors as seen by patients who must certify qualifications for themselves is horizontal at a height $P^s + m$ above the horizontal axis.

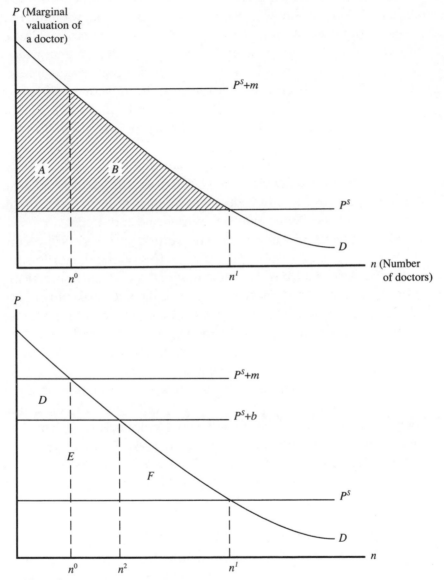

Figure 2.6

c. A lump-sum payment by the government of L is sufficient to identify all qualified doctors who present themselves at no marginal cost.

d^0. (An assumption to be replaced presently.) The licensing procedure is conducted honestly, without bribery and at no marginal cost to the qualified doctor or to the general public.

The costs and benefits of public licensing of doctors are now easily compared. Without public licensing the cost to the public per doctor is $P^S + m$, and the number of doctors demanded is n^0, as shown in the top panel. Introduce public licensing, and the cost per doctor falls from $P^S + m$ to P^S, providing a gain to users of doctors' services equal to the shaded area $A + B$. The area A is the saving on the n^0 doctors already employed, and the area B is the gain from employing $n^1 - n^0$ more doctors at a cost P^S per doctor. The net benefit of licensing is therefore equal to $A + B - L(\Delta W/\Delta R)$, where the term $L(\Delta W/\Delta R)$ is the lump-sum cost of public licensing, scaled up by the marginal social cost per dollar of tax revenue. Public licensing is advantageous if this net benefit is positive.

The effect of malfeasance depends critically on the opportunities for and the constraints on corrupt officials. Two among many possibilities will be examined. Suppose first that the corrupt official can demand as large a bribe from qualified doctors as the market will bear and that he can keep all revenue from bribery. Assumption d^0 is now replaced by assumption d^1:

d^1. The corrupt official can demand a bribe per qualified doctor up to but not in excess of m, which is the cost to the patient of certifying the doctor's qualifications for himself.

Depending on the shape of the demand curve, the optimal bribe from the point of view of the official could be less than or equal to m. Suppose it is just m. Suppose also that income from bribery can be looked on as a mere transfer from one party to another, where the transfer itself involves no social cost because all dollars are counted as equal, in the well-known phrase from cost-benefit analysis, "to whomsoever they may accrue." With a bribe of m, the number of doctors employed is no greater when doctors are licensed than when they are not, for in each case the marginal cost to the patient is $P^s + m$.

Without licensing, the m represents the patients' cost of discovering which doctors are qualified. With licensing the m is part of the fee that the doctor demands to cover the alternative cost of his time, his training cost, and the bribe. The surplus, B, that would accrue if licensing were conducted honestly is now lost, and the net gain from public licensing of doctors is reduced from $A + B - L(\Delta W/\Delta R)$ to $A - L(\Delta W/\Delta R)$. The certification cost, A, to the patient is now converted into a transfer to the corrupt official, but it is still saved because it shows up as somebody's income. (It may even show up as a tax reduction if officials are paid less than the wages they could earn in the private sector because they are expected to acquire extra income from bribes. In that case the net benefit from licensing is $(A - L)(\Delta W/\Delta R)$ rather than $A - L(\Delta W/\Delta R)$. Bribery would be socially advantageous if $(A - L)(\Delta W/\Delta R)$ were greater than $A + B - L(\Delta W/\Delta R)$.)

All this depends on the assumption that amounts paid in bribes represent a pure transfer rather than a social cost. There has to be some truth to the assumption, for otherwise corrupt practices would be profitless to those who engage in them and would not be adopted at all. As stated above, however, the amount of benefit to corrupt officials may be quite small by comparison with the social cost of their activities to the public at large.

Part of the potential gross transfer, A, may be wasted in the following ways: (1) Although corrupt officials as a class have an incentive to avoid licensing unqualified doctors, the average quality of doctors may be lower when officials are corrupt than when they are honest. (2) There may be some cost, to doctors or to the officials themselves, in delivering the bribe. For example, to avoid detection, the bribe might have to be paid through the intermediary of lawyers who would demand a cut. When the maximal physician's wage is $m + P^s$, any transaction cost in bribe taking must reduce the net income of the bribe taker to something less than m per doctor. (3) Bribe takers may bear a risk of punishment, in the form of a fine or of imprisonment. The net gain to the bribe taker is the bribe less the expected cost of punishment. (4) The government may bear a cost of hunting and punishing bribe takers. This cost is converted into a benefit whenever punishment takes the form of a fine. The net cost to the government is the cost of detection of corrupt practices *plus* the cost of imprisonment *minus* the revenue from fines. (The situation is analogous to the government's efforts to stop tax evasion as discussed above.) All four items are genuine costs of the institution of public licensing of doctors, in that they would all be avoided if the government left the licensing of doctors to the market.

In this environment, where bribe taking might be detected and punished, the optimal bribe, b, is likely to be less than the cost of private certification, m. The situation would then be as portrayed in the bottom panel of Figure 2.6, where the demand and supply curves are the same as in the top panel, the number of doctors licensed is n^2 (which is less than n^1 but greater than n^0), the bribe, b, is less than m, and the sum of the three areas D, E, and F is the same as the sum of the two areas A and B in panel A. Assumption d^1 is now replaced by d^2.

d^2. The optimal bribe, b, from the point of view of the officials is less than m, and a fraction f of the doctor's expenditure on bribes, E, is wasted.

Now the net benefit from the licensing of doctors becomes

$$D + (1 - f)E - L(\Delta W/\Delta R)$$

where D is the surplus that remains to consumers from the licensing of doctors because $b < m$ and f is the waste of revenue per dollar of bribes for all the reasons mentioned in the preceding paragraph. The bribery remains advantageous to corrupt officials as long as $f < 1$, but the net benefit to bribe takers, $(1 - f)E$, may be very much less than the social cost of bribery, which in this case is $A + B - D - (1 - f)E$.

Conclusion

That completes the list of the hidden costs of public expenditure. The moral of the story is not that the benefit of any particular public activity is necessarily less than the cost, for benefits of many public activities are surely large enough to justify costs that are many times the dollar value of expenditure. The moral is that the full cost of public activity, including resource cost and hidden cost, should be identified. Hidden costs, which are peppered all over the public and private sectors of the economy, might not be totaled up at all, because each person or department of government is aware only of his immediate cost and nobody keeps track of the whole.

Suppose the government is contemplating an expenditure of $100,000 on, for instance, road construction. The full cost of the road work would be considerably larger than the $100,000 spent directly on it. It would include the cost to the Ministry of Transport in administering that kind of road work, to would-be beneficiaries in maneuvering for road work in their districts rather than elsewhere, to the Ministry of Transport in negotiating with would-be beneficiaries, to the general public in coping with corrupt practices of the contractors and the officials with whom the contractors deal, to the Ministry of National Revenue in collecting the extra tax and in dealing with the extra efforts at concealment by taxpayers brought about by the required increase in tax rates, and to taxpayers in the additional concealment of taxable income made profitable by the rise in tax rates and in ordinary deadweight loss.

Dependent as they are on elasticities that can rarely be measured with any degree of accuracy, the hidden costs of public expenditure are very much more difficult to quantify than the ordinary resource cost of public expenditure. They are too speculative, too theoretical, and too dependent on sheer guesswork for the accountants who would normally be engaged in comparing costs and benefits of public sector activities. But hidden costs exist whether we account for them or not, and such crude estimates as we have suggest that hidden costs, all told, could easily exceed resource cost, perhaps by a very wide margin. Costs that are hard to measure are not necessarily zero, as is implied when such costs are ignored. Public finance may be placed on a sounder footing when hidden costs are measured inaccurately than when they are not measured at all. At a minimum, a listing of hidden costs may serve as an antidote to the tendency on the part of departments of government to justify expansion and promote projects and programs on the grounds that the value of the benefits exceeds the resource cost alone.

Since this volume is about taxes and taxlike measures in the third world, it may be useful to conclude with a few remarks on the applicability of the analysis of hidden costs in that context. A useful starting place is the much-repeated allegation that the tools of economics—especially the assumption that actors in the economy are rational and self-seeking and the models of competition and monopoly—are better suited to the developed economies in which these tools were forged than to the third world, which operates on its own rules and principles. Nothing, in my opinion, could be further from the truth. To be sure, the models with which economists attempt to make sense of events are, like any models in the social sciences, abstract and less than completely representative of the world around us. There is an inevitable and ultimately unbridgeable gap between actual societies and the theories we employ to explain them.

This is true of all theory, no matter where or by whom it is constructed. But, having said that, one should add that our economic models were developed, during the eighteenth and nineteenth centuries, in a Europe that was probably more similar in many respects to the third world as it is today than to contemporary Europe or America. I suspect that Adam Smith would see more that is familiar to him in contemporary Indonesia or Malaysia than in contemporary England or the United States. In particular, I suspect that he would be immediately at home with the peasant agriculture, markets, and small manufacturing of Southeast Asia and that he would have little difficulty in slotting third world trade and industrial policies into the appropriate sections of *The Wealth of Nations*. But, he would, I suspect, be quite mystified by the large, hierarchical, and powerful corporations of the first world, which are neither competition nor monopoly as Smith knew these institutions and whose behavior is imperfectly rationalized by our models. It is at least arguable that the developed economies are to a large extent out of reach of standard economic analysis while the so-called developing economies fit the models reasonably well.

Obviously, each country has its own institutions, customs, and peculiarities that have to be taken into account when drawing conclusions about policy from abstract models and reasoning, and a person analyzing institutions or prescribing policy for a country not his own must be particularly careful to avoid reasoning as though the institutions of his own country were universal. It does not follow that the models per se are country specific or that perfect competition is a better model for Canada than for Thailand.

While the hidden costs of public expenditure are universal, their magnitudes very often depend on the efficiency and honesty of the civil service in each country. In particular, the marginal social cost of tax evasion, tax avoidance, rent seeking, and out-and-out corruption is likely to be very much lower when public administration is effective and honorable than when it is not. From this it follows immediately that the appropriate scope of the public sector depends critically on what the public sector is able to do well. The case for a publicly financed old-age pension is very different in a society where the civil service can immediately identify who is eligible and who is not and where bureaucrats dispensing checks to the old cannot demand compensation from legitimate recipients than it is in a society where these conditions do not obtain. The proposition carries over to unemployment insurance, provision for the very poor, and the subsidization of investment in progressive firms. Thus not only does the classical economic model fit the third world relatively well, but if public administration is, to use the standard euphemism, "developing" along with the rest of the economy, there may be a better case for the classical, laissez-faire prescriptions in the third world than in the first.

Appendix A: Derivation of Marginal Social Cost of Public Revenue for an Excise Tax on a Commodity with an Elasticity of Demand of ϵ^D and an Elasticity of Supply of ϵ^S

There are only two goods in the economy, one taxed and the other not. Let x be the quantity produced and consumed per head of the taxed good, let $P^D(x)$ be its marginal valuation in terms of untaxed goods, and let $P^S(x)$ be its marginal cost in terms of the untaxed good; $P^S(x)$ is the extra amount of the untaxed good that could be produced with the resources released when one less unit of the taxed good is produced. In the absence of tax, the demand and supply prices would be the same. With a tax of t per unit, the market equilibrium output of the taxed good is x^0, such that

$$P^D(x^0) - P^S(x^0) = t \qquad (A1)$$

The market for the taxed good is illustrated in Figure 2.A.1, with price on the vertical axis and quantity on the horizontal axis. As shown in the figure, a tax of t yields a revenue of $[P^D(x^0) - P^S(x^0)]x^0$, which is represented by the area $d + c$. When the tax is increased from t to $t + \Delta t$, the output falls from x^0 to $x^0 - \Delta x$, the demand price rises to $P^D(x^0 - \Delta x)$, the supply price falls to $P^S(x^0 - \Delta x)$, and tax revenue becomes $[P^D(x^0 - \Delta x) - P^S(x^0 - \Delta x)](x^0 - \Delta x)$, which is represented by the area $a + b + d$. The change in tax revenue, called ΔR, is equal to $a + b - c$. The effect on the welfare of the consumer, called ΔW, is the sum of two parts: (1) the increase in tax paid, which is $a + b - c$ and which, with stable demand and supply curves, must correspond to a loss of potential consumption of the untaxed good; and (2) the loss of consumers' and producers' surplus associated with the tax-induced reduction in the consumption of the taxed good. The consumer's marginal reallocation of purchasing power from the taxed to the untaxed good is socially

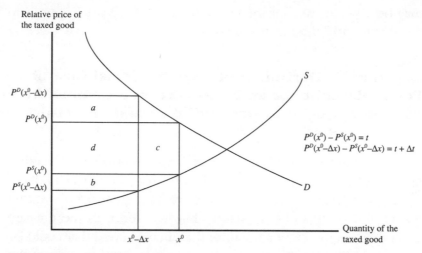

Figure 2.A.1. Marginal revenue $(a + b - c)$ and marginal deadweight loss (c) resulting from an increase in the tax rate from t to $t + \Delta t$.

disadvantageous because the marginal valuation of the taxed good in terms of the untaxed good, $P^D(x^0)$, exceeds its marginal cost, $P^S(x^0)$. This second effect, measured by the area c in the figure, is the marginal deadweight loss associated with the marginal increase in the tax; it is similar to the tax-induced waste of 8 hours of labor in the carpenter and plumber example.

Pulling all this together, we see that the ratio of the full marginal cost to consumers to the marginal revenue generated by a small increase in tax is

$$\frac{\Delta W}{\Delta R} = \frac{\Delta \text{ tax paid} + \Delta \text{ deadweight loss}}{\Delta \text{ tax paid}}$$

$$= \frac{(a + b - c) + c}{a + b - c} = \frac{a + b}{a + b - c} \qquad (A2)$$

the values of a, b, and c can be read from Figure 2.A.1.

$$a = x\Delta P^D$$
$$b = x\Delta P^S$$
$$c = (P^D - P^S)\Delta x$$

It follows that

$$\frac{\Delta W}{\Delta R} = \frac{x\Delta P^D + x\Delta P^S}{x\Delta P^D + x\Delta P^S - (P^D - P^S)\Delta x}$$

$$= \frac{1}{1 - \dfrac{t\Delta x}{x\Delta t}} = \frac{1}{1 + \epsilon_{xt}} \qquad (A3)$$

because $(\Delta P^D + \Delta P^S) = \Delta t$, $P^D - P^S = t$, and a positive Δx refers to a reduction in x. But

$$\frac{t\Delta x}{x\Delta t} = \frac{t}{x\dfrac{\Delta P^D}{\Delta x} + x\dfrac{\Delta P^S}{\Delta x}} = \frac{t}{P^D\left(\dfrac{x\Delta P^D}{P^D\Delta x}\right) + P^S\left(\dfrac{x\Delta P^D}{P^S\Delta x}\right)}$$

$$= \frac{t}{(P^D/\epsilon^D) + (P^S/\epsilon^S)}$$

$$= \frac{t\epsilon^D\epsilon^S}{P^D\epsilon^S + P^S\epsilon^D} \qquad (A4)$$

where ϵ^S and ϵ^D are the absolute values of the elasticities of supply and demand. Equation A4 is reproduced as equation 5 in the text.

Appendix B: Derivation of the Marginal Social Cost of Public Revenue in the Presence of Tax Evasion

In the discussion surrounding Figure 2.1 in the text, deadweight loss was introduced by an example of taxation of water from a well. Reconsider that example with the additional assumption that, although no labor is required to draw water from the well, it is none the less costly to conceal the drawing of water from the watchful tax collector. Let the cost of concealment be $C(v)$, where v is the amount of water on which the tax is not paid. The taxpayer's optimal v is defined by the condition that $C' = t$, where C' is the marginal cost of tax evasion and t is the amount of tax saved. The formula in equation 4 for identifying the marginal cost of public revenue remains valid in the presence of tax evasion as long as the variable x is reinterpreted as the amount of water on which tax is actually paid rather than as the amount of water consumed. Define y to be the amount of water consumed. Necessarily,

$$y = x + v \qquad \text{(B1)}$$

The relation between marginal revenue from the tax, ΔR, and marginal social cost, ΔW, is illustrated in Figure 2.B.1, which is a development of Figure 2.1. The demand for water is the same in both figures. The new feature in Figure 2.B.1 is the marginal cost of concealment, which is shown as increasing with the amount of water concealed. The derivation of the marginal social cost of tax revenue is now almost the same as in the earlier case. As shown in the figure, a rise in the tax per unit of water from t^0 to $t^0 + \Delta t$ leads to a decrease in consumption from y^0 to $y^0 - \Delta y$ and an increase in evasion from v^0 to $v^0 + \Delta v$. Note that Δy and Δv are defined so that positive values signify a reduction in the tax base. Note also that

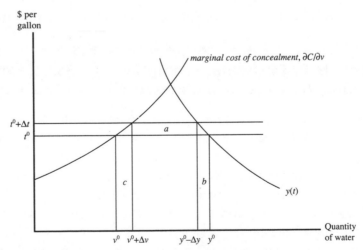

Figure 2.B.1. Relation between marginal revenue from the tax and marginal social cost.

$\Delta x = \Delta y + \Delta v$. Revenue changes from $x^0 t^0$ to $(x^0 - \Delta x)(t^0 + \Delta t)$. Ignoring products of first differences, the change in revenue becomes

$$\Delta R = x^0 \Delta t - t^0 \Delta x \tag{B2}$$

which is the area $a - b - c$. The change in welfare is

$$\Delta W = x^0 \Delta t \tag{B3}$$

which is equal to area a. Marginal social cost per unit of revenue becomes

$$\frac{\Delta W}{\Delta R} = \frac{1}{1 - \dfrac{t^0 \Delta x}{x^0 \Delta t}} = \frac{1}{1 + \epsilon_{xt}} \tag{B4}$$

which is precisely equation 4 in the text. In an economy without tax evasion, ϵ_{xt} was just the elasticity of demand for water. Now it depends on both the elasticity of demand, ϵ^D, and the elasticity of the cost of tax evasion, ϵ^C.

$$-\epsilon_{xt} = \frac{t^0 \Delta x}{x^0 \Delta t} = \frac{t^0 (\Delta y + \Delta v)}{x^0 \Delta t}$$

$$= \left(\frac{t^0 \Delta y}{y^0 \Delta t}\right)\frac{y^0}{x^0} + \left(\frac{t^0 \Delta v}{v^0 \Delta t}\right)\frac{v^0}{x^0}$$

$$= \epsilon^D(y^0/x^0) + \epsilon^C(v^0/x^0) \tag{B5}$$

where $\epsilon^D \equiv |t^0 \Delta y / y^0 \Delta t|$ and $\epsilon^C \equiv |t^0 \Delta v / v^0 \Delta t|$.

Appendix C: Derivation of Q^1, Q^2, and Q^3 in Equations 9, 10, and 12

The key assumption in the derivation of the expressions for Q^1, Q^2, and Q^3 is that the elasticity of the tax base to the tax rate is the same for both groups, the unprosperous, U and the prosperous, P. It follows that the ratio of the marginal burden of tax to the marginal tax collected is also the same for both groups. Define S to be the common value. Specifically,

$$\Delta W^U/\Delta R^U = \Delta W^P/\Delta R^P \equiv S \qquad \text{(C1)}$$

where ΔW^U and ΔW^P are the marginal costs of taxation to the two groups and ΔR^U and ΔR^P are the corresponding tax revenues.

Define T^U to be the transfer per head to the net recipients. Define T^P to be the transfer per head to the net payers; T^P could be zero and must be small enough that transfers received remain less than the group's share of the taxes to finance the transfers. Let ΔT^U be the increase in payment per head to the net recipients, and let ΔT^P be the increase (which could be negative) in payment per head to the net payers. The accounting identity between marginal public revenue and marginal public expenditure requires that

$$n^U\Delta T^U + n^P\Delta T^P = n^U\Delta R^U + n^P\Delta R^P \qquad \text{(C2)}$$

The net marginal benefit to all unprosperous people is

$$B^U \equiv (\Delta T^U - \Delta W^U)n^U \qquad \text{(C3)}$$

The net marginal cost to all prosperous people is

$$B^P \equiv (\Delta W^P - \Delta T^P)n^P \qquad \text{(C4)}$$

The ratio of total net cost to total net benefit is

$$Q = B^P/B^U = n^P(\Delta W^P - \Delta T^P)/n^U(\Delta T^U - \Delta W^U) \qquad \text{(C5)}$$

Note that in the absence of deadweight loss in taxation, the value of S would have to be 1, the values of ΔW^U and ΔR^U would have to be the same, the values of ΔW^P and ΔR^P would have to be the same as well, and it would follow immediately from equation C2 that $Q = 1$. Otherwise—when $S > 1$—the values of Q may be quite high.

The first type of transfer is defined by the property that the net receiver pays no tax and the net payer gets no transfer, specifically that $\Delta R^U = \Delta T^P = 0$, so that ΔW^U is also equal to zero and Q becomes

$$Q^1 = n^P\Delta W^P/n^U\Delta T^U = S \qquad \text{(C6)}$$

because $\Delta W^P = S\Delta R^P$ and $n^P\Delta R^P = n^U\Delta T^U$.

The second type of transfer is defined by the property that the net payer receives no transfer (that is $\Delta T^P = 0$) but both groups are taxed. Assume that each group's tax is proportional to its income, so that $\Delta R^P/\Delta R^U = y^P/y^U$. The value of Q becomes

$$
\begin{aligned}
Q^2 &= n^P\Delta W^P/n^U(\Delta T^U - \Delta W^U) \\
&= n^P\Delta R^P S/n^U(\Delta T^U - S\Delta R^U) \quad \text{(by equation C1)} \\
&= n^P\Delta R^P S/n^U\left\{\frac{n^U\Delta R^U + n^P\Delta R^P}{n^U} - S\Delta R^U\right\} \quad \text{(by equation C2)} \\
&= Sn^P y^P\{n^U y^U + n^P y^P - Sn^P y^P\} \quad \left(\text{because } \frac{\Delta R^P}{\Delta R^U} = \frac{y^P}{y^U}\right) \\
&= S\{1 - (S - 1)n^U y^U/n^P y^P\} \quad\quad\quad\quad\quad\quad\text{(C7)}
\end{aligned}
$$

which is equation 10 in the text.

In the third type the transfer is universal in the double sense that everybody pays the same rate of tax and everybody receives the same amount of transfer. The marginal tax payments are constrained so that $\Delta R^P/\Delta R^U = y^P/y^U$, and the transfer per head becomes $\Delta T^P = \Delta T^U = (n^P \Delta R^P + n^U \Delta R^U)/(n^P + n^U)$. Consequently, the value of Q is

$$
\begin{aligned}
Q^3 &= n^P(\Delta W^P - \Delta T^P)/n^U(\Delta T^U - \Delta W^U) \\
&= \frac{n^P[S\Delta R^P - (n^P\Delta R^P + n^U\Delta R^U)/(n^P + n^U)]}{n^U[(n^P\Delta R^P + n^U\Delta R^U)/(n^P + n^U) - S\Delta R^U]} \\
&= \frac{n^P[Sy^P - (n^P y^P + n^U y^U)/(n^P + n^U)]}{n^U[(n^P y^P + n^U y^U)/(n^P + n^U) - Sy^U]} \\
&= n^P(Sy^P - \bar{y})/n^U(\bar{y} - Sy^U) \quad\quad\quad\quad\quad\text{(C8)}
\end{aligned}
$$

where, by definition, $\bar{y} = (n^P y^P + n^U y^U)/(n^P + n^U)$. Equation C8 is equation 12 in the text.

Appendix D: Rent Seeking

The government proposes to let a large contract at a price that guarantees a profit (a surplus over and above the normal return to the firm) of $1 million. There are n equally eligible firms, and each eligible firm, i, can affect its probability of getting the contract by expenditure on rent seeking, R_i, to persuade officials that it is more eligible than the rest. Specifically, suppose that the probability of success of firm i is

$$p_i = R_i / \sum_{j=1}^{n} R_j \qquad \text{(D1)}$$

Note that the sum of all n of the p_i adds up to 1, as it must when the p_i are probabilities. Each firm chooses R_i to maximize its profit π_i where

$$\pi_i = (1{,}000{,}000)p_i - R_i = \frac{1{,}000{,}000 R_i}{\left(\sum_{j=1}^{n} R_j \right)} - R_i \qquad \text{(D2)}$$

Setting $\partial \pi_i / \partial R_i = 0$ implies that

$$\left[\frac{\sum_{j=1}^{n} R_j - R_i}{\left(\sum_{j=1}^{n} R_j \right)^2} \right] (1{,}000{,}000) = 1$$

which reduces to

$$R = 1{,}000{,}000 \left(\frac{n-1}{n^2} \right) \qquad \text{(D3)}$$

when all firms are alike and R is the common value of all R_i. The value of R must be 0 when $n = 1$ because the single eligible firm receives the prize automatically without the expense of rent seeking. With ten eligible firms (that is, for $n = 10$), each firm's optimal rent-seeking expenditure becomes \$90,000, so that nine-tenths of the subsidy is wasted if rent-seeking expenditure has no intrinsic social product. As n becomes very large, the value of R approaches $1{,}000{,}000/n$, so that the entire prize is wasted in rent seeking.

A different result emerges with a different probability of success function. Suppose each firm's probability of winning the prize is

$$p_i = R_i^\alpha / \sum_{j=1}^{n} R_j^\alpha \tag{D4}$$

where $0 \leqslant \alpha \leqslant 1$. Equation D2 is a special case of this formula where $\alpha = 1$. Profit, π_i, becomes

$$\pi_i = \frac{R_i^\alpha (1,000,000)}{\sum_{j=1}^{n} R_j^\alpha} - R_i$$

Setting $\partial \pi_i \partial R_i = 0$ implies that

$$\left[\frac{\left[\left(\sum_{j=1}^{n} R_j^\alpha \right) \alpha R_i^\alpha / R_i \right] - [R_i^\alpha \alpha R_i^\alpha / R_i]}{\left(\sum_{j=1}^{n} R_j^\alpha \right)^2} \right] (1,000,000) = 1$$

which reduces to

$$R = \frac{\alpha(n - 1)}{n^2} (1,000,000) \tag{D5}$$

where R is the common value of each firm's rent-seeking expenditure. Now, even as the number of firms becomes very large, the proportion of the total rent that is wasted can never exceed α. The remainder, $1 - \alpha$, accrues as a windfall profit to the eligible firms. As α approaches zero, each firm's probability of winning the prize approaches $1/n$, regardless of R_i, so that no firm has anything to gain from rent-seeking activity and there is none. There is no rent-seeking activity unless firms can influence their chances of winning the prize.

Comment   *Joel Slemrod*

I enjoyed reading this paper and was certainly stimulated by it. It is
full of gems. There really are very few academic papers where after
reading them you can honestly say that you learned something, and
I learned something from this paper.

There is both a plot and a theme to this paper. The plot is that the
course of calculating the cost of taxation only begins with the
resource costs, then winds its way through the deadweight costs,
which academic economists are now accustomed to taking seriously,
but then must visit a whole host of other costs. Professor Usher
delineates eight. The implication is that these eight may be as large
as the others, although they are certainly more slippery to quantify.

The theme of the paper is that to understand the effect of taxation
or revenue raising on an economy, a description of the tax rates, the
tax bases, and rules is insufficient. One requires a description of the
entire tax system, which also includes how the tax rules are enforced,
how they are administered, and the institutional mechanism for
collecting revenues. Recognizing the importance of administration

and enforcement often changes our views of what is an optimal or at least a reasonable tax structure.

In my brief remarks I want to try to draw out some of the implications of this change in perspective for tax policy. I want to address three issues. First, how does one measure the total cost of collecting revenue, including all the hidden costs addressed in this paper, or, even more important, what is the total marginal cost of raising revenue? After all, it is the marginal cost that should be set against the marginal benefit of government spending to determine the appropriate size of the government sector.

Second, how does the consideration of these hidden costs change our view of what an optimal tax structure is? Finally, I want to talk a little bit about a research agenda that would accompany taking these hidden costs seriously.

Let me begin with a measurement issue. Professor Usher offers us a cogent argument that in the presence of tax evasion and avoidance, the loss to society—the deadweight loss—of taxing a good is approximated by a triangle the area of which is approximately equal to one-half times the tax rate times the change in (let's say the taxed good is labor supply) taxed labor supply.

This is, of course, the famous Harberger triangle, but the new perspective offered here is the claim that it doesn't matter whether the change in taxed labor supply is due to people's shifting from labor to leisure or to people's simply reporting less labor income to the authorities. It's the change in taxable, or reported-to-the-tax-authorities, labor supply that matters.

In either case (resorting to leisure or resorting to simply not reporting the labor), the taxpayer pursues the alternative to taxable labor until its marginal cost per dollar of tax saved is just equal to one. When the alternative is leisure, the cost to society is an inefficiently large amount of leisure consumed. When it is avoidance, the cost is an excess amount of resources spent on hiding income and avoiding detection.

When the alternative to taxed labor supply is evasion, the way to think about the cost to society may not be obvious. After all, the taxpayer simply doesn't report the labor income to the authorities. But the fact that evasion is limited implies some cost to the individual that offsets the benefits at the margin. A standard way to model this is to assume that by evading tax liability the taxpayer is exposing himself to some risk of detection and penalty. In an economic model of evasion, evasion is pursued until at the margin the tax saving is equal to the disutility of the uncertainty of being subject to a penalty.

What worries me about the enumeration of different costs of taxation is that there is a danger of double counting. Let me try to explain what I mean with an example.

One of the costs of taxation listed in this paper is the administrative cost of running an enforcement system. You need tax collection agents, you need jails, you need judges to decide whether tax understatement is negligence or fraud, and so on.

If you consider that cost, however, I think you also have to consider the fact that the return to evasion is thereby lower than it is otherwise. The higher the probability of detection, because there are more agents and more judges and more jails, the lower is the return to a given act of evasion.

As Professor Usher mentions, one way to limit the deadweight cost of evasion is to have a very high penalty on evasion. There is a line you find in a lot of economic models of evasion to the effect that the way to eliminate evasion with little deadweight or no deadweight cost is to have the death penalty for tax evasion. If people are at risk of incurring the death penalty, even if it's instituted only once a year or even less often, that should be enough to keep people from evading. In fact, it doesn't even matter whether the person executed is an evader or not. You just say he's an evader and put him to death, and that should be it for evading.

The point is that the design of the enforcement system, including the penalties and the probability of detection, reduces the return to evasion. So if you're going to consider the cost of running the enforcement system, you have to take into account how that would affect the amount of evasion.

In fact, you could conceive of using high penalties as a way to reduce the potential deadweight loss of excessive leisure. I think that probably characterizes the Soviet system, where it may be a punishable offense not to work a certain number of hours. Such a system will surely limit the deadweight loss to raising revenue.

Let's take this a step further. Imagine that the enforcement system is appropriately designed so that the more you evade, the higher is the probability that you'll be caught. That's the kind of enforcement system one would want, because it increases the marginal cost to evasion. A potential evader has to consider not only the fact that there's some probability of being caught but also the fact that, at the margin, an extra amount of evasion increases the probability of being caught and therefore the return at the margin to evasion is lower.

Professor Usher notes this problem in his discussion of bribery in the granting of doctors' licenses. He says that if the penalty or the probability of being caught and assessed a penalty is positively related to the amount of bribery, that is an extra marginal cost to bribery and will reduce the amount and the social cost of bribery.

In other words, in calculating the excess burden of an enforcement system and a tax-raising system, one should not assume that the enforcement system is an inefficient one. We are used to thinking in these terms about tax rates. We know that a given amount of revenue can be raised with a high excess burden or with a low excess burden. The higher the marginal tax rates implicit in the tax system, the higher is the excess burden. If we could raise all our revenue with lump-sum taxes, there would be no incentive to hide extra income, and there would be no excess burden. If we raised it with high marginal tax rates, there would be a lot of excess burden. The analogy to a tax enforcement system is that we'll have a higher excess burden if we have a silly enforcement system where the probability of penalty and detection is not related to the amount of evasion. We'll have a lower excess burden if the system is cleverly designed so that the probability of detection and penalty is positively related to the evasion. I think there's a perfect analogy between the design of the tax structure itself and the design of the enforcement system.

The bottom line of all this is that one has to be careful to consider the interaction among these costs. Nowhere in the paper is it said that one should just add up these costs. It is said that we're enumerating the costs. But if we're talking about the total cost of taxation and the marginal costs, a simple adding up of these costs may not be appropriate.

Let me mention a couple of other issues in measuring the marginal cost of raising revenue. If this is to be the beginning of a growth industry, we have to face the tough issue of how to quantify these "hidden" costs of raising revenue.

This is a very tricky issue, because it is often not clear when you have many instruments for a tax system, including not only the rates and the bases but also the enforcement system, whether a particular change in policy will increase or decrease the marginal cost of taxation. For example, if you simplify the tax system in a certain way, will that increase or decrease the cost of raising revenue? Let me try to challenge your intuition. Imagine you have a tax system with a particular tax credit for which the eligibility requirements are very complicated to understand.

Suppose the government is considering making this credit easier to understand. If one of the results of the complexity has been that many people who are eligible for the credit don't bother to take it and now we simplify the instructions so everybody understands it, more people will take the credit, and they will spend time and money to calculate their credit. Thus the resource cost of the tax system goes up.

What this suggests is that we really need a multidimensional measure of the success of a tax system. In my example, simplifying the instructions may increase the cost in taxpayers' time and money in determining how much credit they qualify for, but it may also increase the success of the tax system by some other criterion, such as horizontal equity.

A related random thought on interaction is whether our knowledge of the institutions of certain countries leads us to think that the hidden costs of taxation in some countries are higher than in others.

If so, does that mean that the hidden benefits of expenditures are higher also, or does it mean that they are lower than otherwise, in which case these hidden costs compound to reduce the attractiveness of government spending rather than offset it?

Let me turn to the policy implications of the hidden costs of taxation. The academic public finance community has spent the better part of the past two decades on the question of how to design a tax structure to minimize the first of the eight costs enumerated in this paper, the distortionary costs. This endeavor has been christened the theory of optimal taxation. In some cases minimizing this first distortionary cost is taken to be the only objective of the tax system. In other versions this goal must be balanced against distributional concerns.

Having read this paper, we now realize that the theory of optimal taxation deals only with the tip of the iceberg. A truly optimal tax system should seek to minimize the sum of these eight types of costs (being careful to avoid double counting) subject, perhaps, to distributional concerns. What would an optimal tax system look like when all eight costs are considered?

Unfortunately, we're a long way from knowing the answer to this question. This is just the beginning of a growth industry, after all. But I suspect that in this room there's a lot of knowledge born of experience and thought on this question. So in the spirit of eliciting that knowledge, let me offer some unproven theorems on optimal tax systems in the presence of eight types of costs of taxation rather than one.

My first theorem is that a low-rate, low-allowance tax system is better than a high-rate, high-allowance tax system. Low rates with low allowances reduce the rent or return to any given allowance. If the tax rate is lower, the value of obtaining a special tax break for your particular activity is lower. A lower tax rate also reduces the incentive for evasion and avoidance, at least at certain margins. Going to a low-rate, low-allowance system, however, does not reduce the return to some kinds of evasion: it doesn't matter whether you have a high-rate, high-allowance system or a low-rate, low-allowance system if the decision contemplated is not to file a return at all.

Theorem two. Holding other things constant, the smaller the number and dispersion of tax rates, the better. This is true within a consumption tax, say a value-added tax—the smaller the number of differentiated rates, the better. It's true within a graduated income tax system, where the rates correspond to different brackets. And it's true within a corporation tax system.

The reason I offer this theorem is not because of the directly lower compliance costs of fewer rates. To illustrate what I mean, remember the recent tax reform in the United States, when it was often suggested that moving from fourteen income tax brackets to three would be a good idea because it would simplify the tax system directly, meaning that it would take the typical taxpayer less time to determine his tax liability. Of course, if you think about that, the upper bound to the time saving of moving from fourteen to three brackets is about a second, because the hard part is to obtain the correct figure for taxable income. Once you've got taxable income, you just refer to the tax table, where you don't know or care whether there are three rates or fourteen rates.

The reason I do offer this theorem is because the smaller number of rates reduces the payoff to shifting money across individuals and across firms. It reduces the payoff to having it look as if your kids are earning the family's money instead of you. It reduces the payoff to what's known generally as tax arbitrage, where interest deductions show up in high tax brackets and the receipt of interest and capital income appear in low tax brackets.

The overinvoicing problem is also reduced. My first institutional example for Mexico is that there was a time when a particular sector was subject to a 3½ percent gross revenue tax while other sectors were subject to a 42 percent corporate tax rate on net income. The average tax rate for these different sectors was about the same, but at the margin an extra dollar of reported sales cost three and a half cents in taxes to those firms that were subject to the gross revenue tax, but a dollar of reported expense saved forty-two cents for those firms subject to the corporate income tax. Therefore, there was a tremendous incentive for overinvoicing on transactions between these two different kinds of firms, because a phony invoice could save one firm forty-two cents while costing the other only three and a half cents. There are also many different examples, in a value-added or consumption tax framework, where different rates poison the entire consumption tax system.

Theorem three isn't really a theorem. It's more like an important sentence for a textbook in public finance. The enforcement and administration of a tax system should be given at least as much attention as the statutory rates and bases. A properly designed enforcement system can be thought of as increasing the average tax rate while decreasing the marginal tax rate on declaring tax liability.

Earlier I said that in analyzing the cost of a tax system, you want to make sure you're not assuming a silly administrative and enforcement system. Instead you should assume one as clever as it is in reality, where the more you evade or avoid, the higher is the chance that you'll be caught and subject to penalty. You can think of that as decreasing the marginal cost of declaring tax liability, which we all know will reduce the excess burden of any given tax structure.

How much enforcement should we have? That's a tough issue. The Internal Revenue Service in this country tells us that for every dollar we give to the IRS, it can produce ten dollars more in revenue. The number I heard in Mexico—this is institutional example number two—is 25 to 1. They think that for every extra dollar their enforcement bureau gets, it can produce twenty-five dollars more.

These are tempting numbers in countries where there are deficits. The optimal rule, however, for how much enforcement there should be is definitely *not* to push it until the tax collection agency receives one dollar at the margin for every dollar spent. The reason that's not the optimal rule is that the dollar you collect is a transfer from the private sector to the public sector. That is not a gain to society. The cost, however, is a true resource cost. In calculating the correct rule for how much enforcement there is, one has to calculate correctly the marginal benefit of transferring money from the private to the public sector. That is a tricky issue. One should consider not only the optimal degree of enforcement but the optimal structure of an enforcement system.

My final theorem is that rules are better than discretion. Case-by-case resolution of tax matters invites corruption and also causes uncertainty about true tax liability, which affects long-term decisions. And adherence to rules is arguably less susceptible to special interests. One implication of this theorem is that either an income tax or a consumption tax is better than a hybrid tax where there's no clear concept behind the tax rules.

The last thing I want to talk about is the research agenda. If this is the beginning of a growth industry, we should focus on what our agenda for this growth industry ought to be. In my opinion, the focus ought to be on the technology of collecting taxes. This is an important change in perspective for academic public finance, which, as the empirical counterpart to optimal taxation theory, has focused heretofore on the structure of individual preferences.

The change in perspective to the technology of collecting taxes is an exciting and challenging change in perspective. It's exciting, I think, because technology changes all the time. Just as the technology of making steel has changed a lot in the last half-century, so has the technology of both collecting and avoiding taxes changed.

That means that what was an optimal tax system twenty years ago is no longer an optimal tax system and what is likely to be an optimal tax system twenty years from now is probably different from what it is now. In the United States the technology available to the IRS is very different from what it was just ten years ago. The ability of the IRS to match information from individuals' returns to individuals' reports is much greater than it was. That changes the optimal enforcement structure.

This is also a challenging change in perspective because it requires the rethinking of the entire direction of empirical and theoretical research. The change in the direction of empirical research should be away from the structure of preferences to the technology of collecting taxes, which includes measuring the hidden costs of taxation in total and at the margin and understanding the effectiveness of alternative tax enforcement schemes and how the structure of the tax system interacts with these issues.

The theoretical change in direction is also profound. One should focus on the optimal enforcement structure. As I said, both the level and the structure of a given level of enforcement are important. What is the optimal tax structure when there is a possibility of corruption and rent seeking? How should we design a tax system when we know it's inevitable that there will be some corruption and some rent seeking? These are interesting questions, and we've just begun to think about what the right answers are.

In conclusion, if this seminar does not represent the birth of an academic growth industry, it should.

Discussion

JOHN WHALLEY: I have three comments on the paper. First, I think it would be helpful for Dan to clarify the meaning of his paper's title. Although the paper is entitled "The Hidden Costs of Public Expenditure," 99 percent of both the paper and Joel's comments seemed to be about taxes. This is appropriate, I suppose, if you are simply saying that a hidden cost of public expenditures comes from their financing.

The title of your paper, however, suggests more than this. What it might deliver that is in accordance with its title and the thrust of this seminar is greater attention to *what* the expenditures *are* in developing countries. After all, the distribution of expenditures among categories or expenditure purposes—the form of their public sectors—is strikingly different between developing and developed countries.

In contrast to the public expenditures of industrialized countries, transfer programs are typically quite small as a proportion of the total expenditures of the governments of less-developed countries, which also have quite limited health care programs and spend only a bit more on education but have very large military expenditures. The last are probably the greatest source of deadweight loss in most developing countries. At the same time, in some countries military expenditure might be essential to any semblance of political stability and to the realization of the benefits that stability enables. Suppose that the distribution of a country's public expenditures greatly changed—say, a combination of substantial cuts in military expenditures and sizable increases in transfer programs—and that its total public expenditures, tax revenues, and budget deficit stayed the same. In these circumstances, would the deadweight loss experienced by the country—its hidden cost of public expenditures—have increased or decreased? I cannot discern the answer in Dan's paper.

Second, on the tax side, the discussion was very heavily about formal taxes, but the import of this seminar is its focus on quasi taxes. I would welcome clarification of the reasons for this juxtaposition.

Third, I think it is extremely important to put your discussion of marginal excess burdens and marginal cost of taxes and so on in the developing country context, taking into account the set of taxes that it is feasible for their governments to collect.

In some very low income African countries, for example, 60 to 70 percent of government revenues come from trade taxes. One reason for this—for the relatively low contributions of income and corporate taxes, as well as the absence of a broadly based sales tax—is that they are severely restricted by administrative feasibility. In some instances, of course, political infeasibility is misunderstood as administrative infeasibility. Nonetheless, by ignoring administrative feasibility, your discussion of marginal welfare cost calculations as if they are applicable in that way to developing countries can perhaps be a little misleading.

MAXWELL FRY: I have three short points. First, as a preface, I think Malcolm Gillis, Arnold Harberger, and Adam Smith would disagree that this is the birth of something new. Mention of Adam Smith brings me to one of the two principles Joel enunciated. In *The Wealth of Nations* you'll see quite clearly that Smith enunciated the principle that tax certainty is a very important key to an efficient tax system.

In his evaluation of all the tremendous amount of work that economists have put into calculating effective rates of protection, Harberger suggests that all these calculations show that a uniform import duty is the only sensible tax system for imports. Even a very few different tax rates produce different rates of effective protection that one cannot foresee. With any new product, there will be a different product mix; so there is no way of forecasting what the effective rate of protection will be. Those two principles have been rather well established. My third point concerns bribery. One of the things that I would like to know, because I'm not in public finance, is how you evaluate the social benefit, if any, of the legal profession. It seems to me that there's some trade-off here. You can try to avoid bribery, and then you have to go to a lawyer to fix your problems, and in my mind that's a fairly negative type of expenditure. Furthermore, and I think this applies to the federal government in the United States at the present time, salaries are so low that you might be improving the quality of employees if you had direct payment to them rather than to the legal profession.

MICHAEL McKEE: Something John Whalley said anticipated something I had planned to talk a little about this afternoon, which is that there is a link between the hidden cost of explicit taxes and the hidden cost of hidden taxes.

John said that explicit public expenditures in developing countries are largely military, but much of the public sector in these countries does not appear in their budgets. Included among these, for example, are state enterprises and goals of the public sector that are met through regulation and interest rate controls.

There are two questions about that, it seems to me. One is, Are these goals sensible? The second is, Assuming for the moment that they are sensible, is there a better way to achieve these goals? Presumably the alternative to achieving the goals through hidden means is to achieve them through explicit taxes and expenditures.

In that case, we are really trading off, in a sort of comparative, "function-neutral" analysis, between achieving goals through hidden spending and hidden taxes and achieving them through explicit taxes and spending. In that case, we're going to get into calculations not of the deadweight loss or the total losses but of the net gain or loss in deadweight loss and what-not of these eight different costs from shifting from one sort of public sector to another.

MR. WHALLEY: It seems to me that the magnitude of tax evasion in a country will very much affect which sort of public sector is opted for and thus the extent to which the government employs hidden rather than formal taxes. This point is exemplified by the sizable literature on how disastrous the income tax is in India.

Surveys suggest that 75 to 80 percent of all income tax auditors in India take bribes. In consequence, the amount of revenue raised from the tax is so small that the government does not even factor it into its budgets. So it's just as though that formal tax has been entirely plucked out of the system. The attitude that now seems to prevail is that we don't really need to worry about it because it's a nonimportant tax.

RICHARD BIRD: We have to be careful not to confuse the fact that we may not collect any revenue from some tax with the fact that there may be an enormous amount of distortion introduced into the system because of the existence of this tax that produces no revenue and from all the efforts and maneuvers people go through to make sure that we don't have any revenue. Just because something is not important in revenue terms does not mean it's not important. That's the whole point of this conference.

CHARLES McLURE: I just want to make a small technical correction to Joel's comment about the importance of reducing the number of tax rates. It's not really the number of rates that matters but the spread of the tax rates. If you have a very smooth progression of rates of one percentage point at a time from 10 to 50 percent, there's not much incentive for moving between the 10 and 11 percent rates.

If you have a rate structure of 10 percent, 35 percent, and 50 percent, however, and you can move between the 10 and the 35 percent rates or the 10 and the 50 percent rates, there is lots of money to be made. With few rates, over some range, it's going to be like a flat-rate system. But over the range where it jumps, the jumps are big. It's really the compression, not just the number of rates, that matters.

JOEL SLEMROD: I accept that amendment to my theorem.

DWIGHT LEE: There's a comment in the paper to which I'd like to respond. The comment is that "a listing of hidden costs may serve as an antidote to the tendency on the part of departments of government to promote activities on the grounds that benefits exceed resource costs, ignoring hidden costs that may exceed resource costs by a significant margin."

I think there's some truth to that, but I want to be a bit of a pessimist and say that most political decision makers know about these costs, see them as benefits, and have exploited all the opportunities they offer. But to the extent that they don't, telling them about these costs may actually encourage them to spend more, again because many of these hidden costs offer benefits to political decision makers.

Rent seeking is the most obvious example; bribery and corruption also constitute profitable opportunities for political decision makers. Politicians have probably already exploited most of the opportunities available. But if they haven't, it's not clear that informing them will make things better.

MR. BIRD: The public choice, political economy perspective is extremely important in this seminar, but I would just raise the question whether what we're talking about is informing politicians or informing society. It seems to me there's quite a difference.

ALVIN RABUSHKA: Dan Usher has written two papers. From the standpoint of this seminar, particularly with respect to its focus on the developing world, we might be better served if he had written only one paper. The first paper enumerates the hidden costs of expenditure, chiefly taxation, and the second paper enumerates Usher's social philosophy about government activity. The deletion of some sections could result in a better paper. I'll mention these in order of their appearance in its first several pages.

First, he says that civilized society requires a large public sector. Absolutely false. It does not. Hong Kong, Taiwan, Singapore, and Korea are all very civilized societies. They all have small public sectors. Indeed, they're more civilized than several Western European societies that have very large public sectors.

The four Asian tigers may have large public sectors in absolute terms, but this results from 10 percent growth in real terms over several decades. By taxing a constant portion of 15 to 20 percent of gross national product of a rapidly expanding economy, the public sector grows quickly in dollar terms. But when you try to finance a society you can't afford through massive redistribution, you end up with lower growth rates and, in the long run, a less civilized public sector.

Second, Usher tells us that citizens demand redistribution. I don't believe that citizens demand redistribution. A class of people who hold to a certain social philosophy demand redistribution. I believe that what citizens demand is rising after-tax incomes to maximize their discretionary purchases. This result is maximized by high rates of economic growth. Usher argues convincingly in his paper that distribution that entails high taxes adversely affects growth through these deadweight losses.

I would also quarrel with his notion that speculation makes little else but millionaires. A large body of literature exists that suggests that speculation plays a vital role in creating economic opportunities.

In addition, Usher states that the distribution of income is an important benefit of public expenditure. I regard that statement as a personal value. I don't think that government attempts to equalize the distribution of income constitute an important benefit of public expenditure. In the developing world, which is what we're focused on, the two best examples of long-run improvement in income distribution are Taiwan and Korea, which have emphasized high rates of growth and low rates of public expenditure, emphasizing infrastructure over transfers.

Then Usher mentions that nothing in his paper should lead one to presume that the growth in the public sector is unwarranted. I think the whole paper repudiates that doctrine.

Usher tells us that the bigger government gets, the greater the wedge that is driven between the marginal cost to the taxpayer and the marginal tax rates, particularly as rates increase. But then he says this wedge may be acceptable because there's so much a modern government must do.

The 1980s reveal all over the world that governments have done too much. Whether you look in Western Europe or a number of developing countries, it's quite clear that governments today are trying to do less rather than more. As long as you have high rates of growth, the government can painlessly afford to do more. But when the economy grows slowly or stagnates, it absolutely can't.

Now to some more controversial items.

Where Dan refers to the possibility of humiliating recipients of welfare, I think that such a raising of the price of getting a free ride in society is warranted. It would lower the demand for transfers, thus lowering the requirements for public expenditure and taxation and lowering deadweight cost. His description of the adverse effects of welfare is a gross underestimate. The literature on that topic reveals the growth of a welfare dependency culture with very high adverse effects.

Finally, I would strongly disagree with the notion that there's any justification for investing in a depressed region because that is an alternative to welfare. Let people move from low-value-added to high-value-added activities.

In some sense Usher redeems himself on the last page, in the very last sentence of his paper, when he says that laissez-faire is more appropriate in the third world, even though the major thrust of the paper revolves around the welfare norms of the first world.

My recommendation is to blue-pencil out the areas I've mentioned, leave the rest of the analysis intact, and the paper will be significantly improved.

DAN USHER: There is an unfortunate tendency for debate about the size of the public sector to polarize into left and right camps. The left, in this caricature, places the entire emphasis on the benefits of public sector activity—on "needs" that "must" be met—the implicit assumption being that the costs are borne by a shadowy class of filthy-rich taxpayers whose consumption can be greatly reduced with no ill effects on the rest of society. The right points to the money that taxpayers can expect to save if tax rates are reduced, without reference to the accompanying reduction in public services, the implicit assumption being either that the reduction in revenue would be matched by an elimination of waste in the public sector or that society is already on the wrong side of the Laffer curve. One side sees benefit and no cost. The other sees cost and no benefit.

I see little merit in either of these positions. One way or another everybody pays taxes. If there is large-scale waste in government, it would be unreasonable to suppose that reductions in revenue would lead to the elimination of waste rather than of useful public services. Nor is there evidence that I am aware of that the American economy, for example, is on the wrong side of the Laffer curve. Greedy bureaucrats would be the first to lobby for tax reduction if that were so.

The polarization of the debate is unfortunate because the size of government should be determined as a byproduct of an analysis of expenditures one by one. Just as it should be incumbent on those who advocate increases in public sector activity to couple their advocacy with a statement of which taxes might be raised (and by how much) to pay for the new services, so should it be incumbent on the tax reducers to say what public sector activities they are prepared to give up.

My task for this seminar was to write about the cost of public expenditure. In discharging this task, I was particularly concerned to avoid being seen as adopting a style of analysis in which government is treated as a parasite gorging funds from the productive economy and providing nothing in return. That is Alvin's social philosophy. It was not part of my task to say how large the government ought to be. The central proposition of the paper is that the hidden cost of public expenditure can be large in relation to the overt or resource cost. In making this point, I need not belittle or deny the benefits of public expenditure. In fact, marginal benefit must be as large as marginal cost when the size of the public sector is appropriately chosen, regardless of whether the appropriate share of government in the GNP is 16 percent, as Alvin believes it should be, or approximately 40 percent, as it is in the United States today. My list of the appropriate functions of government is perhaps a little longer than Alvin's list, but we would, I presume, agree that some core of public expenditures are worth the price.

Although the issue does not bear directly on the enumeration and quantification of the costs of public expenditure, I should say a word in defence of the proposition that "citizens in a democracy demand a certain amount of redistribution." I use "demand," of course, in the economists' sense of the term. I do not mean that the majority of voters are clamoring for more redistribution than is currently provided. I mean no more than that citizens "demand" redistribution in the same sense that they "demand" food and clothing. They demand redistribution in the sense that they are prepared to pay the price. They demand redistribution by voting for political parties committed to maintaining redistributive programs. I see no majority in Canada or the United States that is committed to the abolition of the old-age pension (redistribution from young to old), unemployment insurance, welfare to the destitute, and a degree of public provision of medical care. If a substantial majority of voters disapproved of such programs, then surely one of the major political parties would have come out against them.

Against this view of mine that a majority of voters get more or less what they want, one might adopt, as Alvin appears to do, the essentially Marxist position that voters, deluded with false consciousness or thwarted by the special interests of dominant classes in society, are incapable of perceiving or incapable of acting on their true interest as identified by those who understand the course of history. Though unsympathetic to this position, I cannot assert that it is entirely wrong, for the study of the hidden cost of public expenditure is an attempt to replace ignorance with knowledge (or with less complete ignorance) within a limited domain. Nor can I deny that bureaucrats seeking to expand their empires or well-financed interest groups can put one over on the general public from time to time. It is quite another matter to suppose that ordinary voters are cheated, pressured, or bamboozled by secret forces into a public sector of 40 percent of the GNP when 16 percent is all they really want. The proposition is especially hard to swallow when one allows for the possibility that public programs beneficial to and desired by the poorer half of the population may have been forestalled by the political influence of the rich.

A distinction should be drawn in this context between size and growth. Like Alvin, I see a trend of public opinion against redistribution, but I interpret the trend as meaning that many voters would like to stop the growth of redistributive expenditure as a share of GNP or would welcome some reduction in the share. I do not see a majority in favor of eliminating such expenditures altogether, as would be necessary to reduce government's share to 16 percent. As I said, no major political party has espoused such a program. My reading of the history of public finance over the period since the second world war is that public expenditure in general and redistributive expenditure in particular grew substantially because most voters wanted them to grow, because they preferred to have what the government could supply rather than what their tax dollars would have bought instead. The change of opinion, as I perceive it, might be a consequence of the growth of the public sector. It does not imply that redistribution was never popular. It does not augur for the complete elimination of redistributive expenditure. I see no reason to modify my statement that citizens demand redistribution.

Alvin chides me for not devoting enough attention to the adverse effects of welfare. I did mention the problem and refer in a note to as lurid an account of the evils of welfare dependency as anyone could wish for. I take the problem seriously and fear we may be doing our society considerable harm by encouraging illegitimacy, idleness, and crime. This is an area, however, where what I have been calling left-right analysis can be especially misleading. The costs of welfare are undoubtedly real and substantial. That does not imply that the benefits are spurious. The alternative to welfare is—to put the matter bluntly—the abject poverty or death by starvation of the widow or unmarried mother with three kids, in the event that the sympathy and condescension of the likes of Alvin Rabushka and Dan Usher prove insufficient to provide the private charity required to keep all such people alive. Reform of welfare requires consideration of costs *and* benefits.

Like most participants at this seminar, I have a personal hit list of public expenditures I would like to see eliminated because they are not worth the costs or because I see them as corrosive to democratic government. To have such a list does not commit one to denying that many public expenditures are worth the costs, that there are many potential departures from efficiency in the private sector that can only be rectified by the government, or that the majority of people in most democratic countries do favor a certain amount of redistributive activity. It is one thing to weigh benefits of public expenditures against cost. It is quite another to assert that there are no benefits at all.

MR. BIRD: I think that was a helpful interchange. May I note, also coming from up north, that even though we don't have an army, we do manage to spend it somehow.

MR. USHER: Yes.

[Laughter]

WARREN BROOKES: Complementing, I think, Alvin's observations are Colin Campbell's recent analyses of two neighboring states, Vermont and New Hampshire. They started out from approximately the same income picture twenty years ago, one pursuing a more central government approach, the other pursuing the traditional local government nontax approach; one state, Vermont, with all the panoply of taxes, sales tax, income tax, the other one with none.

What intrigues me is that while income has been falling and the inequality of its distribution has been rising in Vermont, the opposite has occurred over the twenty years in New Hampshire. In fact, New Hampshire, with the lowest tax burden of this country's fifty states— in which there are no state income taxes and no state sales taxes— has the fastest rising per capita income in the country.

MR. BIRD: So New Hampshire is the Hong Kong of the United States?

MR. BROOKES: Yes.

MR. BIRD: And like Hong Kong, it is right next to a large and growing market.

More generally, I think it is important to recognize what Dan's paper did, and did not, attempt to do. Each of us might wish he had addressed our favorite topic within the confines of his paper, but had he satisfied all our desires he would have presented a book, instead of a paper, to this seminar. For instance, part of Alvin Rabushka's comments reflect a belief that dynamic, rather than static, welfare analysis is what is most important. Although Dan's paper is confined to essentially static welfare analysis, he certainly sets the stage for anyone wishing to expand his analysis by introducing the dimension of time.

Likewise, Warren Brookes's remarks raise another aspect not explicitly discussed in Dan's paper—whether the economy is open or not. Would it make much difference if we had an open economy? Let me illustrate the point. Suppose we have an open economy. We impose some sort of a tax on capital. All our capital flees. We do not collect any revenue from the capital tax. Is there then any excess burden—or any of the excessive burdens discussed by Dan? Does capital flight increase or decrease the excess burden in any meaningful sense in this society?

Another aspect that might warrant greater attention is that there are not only efficiency effects of these excess burdens but distributional effects. How the system adjusts to particular policy instruments can have strong distributional as well as allocative effects. Both distributional and allocative effects underlie one piece of advice I used to give people in developing countries—that you always have to have some loophole, so to speak, some place where avoiders and evaders can go, and it's better if it's not offshore, because if they go offshore, you've lost everything. I don't know what Dan's analysis says with respect to that rather pragmatic piece of policy advice, but I just wanted to throw it in.

MR. LEE: One hidden cost of government spending that might be given greater emphasis in the paper arises from the sheer ineptitude of government spending.

It's extremely costly to transfer income. If you're more precise about the objective and want government to transfer income from the wealthy to the poor, you might argue that the cost is near infinity. There just doesn't seem to be any compelling evidence that, despite massive government programs that at least purported to equalize the distribution of income, there's been much if any effect on the distribution of income at all over the past twenty or thirty years. So another aspect of the costliness of achieving certain objectives through government is simply the inability of government to achieve those objectives.

CHRISTOPHE CHAMLEY: The statement that the government cannot redistribute income to the poor efficiently may be true in the long run. But in the short run it warrants closer examination. Each time governments have tried to reduce subsidies, food subsidies, we have riots; obviously there is a little bit of transfer occurring that can be efficient in the short run.

MR. LEE: Yes, but of course that doesn't mean you've effected a transfer to those people. It just means you've changed the incentives. They've responded to them. Maybe there's no net transfer, but they responded to the rules that exist, and there are certainly going to be losses if you change those rules.

MALCOLM GILLIS: Or at least the *perception* of losses. Not all the losses perceived are in fact incurred. In a lot of countries, you find that urban transport subsidies in state-owned enterprises result in services so unreliable that the poor don't use them. In the Philippines and other countries they use private lines, because they get better service.

MR. CHAMLEY: I started by saying that there's a difference between the short run and the long run; I agree that in the long run it's a debatable issue.

MR. FRY: I want to comment on Richard Bird's point about capital flight. If you go through David Ricardo's *Principles* to find out what he had to say about Ricardian equivalence, which he clearly refutes, he has a very nice point about tax burdens in an open economy. In it he says that if government expenditure rises too much and the "burthen," as he calls it, becomes too great, people will reluctantly leave the place of their birth and move elsewhere. That's fine. The problem in this world today is that there are some restrictions on labor mobility, and that's where the problem of capital mobility comes in. If you can't move labor along with capital out of the country, then there is inefficiency that may not exist if everybody is free to leave.

MR. BIRD: Let me give you two quotations in reply. One is my own: The rise of the income tax is directly correlated with the rise of the passport. The second one, from Adam Smith, is that of all pieces of luggage, none is more difficult to transport than man.

MR. WHALLEY: Returning to Dwight Lee's statement that all the evidence shows that attempts to redistribute income have no effect, I'd like to know just what evidence you're referring to.

The papers I've heard on U.S. income distribution statistics show fairly clearly that with cuts in expenditure programs during the Reagan years, there has been a rise in Gini coefficients, reflecting increased inequality. It may not be that huge, but it's clearly discernible in income distribution data.

There's also a change in the nature and concentration of poverty, which is increasingly in single-parent households with children. This pattern of poverty does appear to have changed, and you can find similar outcomes in other countries over periods of ten, fifteen years, where there have been comparable policy changes.

MR. LEE: The evidence I've seen is that if you look at the percentage of total income going to the different quintiles, it's almost stationary over long, long periods of time. If you look at particular programs or particular groups, you might find that in particular programs of transferred income, particular groups have benefited. But if you look at the overall transfer activities of government, they don't seem to have had any noticeable effect on the distribution of income, at least as shown by these quintile figures.

In a way, that's not surprising. If you think of the political process as just another competitive arena, there's no reason to believe that people who haven't been able to compete effectively in the market are going to be any more capable of competing effectively in the political arena. For every program that helps the poor or is put forth in the name of helping the poor, a whole host of other people come in and, through legislative log rolling, get programs that have absolutely nothing to do with helping the poor and in fact do exactly the opposite. So the political competition that results doesn't seem to be biased in favor of the poor.

MR. GILLIS: I would have thought that by now we had no excuses for talking about income distribution across all income groups in this country and Canada. I would have thought that we would be focusing on income distribution among age cohorts, instead of what we fiscal economists have been doing for years, in looking across the entire distribution. When somebody shows me convincing income distribution data across age cohorts I'll be more interested in the evidence.

MR. BIRD: In his paper Dan cites many quantitative estimates of different costs and tells us how shaky they are. Joel, in turn, raised some good questions about the interaction of these costs and therefore the appropriateness of adding them together. And of course all these estimates were done for first world countries.

The conclusion of Dan's paper contends that his analysis may be more appropriate in the third world than in the first, that Adam Smith would feel much more at home in the streets of Taipei than in New York. I think that's true. But the question is, if we think about making estimates like this in the third world, what would be our a priori expectation? Would we expect these numbers to be higher or lower? I can think of things going either way in any one country and both ways in a set of countries.

Another point, which was raised earlier by John Whalley, is that Dan's paper and this discussion have largely been about what we can see, feel, and taste—taxes—and not about what we're really supposed to be focusing on here, things that are much like taxes but we don't know they're there unless we make a real point of thinking about it, the so-called implicit or hidden taxes. Most of the costs Dan discussed related to the explicit tax system. If one tried to measure similar costs with respect to implicit taxes, would we expect to see the same pattern? Would we expect to see rising marginal costs from exploiting each way, whether explicit or implicit, of achieving policy objectives? To put the argument back into the political economy context that Dwight Lee was trying to get us in earlier, suppose you have a government that's trying to do something like stay in power or keep the state together or pay off its friends. It doesn't matter what they're trying to do. They have a set of governing instruments or tools they can use to accomplish these different objectives. Some of these tools are obvious and explicit, some of them are not. The government is facing a set of marginal political costs of raising revenue, spending money, or regulating in various ways, and they're calculating what to do.

If that's what's going on, then one would expect the mix of policies in different countries to reflect the basic problems of achieving political balance in each country. Perhaps we should get these economists out of the room and get some political scientists in here who are supposed to know something about such matters. But if this is the case, do the quantitative measures emphasized by Usher matter terribly? Are the right marginal costs being measured? The marginal political cost of decision makers can be quite different from the marginal social costs discussed in Dan's paper.

ROBERT HIGGS: I'd like to follow up on what you're saying. I have great sympathy with what Dwight Lee and Alvin Rabushka had to say a while back, but the focus on rent seeking and the recognition of its prevalence in all societies—subject to different constraints because they have different institutions—leads most people to emphasize the waste, losses, harms, and hurts of various kinds that people with more political clout are able to impose on those with less. Although I accept that general picture of the workings of any polity, it's important at the same time to realize that what may appear to be rent-seeking behavior may take on a quite different coloration if we understand the political context differently.

Consider, for example, that some organized group might go to the government, officially or unofficially, in search of what amounts to self-defense. That is to say, for every exaction, hidden or explicit, laid on a group by government policy, those who suffer from it may be viewed as having a right—or at least an inclination—to attempt to gain relief.

If they then bear resource costs, in an attempt to avoid what they view as an unjust exaction, should that resource cost be counted as rent-seeking waste? This kind of example points up the inevitable ambiguity surrounding the concept of rent seeking, which Professor Usher touches on in a note when he discusses the meaning of rent seeking.

I think, as he does, that it's a singularly unfortunate term and that the way that most people in the public choice field use it is unfortunate, because it fails to make this distinction. What is overlooked is that every notion of efficiency—which is at stake here, underneath the rent-seeking concept—requires a rights benchmark.

In the third world, as in every other world populated by human beings, politics goes on; and politics, as Lord Bolingbroke told us centuries ago, consists in helping your friends, hurting your enemies, and lining your pockets.

How one may best achieve these objectives is contingent. It depends on the society in which one works, on the institutions that exist and establish the incentives and constraints under which people may operate only at various costs. In this connection it would be a useful extension of Professor Usher's effort to apply a bit more methodological individualism to the concept of government.

Usher's paper is about actions taken by governments. Governments are people, and the individual people who compose government have interests of their own. They have friends and enemies. It might be worth pausing to ask in each individual case who composes the government and what these people are trying to do.

In many third world countries the regimes are essentially military. The government consists of more or less organized bands of armed thugs. They are trying to practice optimal predation. That is, they are trying to follow Lord Bolingbroke's maxim, perhaps with considerable inefficiency but trying nonetheless.

Along the way they have incentives, as Dwight Lee mentioned, to create salable privileges, as long as the transaction costs are not so great that there's no net gain from creating and selling those privileges. The drift of Professor Usher's paper is that the creation of public taxation and expenditure schemes, tied up with the sale of privileges, imposes a whole array of other costs on the society. But those would have to be, as I said a minute ago, set against the costs being borne by people who are seeking what we might call self-defense or justice.

In one sense they cancel out; in another sense they're additive. We simply have an enormous amount of resources being consumed unproductively in a society that's thrashing around in a process of extensive political conflict.

The bribery and the corruption to which a number of people have alluded, which are endemic to societies with so little established, civilized order, have even greater costs than those that have been enumerated. In a sense, what happens in such societies is a decay of the most precious of all capitals, cultural capital.

When dishonesty, violence, and predation are practiced cheaply by armed thugs who constitute the government, it's not surprising that other people who can act similarly begin to do so. The past twenty to twenty-five years of the history of some regimes exemplify the general decay and deterioration of whole societies, not only economically but politically, socially, and in other respects, that can occur when governments attempt to practice optimal predation in circumstances where the social capital cannot sustain the society's productivity in the face of this assault. Advanced societies are fortunate, because they can have an enormous amount of predation and their productivity is so huge that they're still relatively well off. But when we have "politics as usual" in many third world settings, the costs may become overwhelming.

MR. WHALLEY: Dan's paper suggests that we have to correct our use of the expression "rent seeking." As Bob Higgs just said, many of the things we're talking about are penalty-avoiding activities. People will use resources to prevent a penalty from being imposed on them, and once you've got a tax system, you can have huge amounts of resources being so used, when in fact no rents are really being created. So the original Krueger proposition—that the total value of resources wasted in rent seeking is equal to the value of rents created—is clearly false in many of the contexts we're talking about, because people will use resources to avoid the penalty.

With respect to this, some of the literature on tax evasion in India is quite suggestive. One estimate is that the bribe rate in India is about 20 percent of total taxes owing and that, furthermore, over time there has been a secular increase in the bribe rate. The rate of a first-year bribe reflects the value to the erstwhile taxpayer of not paying taxes in that year. In the second year, however, the auditor (who accepts the bribe) has more leverage. The bribe rate is responsive not only to the value of any given year's nonpayment of taxes but to the accumulation of all the preceding years' bribes.

A static analysis, looking at any one year's bribes and taxes not paid, may have value in itself, but a dynamic analysis, introducing the dimension of time, permits recognition of qualitative change in addition to quantitative consequences. First, in any year but the first, the bribe payed by the nontaxpayer in India cannot be understood as simply "rent seeking." Second, and more critically, the institutional growth of an alternative "tax system," more complementary to the black economy than to the formal economy, may be discerned and understood. Such emergent institutions, because they are alternatives, mean that the policies and institutions of the formal government and society will have quite different effects at different times within a single country.

MR. RABUSHKA: Two brief comments. The first is that in the list of things to look at, it might be worth considering the diminution or reduction in entrepreneurial activity—a tough item to measure but still worth looking at.

The other thing I wanted to say is a great complication, especially for economists. As Dan defines the hidden costs of public expenditure or taxation, which reduce real national income (using as his norm the simple maximization of national income), there is another dimension to consider—the reduction in individual economic liberty, or the reduction in individual freedom broadly defined, from the rising activities of government.

MR. GILLIS: Estimating the price of corruption is an underexplored topic in all of this. How much will tax administrators give up in state revenues to achieve any given dollar or peso for themselves? In Colombia, Jaime Vazquez showed that for every one peso received as a bribe by the tax collector, the government gave up twenty. In Indonesia I had access to income tax returns of corporations, and strangely enough I found in many cases that when you go back over the audit, for each rupiah in bribes about twenty rupiah were lost to the government. I'd like to see this expanded to Argentina—and also Massachusetts, Maryland, New Jersey.

[Laughter]

MR. BIRD: The "Gillis constant" may enter the literature. Joel, do you have one quick comment before we turn to Dan at the end?

MR. SLEMROD: I just had a comment on the public choice perspective on tax systems. I agree that we should take seriously the proposition that government is composed of people too. That's important when you consider the role of the economists in recommending economic policy that may not be in the interest of the people in power.

I wonder if people from that perspective are challenging what I think is an underlying theme of Dan's paper, which is that if we could, we *should* reduce the costs, hidden and overt, of taxation. Do you think there are cases when that's the wrong way to go? What if the government is spending too much money for its own purposes—lining its own pockets or for whatever reason—and the cost of taxation serves as a limiting factor on that overspending? Do you think this is a case when increasing the costs of taxation may be optimal, as a way to constrain the overspending government?

Response

Dan Usher

Are legal expenditures social cost? Does the use of time and resources by litigants, lawyers, courts, and prisons count as part of the overhead cost of the public sector and of the marginal cost of public expenditure? My answer is yes. Look at any textbook of microeconomics, and you will see in the proof of the optimality of the competitive equilibrium that the human and physical capital is assumed to be apportioned among people. No mention of how property gets apportioned or of how people are prevented from fighting over the allocation of property rights. Lawyers are assumed away because there is nothing for them to do in such a world. Drop the assumption of costless maintenance of property rights, and we acquire what Adam Smith saw as the first task of government, which is to protect people from one another. The task includes the obligation to define property rights, to resolve disputes, and to punish those who try to take what belongs to others.

On the question of double counting, I have revised the paper in the light of Joel Slemrod's remarks and have specified, as exactly as I can, when and to what extent double counting is likely to occur. As

I see it, double counting occurs if and only if punishment is in the form of a fine that benefits society as it harms the criminal. Otherwise the marginal costs of detecting and punishing tax evasion—costs borne by the taxpayer himself in evading the tax collector, by the tax collector in hunting down the tax evader, by everybody in hiring lawyers, by the courts in trying the tax evader, by the state in imprisoning him—are additive.

In some circumstances all possible tax sources should be exploited to some extent. If full income could be measured accurately and were invariant to the rate of tax, then the ideal tax system would consist of one tax only—an income tax as recommended by Haig and Simons, a consumption tax, or a wealth tax. In an imperfect world where no tax is free of deadweight loss and where the marginal cost of taxation per unit of tax revenue increases with the rate of tax, there may be a case for taxing everything in sight. When an income tax has a deadweight loss associated with the labor-leisure choice, a corporation income tax has a deadweight loss associated with the rate of investment, a gasoline tax (ignoring its role as a corrective tax) has a deadweight loss associated with road use, and an inheritance tax has an entirely different set of hidden costs, there is a case for employing each source of revenue up to the point where the marginal hidden cost per dollar of revenue is the same.

The analysis applies to trade taxes just as it does to any other tax. Trade taxes can be looked on as taxes on imports procured by exporting. The distinction between average and marginal deadweight loss is as valid for trade taxes as for domestic taxes. There are, however, special difficulties in measuring marginal deadweight loss when exchange rates are rigged, when there is exchange control, or in the presence of international monopoly power. On the dynamic context: I touched on the matter in the discussion of the double taxation of saving under the income tax. I am confident that the story of the hidden cost of taxation does generalize to a dynamic context; but the subject is quite complex, and I have not studied it thoroughly.

Let me conclude by explaining why I changed the title of the paper. The explanation may be responsive to several questions expressed during the discussion. The paper was to have been called, "The Hidden Cost of Taxation." I changed it to "The Hidden Costs of Public Expenditure" to emphasize the fundamental trade-off in public finance between stuff acquired through the public sector (guns, roads, public administration, and so on) and stuff forgone in the private sector (food, clothing, housing, and so on) as resources are shifted from one use to another. Payment of tax is a cost to the taxpayer. Hidden costs are like additional taxation unrecorded in the public accounts. Both costs are borne to procure what the government supplies.

The overt cost of public expenditure is the loss of output in the private sector as resources are diverted to the production of what the government supplies. The hidden cost is a side effect of taxpayers' attempts to rearrange their affairs to minimize their tax bills or to make themselves eligible as beneficiaries of public expenditure. The hidden cost of maneuvers to minimize one's tax bill is studied under the heading of deadweight loss. The hidden cost of the attempts to position oneself to benefit from public expenditure is exemplified by lobbying for lucrative contracts, by the effect of unemployment insurance on the willingness to work, and by the effect of welfare on the incidence of illegitimacy.

On the paper itself, I would like to emphasize two points. The first is the significance of the distinction between marginal and total deadweight loss. Early studies of deadweight loss emphasized the ratio of *total* deadweight loss in taxation—the Harberger triangle— to *total* tax revenue. Recently the emphasis has shifted to the ratio of *marginal* deadweight loss to *marginal* tax revenue in response to a small increase in the tax rate. It is the latter ratio that is appropriate for the evaluation of projects or programs in cost-benefit analysis. The net cost of a project or program is the effect on the economy of the marginal increase in the tax rate that is required to procure the extra revenue to finance the project or program. Furthermore, the ratio of marginal deadweight loss to marginal revenue must—as an accounting identity—be larger than the ratio of total deadweight loss to total revenue. Estimates of marginal deadweight loss have varied considerably from one study to the next. Authors have estimated it at a quarter, a half, or even a multiple of marginal revenue.

I would also like to recommend caution in imputing cost to rent-seeking behavior. The general idea of rent seeking is that one should beware of governments bearing gifts, not because the gifts themselves are spurious but because gifts are dissipated in the squabble among would-be recipients, each hoping to grab the lion's share. Potential recipients devote resources to staking their claims in ways that are always privately advantageous but are often socially wasteful. The gift might be a license to import certain goods, or an investment grant, or water rights, or public housing, or a lucrative defense contract.

The value of the gift to the recipient may be entirely wasted in rent-seeking activity, but this need not be so: First, there can be no rent-seeking activity if it is obvious from the start who the fortunate recipient will be. The percentage of the gift that is wasted can vary from nothing to 100 percent depending on the initial probabilities of each possible recipient and how these are affected by rent seeking. Second, competition for favors at the disposal of the government can be socially beneficial. For example, a patent is a gift of monopoly by the government to a private firm. Would-be recipients compete for this gift, exactly as the rent-seeking literature says that they would. But the form of competition is to conduct research that is beneficial to society as a whole and might not be profitable in the absence of patent rights. Third, rent seeking may be a cover for bribery. The ultimate beneficiary of an import license or valuable contract may be the official whose task it is to dispense this gift rather than the agent in the private sector who receives it. The economics of bribery is complicated, for the social cost of bribery can vary according to the circumstances from nothing to over 100 percent of the face value of the bribe. What we call bribery may be functionally equivalent to the ordinary wage of public officials, but it may, alternatively, be the occasion of huge social loss that is not reflected in the amount of money changing hands. The term "rent seeking" can cover a broad spectrum of activities from research to lobbying to bribery. Some rent-seeking activities are wasteful, others not.

3

John Whalley

Taxlike Features of Developing Country Trade Regimes

The aim of this paper is to explore the taxlike effects of the trade regimes in developing countries. The term "taxlike" refers to unintended effects of trade-related policies on resource allocation, income distribution, growth, and other aspects of economic performance—the same effects often attributed to taxes as inevitable, and usually undesirable, byproducts of their revenue-raising function.

With most of the key elements of the trade regime, such as quotas, rationed foreign exchange, export bans, free-trade zones, and the like, no direct revenue-raising functions are involved. The paper tries to identify some of the more important of these taxlike effects, to analyze how they compound or offset effects attributable to formal taxes in developing countries, and to assess what implications the current trade liberalization under way in many developing countries may have for these interactions. The paper draws on the experience of eleven developing countries that have been the subject of a recent Ford Foundation–supported project on trade policies in the developing world.[1]

A number of themes emerge from the paper. One is that both the form that taxlike effects of trade regimes take and their importance depend critically on the wider policy system within which they operate, including conventional tax policies. Policy instruments compound and interact with one another, making some redundant as far as resource allocation is concerned but elevating the effects on income distribution of others. Thus a tariff in the presence of a binding quota has no effect on trade flows or resource allocation but does take rents away from the owners of the quota. If, however, a quota affects trade, it also affects domestic production and consumption through its trade effects. If rent-seeking effects are associated with quota allocation schemes, even in the presence of quotas, tariffs can reduce the value of quota rents and hence the amount of resources devoted to rent seeking. These policy interactions are central to assessing what the taxlike effects of individual policies are. Moreover, the model chosen to analyze them further determines their perceived effects (such as the choice between models with or without rent seeking). Generally speaking, the paper suggests that binding instruments have their largest effects on resource allocation; nonbinding instruments have larger distributional effects.

The paper also emphasizes that it is often difficult to determine the precise effects of policy systems in various countries. Information is sparse, and what the effects are depends on the structure of the model used to analyze them as well as on parameter values. Often these are little more than guesses, and the substantial and continual change over time in policies in most of the countries at issue makes assessments of effects even more difficult. All of this makes it that much harder to know precisely what the taxlike effects of trade policies are and how substantial is their influence on economic performance.

Key Concepts

Before elaborating what the taxlike effects of developing countries' trade regimes are and how they interact with formal tax systems in these countries, it is helpful first to clarify a few key concepts.

Taxlike effects. The term "taxlike effect" may seem relatively straightforward but has hidden subtleties when applied to a discussion of policies that impinge on developing countries' trade performance. Taxes themselves have a range of effects. Primarily they raise revenue, but in the process they also affect economic performance. A convenient way of categorizing these effects is in terms of the three branches of justifiable policy intervention developed by Richard Musgrave in his classic public finance text (1959).

He suggested that allocation, distribution, and stabilization objectives provide legitimate arguments on which to base government intervention in the economy. Allocation-driven justifications cover externality, market structure, public good (jointness of consumption), and other areas of policy, where improvement of resource allocation is the goal. Distributional justifications rationalize those policies (such as a progressive income tax) whose main objective is to align a market-determined distributional outcome more closely with a socially desirable outcome. And stabilization justifications cover anti-inflationary policies, proemployment and progrowth policies, balance-of-payments-driven policy actions, and other macro-objectives.

In adopting this classification to group the taxlike effects of trade policies, I assume that each of the Musgravean branches of government objectives can also be used to categorize broad classes of effects of trade-related policies. I further assume that the taxlike effects of trade policies ensue from the use of instruments that either have no direct revenue implications for government or, if they do have an effect on revenue, have taxlike effects as their central focus. To complicate matters further, some of the instruments discussed here have taxlike effects that feed back on revenues, because they

indirectly increase or decrease a revenue source for government.
Thus, for instance, an import quota may increase the profits of a
protected industry and therefore increase collections under corporate and other taxes.

Hence using this classification of taxlike effects of trade policies
suggests that policies can change the use of factors by and outputs
from the various sectors in the economy (allocation effects), change
the distribution of income (distributional effects), and affect macro
performance (stabilization effects). Individual policy elements of the
trade regime may simultaneously have all these effects; one may
dominate the others or may have only mild effects in all three
categories.

While the approach is different from Musgrave's original classification of policy objectives, considering the effects of policies in this
way provides a convenient organizing framework for the discussion
that follows.

Trade regimes. Like many policy subsystems, trade regimes in
developing countries are both complicated and substantially more
so than those in developed countries. Table 3.1 sets out some of the
more central elements that can be found in typical trade regimes in
developing countries and outlines some of their more important
taxlike effects.

Our discussion of trade regimes begins with the tariff, the form of
trade intervention most widely addressed by trade theorists.[2] A tariff
is an ad valorem tax on importation and has traditionally been a
major source of revenue in all countries at early stages of development. In developing countries, tariffs currently range from very high
levels, as in India, where tariff rates of 300 percent are not unknown,
to much lower rates, as in Korea and, more recently, Mexico.[3]

Tariffs and trade taxes are a major source of revenue in developing countries, but the picture is varied and rapidly changing. It is
typical for countries to rely heavily on trade taxes at early stages of
development. In the United States in the 1920s, for instance, the tariff
still accounted for well over 30 percent of central government

revenues.[4] And in low-income developing countries today, tariffs remain a significant source of revenue.

Table 3.2 presents recent International Monetary Fund data for a sample of developed and developing countries, reporting the share of trade taxes (tariffs and export taxes) in government revenues. For lower-income countries in Africa (Gambia, Benin, Rwanda) shares in the 40–70 percent range occur; in African countries with a small or modest manufacturing base (Kenya, Tanzania, Nigeria) the range is smaller, 10–20 percent. In Asia countries in the Indian subcontinent are in the 20–30 percent range; higher-income newly industrialized countries (NICs) such as Korea are about 15 percent. Latin America reports the lowest ratios, with Brazil and Mexico below 5 percent.

After the tariff come quotas (quantitative restrictions). These are outlawed under the General Agreement on Tariffs and Trade,[5] but developing countries use them widely nonetheless, because of special rules that apply to their use by developing countries under Article 18-B of the GATT.[6] This GATT article allows developing countries more latitude than developed countries in using quantitative restrictions to deal with their balance-of-payments problems, including the use of product-specific restrictions. The use of quantitative restrictions has been in relative decline in many of the faster growing Asian economies for some years, and their use in Latin America is also in a state of flux, with significant current reductions.[7]

The trade-restricting components of trade regimes in developing countries do not, however, end with tariffs and quotas. Most countries have fixed exchange rate regimes, nonaccommodative domestic monetary policies, and foreign exchange shortages. As a result, foreign exchange is usually rationed, and the rationing scheme used, like the forced surrender of foreign exchange earnings of exporters, has major effects.

The rationing of foreign exchange typically works in the following way.[8] Any firm generating export earnings through export sales is required to surrender the resulting foreign exchange to the central bank at the official exchange rate, even though the same firm

Table 3.1
Taxlike Effects of Trade Regimes in Developing Countries

Policy element in trade regime	Resource allocation effects	Distributional effects	Stabilization effects
Tariff	If quotas or FER binding: none. If quotas or FER nonbinding: draws resources into protected industries withdraws resources from export and nontraded good industries.	If quotas or FER nonbinding, raises prices of protected commodities (typically luxuries). These are typically propoor, antiurban effects.	If trade taxes are significant revenue source, expenditures on luxury imports are procyclical, and revenues are destabilizing, not stabilizing.
Quotas (quantitative restrictions)	If FER binding: none. If FER nonbinding: draw resources into protected industries; withdraw resources from export industries. Under either regime, resource loss from rent-seeking behavior.	Raise prices of protected commodities (typically luxuries). Typically propoor, antiurban effects, but benefits/rents received by those who receive quotas.	Quotas usually adjusted during periods of import compression. Thus, they are a direct instrument of stabilization policy.
Rationed foreign exchange (FER)	Effects are similar to those of a tariff, except that (1) typically zero revenue raised since exporters are required to surrender foreign exchange at below-free-market exchange rates and foreign exchange received by importers is also at below-free-market rates (effectively a zero-revenue-raising tax or transfer scheme), (2) rent seeking for foreign exchange allocations occurs.	Effects broadly similar to those of tariffs and quotas. Rent transfers to recipients of quotas; losses to exporters forced to surrender foreign exchange.	FER tightened during periods of import compression. Severity of FER tightening, if any, depends on whether devaluation also occurs.

Advanced import deposit schemes	Effects similar to those of a tariff, but if rationed foreign exchange is the binding import restriction, advanced import deposit schemes act as a tax on recipients of foreign exchange and as a quota.	Effects broadly similar to those of rationing of foreign exchange, since advance deposit acts as a rationing device. Cost of compliance acts as tax on recipient of foreign exchange.	Length of deposit adjusted during times of import compression or liberalization.
Export taxes	Force resources out of taxed industries. Encourage resource flow into import competing and nontraded good industries. Effects typically not offset by quantity constraints. Effects typically compound those of tariffs.	Typically depress prices of taxed commodities. Frequently primary commodities heavily purchased by poor, but workers in taxed industry partly bear burden through lower wage rates.	Can have stabilizing effects on sectoral prices (see export bans).
Export bans	Used sometimes to encourage more fabrication in local market (rattan in Indonesia). May or may not increase export earnings and pull resources into export sector.	Typically depress price of banned item. Other income distribution effects uncertain, since these are often intermediate items.	Occasionally used as stabilization device (tea in India) to stabilize domestic price if world prices are volatile.
Export promotion policies (import duty remissions/ free-trade zones)	Various schemes are used to promote exports and if successful pull resources into export industries from nontraded good and import-competing industries.	Typically raise prices of nontraded goods and import substitutes. This is typically propoor if these are luxuries.	Not used for stabilization purposes. Commitment to these instruments is usually for longer-term developmental reasons.
Export prioritization (credit rationing)	Prioritization in favor of exports pulls resources from nontraded good and import industries into export industries. Under credit rationing, rent-seeking effects may follow.	Similar effects to export promotion schemes.	Stabilization programs (especially under World Bank or IMF auspices) may well involve change in prioritization of credit rationing and favor or hurt export industries.

Table 3.2

Trade and Other Taxes as a Percentage of Government Revenue, Selected Countries, 1986

Country	General sales turnover or VAT	Taxes on international trade	Individual	Corporation	Other
OECD					
United States	—	1.56	42.27	7.76	48.41
Canada	9.06	5.26	36.34	10.96	38.38
New Zealand	11.39	4.78	52.43	8.12	23.28
Germany	12.26p	0.02p	13.48p	3.52p	70.72p
Sweden	16.86	0.54	15.22	3.33	64.05
United Kingdom	14.74	0.01	26.83	11.53	46.89
Africa					
Benin	2.85	53.44	3.28	5.82	34.61
Gambia	—	68.73	9.84	6.07	15.36
Kenya	28.55	20.40	—	—	51.05
Madagascar	22.86	20.01	7.88	6.07	43.18
Nigeria	—	22.35	0.06	59.71	17.88
Rwanda	—	42.39	6.91	9.80	40.90
Tanzania	52.38p	10.81p	12.23p	19.86p	4.72p
Zaire	16.63	25.70	15.93	17.42	24.32
Pacific					
Bangladesh	8.57p	32.20p	11.80p	0.01p	47.42p
India	0.93p	24.07p	6.00p	9.37p	59.63p
Indonesia	4.69	3.32	2.41	63.35	26.23
Korea	20.84	14.01	13.25	11.71	40.19
Pakistan	6.51	30.94	—	—	62.55
Philippines	7.72p	23.72p	8.30p	13.65p	46.61p
Latin America					
Argentina	11.95	13.31	0.11	0.48	74.15
Brazil	2.22	4.22	0.81	6.13	86.62
Chile	29.36	10.81	3.37	7.89	48.57
Colombia	15.27	11.58	—	—	73.15
Costa Rica	16.61	22.38	13.94	3.00	44.07
Jamaica	18.23	4.13	17.45	8.19	52.00
Mexico	18.96	2.73	11.29	13.23	53.79
Uruguay	27.56	12.19	3.04	3.73	53.48
Venezuela	—	18.00	3.63	55.51	22.86

NOTE: Owing to adjustment items and unallocated transactions, components may not add to 100 percent. Percentages are for *central* government only.

p. Data are in whole or in part provisional, preliminary, or projected.

SOURCE: IMF, *Government Finance Statistics Yearbook* (1988).

could, in all probability, obtain a better rate were it to sell the foreign exchange (albeit illegally) on the black market.

The foreign exchange generated in this way is then allocated by the central bank on a priority basis to importers of particular products. Usually an import license justifying importation of specified products is required before any foreign exchange can be allocated, and the rules are such that anyone receiving an allocation of foreign exchange is supposedly not allowed to resell either the foreign exchange or the items they are authorized to import (typically intermediate raw materials or capital goods and machinery).[9] Advanced import deposit schemes are widely used as part of this rationing process.[10]

Besides these, other policy elements often appear in the trade regime in developing countries, as Table 3.1 indicates. Export taxes,[11] for instance, are employed in many countries.[12] These typically apply to agricultural items and raw materials and often reflect the rationale that ownership of agricultural land is heavily concentrated in a relatively small number of landowners.[13] This is the case in many Latin American countries and in parts of the Pacific.

Beyond export taxes, there may be export bans. India, for example, bans the export of tea from time to time to stabilize domestic prices in the internal market.[14] Export bans are sometimes justified by developing countries as helping to encourage higher domestic production and processing in their own economies, hence increasing the value-added content of their trade. Thus does Indonesia ban the export of rattan in raw form to encourage processing of rattan into furniture in its own economy rather than abroad.

A further commonly used set of instruments, opposite in intent to export taxes and bans, consists of various schemes used to promote exports. One widely used scheme is to remit duties on imports used for processing and reexport or to remit indirect taxes (often cascading turnover or wholesale taxes) applying to exports.[15] Such remission schemes were widely used by Korea in the early to mid-1960s as part of its initial thrust toward an outward-oriented trade policy and are widely believed in Korea to have been highly successful in propelling the economy toward a more outward-oriented stance and higher growth rates.[16] This change in policy stance has generated substantial increases in export volumes.

Export zones are a further export promotion device now in wide use in China,[17] India,[18] and other countries. Generally speaking, however, free-trade zones have not been so successful as the Korean remission schemes.[19] Under these schemes imports into zones are duty free if used for further fabrication for export. It is also common to allow exporters to retain a portion or even all of the foreign exchange they generate for use in importing raw materials and capital goods for production.

In addition to these elements of a typical developing country trade regime, others, not usually considered part of the trade regime, link it to policies affecting the rest of the economy. It is common, for instance, for the banking system to be under central-ized control and for credit rationing to be used to generate export-oriented activity in the economy.[20] This is akin to a form of forced mobilization, which drives resources into export-oriented produc-tion. The effects that follow are taxlike insofar as a significant reallocation of resources can result. At the same time, they are nontaxlike in the sense that there is a forced mobilization rather than a market-driven inducement component to such schemes, that is, central direction rather than market-driven changes in behavior in the economy.

Registration schemes have also been used at various times in some economies, such as Korea.[21] Under these, to qualify for import licenses and allocations of foreign exchange, one has to export a particular target value of production. Continuation of registration has then been conditional on export performance.[22]

Together, all these policy elements make up the trade or external sector regime in developing countries. They all have taxlike effects through resource allocation, income distribution, and stabilization. Their precise form, of course, differs from country to country, but complexity and interaction between the policy elements is the norm.

Taxlike Effects of the Trade Regime in Developing Countries

The various elements identified above, which together define the trade regime in developing countries, have many taxlike effects. These are summarized in Table 3.1, which also emphasizes that the precise effects attributable to any one policy element depend on the form other policy elements take and how they interact.[23]

There are, for instance, overall effects on trade performance that can be attributed to various elements in the external sector policy mix. Those that tend to limit import volumes, such as tariffs, quotas, and rationed foreign exchange, draw resources from elsewhere in the economy into protected industries, making fewer resources available for exports and ultimately reducing exports.[24] In that sense these devices operate to some extent as a tax on exports, although these effects are weaker if resources can also be drawn from nontraded goods industries.

Other taxlike effects are also antitrade in their bias, because the objective of the instrument used is to insulate the economy from external sector shocks. Many developing countries have exports that are concentrated in a relatively small number of product categories and have exchange markets that, if allowed to find their own level, would do so in an extremely thinly traded environment. Much of the desire for insulation from external shocks that one sees in developing countries is, therefore, a reaction to the perceived instability of their external environment and the large adjustment costs that they would otherwise see themselves as facing.[25] Developing countries often have such restrictions as rationed foreign exchange and quotas in their trade regimes because, in the past, they have been directly affected by terms of trade and other external sector shocks that, if left unattended, would imply major adjustment costs for the economy.[26] In evaluating the taxlike effects of a trade regime in terms of the Musgravean stabilization category stressed above, therefore, one must recognize that a principal objective embodied in the regime may be to insulate key domestic industries from external shocks.

Other taxlike effects of these policy elements reflect the limited availability to governments in developing countries of other instruments for achieving particular ends. One can, for instance, partly justify the structure of the Philippines' foreign trade regime as being a partial redistributive scheme, which reflects the inability of the government to use a wider tax transfer system to redistribute income in favor of rural households.[27] The Philippines is often characterized as having a large and restive urban population that can potentially destabilize the regime in power. Governments have to keep the support of urban groups and do so in part through price controls on agricultural production from the rural population. Bans of luxury import items in the trade regime are, therefore, in part a quid pro quo for these arrangements, since conspicuous consumption of luxury imported items in urban areas would lose political support in rural areas. In turn, setting priorities for imports targeted toward basic necessities more heavily purchased by the rural population can partially correct for redistribution taking place elsewhere in the policy regime through price controls.

Taxlike effects emanating from trade regimes also have clear sectoral effects. The usual effect is a substantial bias in favor of manufacturing industries, through protection applied to imports of manufactures. Thus imports of consumer goods are either effectively banned or at least sharply restricted, leaving consumer goods as the most heavily protected industries in these economies. The effect is to draw significant amounts of resources into manufacturing behind the protective barrier.[28] Capital goods industries are typically less heavily protected, since priorities set in import licensing usually operate in favor of capital goods and raw materials. Although preferentially treated compared with other manufactures in allowable import volumes, they are still protected compared with agriculture, resource, and service industries.

Related to all these broad-ranging taxlike effects is the issue of urban-rural bias in the trade regime (already alluded to in the Philippine case) and induced effects on both production composition and urban-rural population composition and migration. In the well known Harris-Todaro (1970) model of urban-rural migration, for instance, migration occurs up to the point where the expected wage across urban and rural sectors is equalized. An important tax-like effect of the typical developing country trade regime is to protect manufacturing, raise urban sector wages, and encourage additional migration into urban areas. Taxlike effects on resource allocation from the trade regime can be some of the most serious because of the added unemployment in urban areas that can result.[29]

Taxlike effects from the trade regimes can also show up in the growth performance of various countries. Duty remission schemes, credit rationing, export-related import licensing, and other devices are widely believed to have been central to both the sharp growth in exports in Korea in the 1960s and 1970s and the higher GDP growth rates.[30] High growth in Korea is generally thought not to have been significantly affected by the tax policies used.[31]

The taxlike effects of these various elements of the foreign trade regime are set out in more detail in Table 3.1. The effects of tariffs are well known and widely discussed in the literature (see Bhagwati and Srinivasan 1983). They increase the prices of products produced in protected industries, drawing resources into these industries and reducing the volume of imports. An important taxlike effect of a tariff is that, where there are no nontraded goods, it operates as a tax on exports. In the presence of a nontraded goods sector, however, if it is large enough, the main effect can be to draw resources from the nontraded goods sector rather than from the export industries.

The income distribution effects of the tariff reflect any changes induced in relative prices domestically. Since tariffs in most developing countries are heavily concentrated on luxury items rather than on basic necessities, these effects are usually taken to be antirich and also antiurban, terms that are frequently assumed to be synonymous.

Quantitative restrictions are widely thought to have taxlike effects similar to those of a tariff. They raise prices of protected products in the domestic economy. This yields higher prices for domestic producers, draws more resources to protected industries, and ultimately, like a tariff, also operates as something akin to a tax on export industries. The interactions between quantitative restrictions and tariffs are important, because with binding quantitative restrictions, the main effect of the tariff is to operate as a redistributive device taking income away from recipients of quota rents. With quotas the income-distribution effects depend on whether quotas are auctioned or sold by government and, therefore, whether the revenues from quotas are received by government or directly allocated to individual citizens or firms. Related to this is the issue of whether rent-seeking activities are thought to accompany whatever quota allocation scheme is used.[32]

Foreign exchange rationing, a further import-restricting element of the trade policy regime, has pronounced taxlike effects. Foreign exchange rationing operates, in effect, as a tax transfer scheme that raises zero revenue for governments. It taxes exporters and transfers rents to importers through the allocation of foreign exchange. Its effect is much like that of a tariff or a quantitative restriction. It raises prices in the domestic market. This draws resources to industries that are protected in this way, with differential protection reflecting the way in which priorities are set for foreign exchange among different import categories. In the long run it also has the effect, like a tariff, of operating as a tax on exports in the economy.[33]

Foreign exchange rationing can also make both quotas and tariffs redundant instruments of trade policy. Thus, with binding foreign exchange rationing, quotas and tariffs may have no effects on trade volumes, since rationed foreign exchange becomes the effective restriction within the trade regime. Tariffs are then on rents and hence are borne by importers who receive quotas. In periods of major foreign exchange shortage in developing countries, such as the early 1980s and after the onset of the debt crisis and higher oil prices, foreign exchange rationing schemes typically become the most crucial part of trade regimes in developing countries. If there is growth in the developed world, however, such as has taken place more recently, and devaluations occur, then a weakening of the foreign exchange constraint will eventually imply that other elements of trade policy become more critical.

The taxlike effects of export taxes and bans are much the same as those associated with tariffs. These reduce export volumes and, through the displacement of domestic resources, pull resources from those sectors into import-competing industries. The effect is to raise the relative price of import-competing products through the depressing effect of the export tax, since, in the small open economy case that characterizes most developing countries, these taxes are typically fully borne by producers of export items. Export taxes and bans, therefore, compound those taxlike effects attributable to the tariff. With binding quotas or rationed foreign exchange, taxes on exports reduce prices received by exporters and hence export volumes and make the rationing of foreign exchange more severe through lowered foreign exchange earnings.

Operating in a way opposite to that of tariffs are export promotion schemes such as import duty remissions, free-trade processing zones, and other similar devices. These are sometimes employed in economies that want to move closer to trade neutrality while leaving the structure of protection in the form of tariffs in place. This approach has been widely used in the Asian economies and has been adopted by them as a means of consciously moving in a trade-liberalizing direction while not removing politically sensitive protection. The taxlike effects of these instruments operate in a direction opposite to those of trade-restricting measures. Things become somewhat more complex when licensing schemes and credit rationing come into play since the taxlike effects here operate in ways that tend to offset the quantity rationing components associated with the foreign exchange and quota regimes. Which effects dominate depend on which constraints are binding and which are larger.

All these taxlike effects, however, have to be understood in the context of the overall policy system that operates in developing countries. The taxlike effects of any individual element depend crucially on what the other components of the trade regime, and indeed the wider policy regime, are. The taxlike effects of a tariff in the presence of a quota differ depending on whether the quota is binding or nonbinding. Similarly, binding foreign exchange rationing will change the taxlike effects of both a quota and a tariff and also affect the taxlike effects attributable to export promotion, export tax, and prioritization schemes.

Indeed, it is the taxlike effects attributable to these instruments that, in many cases, have made them the binding instrument in the trade regime and the policy instrument most widely used to effect change. Thus those economies that have recently used alternative foreign exchange retention programs, under which exporters can retain a fraction of their foreign exchange earnings and keep them in foreign currency accounts to finance imports, have revealed the clear appreciation by their policy makers of their own trade policy regime, as well as an understanding of which are the key instruments to affect performance. Recently these schemes have been used as means of promoting exports in a series of countries.[34]

Thus taxlike effects attributable to individual elements of a trade regime must be evaluated with some caution because of the interactions that take place among all these elements and between them and nontrade policies. Disentangling this network of interactions and examining one policy instrument in isolation can be both misleading and potentially dangerous.

Taxlike Effects of the Trade Regime in the Wider Policy System

It is desirable, then, to consider the taxlike effects of trade policy regimes in a broader context to obtain a more complete sense of how they operate and where they may be headed. This accounts for the discussion in this section of trade regime interactions with formal tax systems in developing countries[35] and what may be happening on the trade liberalization front.[36]

Compounding effects between tax and trade regimes. Generally, interactions between tax systems and the taxlike effects of trade regimes tend to reduce the distorting effects of trade taxes. In lower-income countries trade taxes are especially important in accounting for a large and significant portion of revenues raised.[37] To the extent that other elements of trade policy come into play, such as quotas and rationed foreign exchange, they tend to cause trade taxes to have largely lump-sum effects. These apply more to imports, where quotas and rationing of foreign exchange apply, than to exports, where export bans and restrictions are less pervasive.

Another taxlike effect reflecting the compounding of taxes with the trade system involves the intersectoral agricultural-manufacturing balance, a major issue in many developing countries. In most countries agriculture is largely or wholly tax free while protection tends to benefit the manufacturing industry. The agricultural-manufacturing terms of trade in many developing countries are a continuing topic of policy debate, as illustrated by the active debates on this issue in India since independence in 1947.[38] To the extent that the manufacturing sector is more heavily taxed, the taxlike effects of the trade regime in generating higher prices of protected manufactured products tend to offset the effects of the tax regime on the intersectoral terms of trade. And in combination the trade regime effects greater revenues under the tax system.

A third effect of the trade regime that compounds with effects of the tax system is that the trade regime typically creates taxable rents. This raises revenues for the government but at the same time may generate increased evasion because the incentives to evade taxes are higher. Black-market activity in countries such as India may be heavily tax generated, but its size and scope are influenced by the trade regime.[39]

A fourth compounding effect between taxes and the trade regime affects both recent tax reform and trade liberalization efforts. Trade liberalization has accelerated rapidly in developing countries in recent years. As trade liberalization occurs, the effects of tax policies on resource allocation become more important than taxing rents associated with forgone policies. As tax reform occurs through such moves as broadening of the base of sales taxes and lowering tax rates, it tends to weaken the interaction between tax and trade policies.

Some implications of recent trade liberalization. The taxlike effects of trade policies are also changed by reform and the ebb and flow of policy change in developing countries. Developing countries have experienced wide oscillations of policies in recent decades, with attempts at liberalization frequently regressing into arrangements closer to the original form, simultaneously with changes elsewhere in the policy system.[40] Because so many policy elements affect the taxlike effects of the trade regime and because change is so rapid, disentangling the taxlike effects is especially difficult. Thus, where domestic price controls apply, the taxlike effects of tariffs can be quite different because the resource misallocation effects induced by an increase in prices that follow from the introduction of a new protective barrier can be offset through effective price controls.

One of the more remarkable sets of changes currently going on in developing countries is liberalization in the external sector. The recent Ford Foundation–supported project on developing countries has tried to document how extensive this is.[41] An appendix to the final report of that project attempts to summarize the liberalization experiences of the eleven participating countries. What seems to emerge is that a series of pressures has grown in developing countries in recent years that has forced them to reevaluate their trade and development strategies. In some cases dramatic change has resulted. In others changes have been confined to reevaluations of strategies, evidence, and thinking. But in all cases change is evident.[42]

Many developing countries that through the 1950s and 1960s were strongly wedded to the ideas associated with import substitution trade strategies, emphasizing growth behind a domestic protective barrier, have seen the relative success of the more outward-oriented economies, such as the Asian NICs, and the relative lack of success of countries opting for the import substitution route. As a result, many have begun to reevaluate the desirability of their own import substitution strategies, and the intellectual climate has changed substantially. Economists and key decision makers in many countries no longer closely reflect the tradition from the 1950s and

1960s in which the ideas of Prebisch and others associated with import substitution were particularly influential.[43]

Furthermore, the trade performance of most developing countries suffered substantially during the 1981 recession. Many of them became convinced in the mid-1980s that they had to prevent any future wherein closing of the international trade system might be threatened. Genuinely concerned about threats to their access to markets for manufactures in developed countries, most were more willing than before to consider liberalization as a way of ensuring access abroad through a bargained approach, as in the GATT. There have also been pressures for liberalization operating through conditionality from the IMF and the World Bank, particularly in the African economies but also in some of the Asian and Latin American economies.[44]

All these factors, combined with the strong growth of developed countries from 1982 onward and the growth in export earnings of developing countries that this has generated, have created a new climate of trade policy in the developing world. This has allowed for liberalization of foreign exchange arrangements in many countries.

Liberalization is now extensive in the developing world. It ranges from dramatic cases (such as Mexico, Nigeria, and Korea) to intermediate cases where clear steps have been taken (as in the Philippines, Costa Rica, China, and elsewhere) to cases that are more tentative but in which a direction in favor of liberalization is clearly emerging (such as India, Brazil, and Argentina). In most of these countries there has first been liberalization of foreign exchange arrangements, followed by a slow relaxation and withdrawal of quota restrictions, followed finally by reductions in tariffs. Mexico, for instance, now has less than 24 percent of its trade covered by quantitative restrictions, compared with 80 to 100 percent in the early 1980s. The maximum tariff in Mexico is 20 percent, compared with 50 percent when Mexico first came into the GATT in 1986.

This wave of liberalization clearly changes the taxlike effects of the trade regime in developing countries. Because of the sequencing implicit in this liberalization process, what were previously nonbinding instruments of trade policy become binding.[45] As foreign exchange arrangements are liberalized, first quotas and then tariffs become the binding restrictions on trade. The taxlike effects of the trade regime, therefore, are rearranged in light of these developments. Policy elements with large taxlike effects, such as rationed foreign exchange, can disappear over time; and instruments such as tariffs change from lump-sum redistributive arrangements to price-driven resource allocation policies.

Is this trade liberalization sustainable? The report of the Ford Foundation–supported project discusses this in some detail and suggests that, despite their progress, in the medium to longer term these liberalizations could prove somewhat frail. They are still lacking widespread domestic support, since few of them have yet demonstrated enough concrete positive results through improvements in economic performance in the economies involved. Moreover, political support is strongly needed for these reforms in the guise of reciprocated actions by developed countries in the current GATT round, especially in the areas of tropical products, provisions for credit in GATT negotiations for liberalization made before the negotiations, and implementation of standstill and rollback provisions. Wider issues such as textiles, safeguards, and agriculture also need urgent attention from the point of view of developing countries.

The sustainability of liberalization of trade regimes in developing countries is also clearly dependent on macroeconomic conditions in the developed countries. A recession in the developed world and an elimination of the current U.S. trade deficit would undoubtedly adversely affect the trade prospects of developing countries and might reverse much of the liberalization that has been under way in the past few years.

All of this, therefore, indicates how policy arrangements in developing countries are in constant flux; as this occurs, instruments that were previously nonbinding on decision making become binding and vice versa. As a result, the taxlike effects of components of trade regimes can change quite remarkably. This emphasizes the difficulties of disentangling and firmly demonstrating what the taxlike effects of individual trade policies actually are.

Conclusion

This paper evaluates the taxlike effects of the trade regime in developing countries. The key effects are those on resource allocation, income distribution, growth, and other performance criteria of economies. The paper discusses what is meant by the term "taxlike effects" and traces how these effects arise with tariffs, quotas, rationed foreign exchange, advance import deposit schemes, export bans, export taxes, free-trade zones, credit rationing, and other components of trade regimes.

It suggests that the taxlike effects of trade regimes can be pronounced but highly variable—among both regimes and their policy components. It indicates how the taxlike effects of one or more trade policies can compound or offset the effects of trade taxes. It establishes their importance in the context of their more inclusive policy systems, in which only binding instruments have major and significant effects on resource allocation. Such instruments as tariffs, for instance, are shown to have income distribution effects only to the extent that foreign exchange restrictions are operative.

Finally, the paper notes that recent trade liberalization seems to be accelerating in the developing world, making tax design more important as the taxlike effects of trade policies become weaker.

Comment

Jesus Seade

John has presented a very comprehensive, very deep analysis and discussion of how different elements of trade policy, broadly defined, interact with one another, with domestic tax policy, and with other areas of policy. I found very illuminating his discussion of the different tax effects that result from any given policy change, depending on whether there are other items of policy in place or not, such as quotas, exchange controls, or credit controls.

I find the paper extremely convincing and readable, and I will make just two main points. The first is that in my view the analysis is largely positive—positive not as opposed to negative but as opposed to normative. He discusses very convincingly the complementary interactions that exist in the results from different tools, how they jointly affect allocation, how they jointly affect incidence. But we also want to know how these interrelated effects might affect our assessment of the policy instruments: in other words, what should we be doing with them? We want to know what to do with tariffs, with other instruments that have similar characteristics, such as other areas of trade policy or certainly taxes.

Let me give you three specific examples and then a broader one. The first one almost flows from what John has described in his paper, although it's not put in those terms. Decreased or increased tariffs, if other controls are already in place, not only will not have an effect on allocation but will often be like lump-sum transfers. In that case what is relevant is the effect on normative views on distribution. Another example, which again goes in the same direction with respect to the commercial policy from a fiscal or tax viewpoint, is to note that quite often instruments that are normally thought of as being negative, as being bad, can be good.

Consider export taxes. People are normally against export taxes, and our gut reaction when we see a context where exports are being taxed is to say that's a no-no. Most of the time that's right. But in terms of tax policy, export taxes can be a very good and reasonable alternative to nonexistent taxes that you would like to have. This happens, for example, with mining where you have royalties in place. More likely it can happen with agriculture, where you cannot have a proper income tax for whatever reason—although, if the issue is political, maybe you will not be able to get away with an export tax either.

Tariff and export tax policy can thus interact very directly. For example, you might want to have export taxes that can be credited against income taxes, so that for those who are liable to income tax, the export taxes apply; for those who don't, forget it.

The third specific example is also appropriate to the discussion of evasion in Dan Usher's paper. Let us suppose that we do not want to tax intermediate goods but only final consumption. In that context the value-added tax has a big advantage, since in effect it frees inputs from tax when the user of inputs sells final products within the formal (taxed) sector. As soon as you have some producers outside the control of tax authorities, however, the value-added tax at least ends up taxing the inputs that they buy. So in that sense, too, the value-added tax is attractive.

The counterpart on the trade side of the value-added tax is not to tax imported inputs or imported capital goods. But if imported inputs are exempted, they are exempted also for producers in the underground economy and so on. In this case a country may want to tax those imports in spite of the principle of not taxing inputs because this is the only handle it has on some part of its economy.

This third point takes me to my second broad remark. I want to talk a little bit about structure, the structure of tariffs and commercial policy generally, which is much easier to talk about in the light of what's going on with the rest of the economy—the tax side.

In that context two positions are often adopted. On the one hand are those who say we do not want to tax capital inputs, and therefore we don't want to tax imported capital inputs, we don't want to subject them to tariffs, because that adds to costs and creates inefficiency in production. On the other hand is a school that takes more of a trade perspective—protection. In this view we don't want to discriminate against final goods sectors, because this will give rise to unintended protection and therefore to all kinds of distortions in resource allocation. This prescription is therefore for uniform tariffs—uniformity in effective protection.

Both these positions seem lacking in principle. Let me start with the uniformity idea.

The basic idea can be defended, but only if you can actually apply the uniform tariff to all trade, which implies also granting an equal subsidy to exports. Then you do have uniformity, which is actually zero protection. It's not a very relevant case.

Just having uniformity on the import side without touching exports is equivalent to the neutral uniform structure combined with a tax on exports, and therefore it penalizes exports. Duty drawback provisions or other forms of credit mechanism can undo much of the damage to exporters, but through domestic inputs you will always have some kind of penalty.

This takes me to the other argument. Do we then not want to tax capital goods or to place tariffs on capital goods? This is sometimes taken almost as an article of faith. One of the central tenets of modern public finance is that we don't want to disrupt efficiency. Again, this is one of the intellectual merits of the value-added tax.

I find this kind of argument difficult to understand because it requires a highly sophisticated world with lots of different tax rates chosen at random and so on—a world that has nothing to do with what we can really consider seriously for application as policy.

That is one way in which the argument is not satisfactory. Suppose that we start from a highly sophisticated world where we have optimization and are restricted to a world that is closer to reality with one or two rates. Is the best answer likely to be a zero rate on inputs, a zero rate on capital? Not necessarily. We don't know exactly where we would come out, but chances are that the answer would be some kind of tax on inputs that bears some relation to the greater differentiation we would want to have on the consumption side, where we are forcing a single rate on a group of commodities. So, in principle, the argument for zero taxation of capital goods doesn't really hold water.

Another argument that is perhaps related to this one and more interesting is the following: Another reason why the value-added tax is a good tax is because if you want to tax production, as many countries used to do on a turnover basis with cascading, cascading will result in overtaxation in some sectors and undertaxation in others and a general lack of transparency so that you don't even know what you're doing. That's why we don't want to tax inputs.

Imported capital goods, however, imported inputs, do not give rise to any cascading. When you levy a tax of 3 percent on imported goods or 10 percent, you know exactly what you're doing. You know exactly how much that good is going to cost the economy, and that doesn't create cascading. What will determine whether there is cascading or not is what you do with the taxes and tariffs of downstream sectors. So, again, the argument against taxing imported inputs because inputs are not taxed by a value-added tax does not apply.

Finally, I go back to the previous argument, the one that I used in relation to the uniformity proposal. What we want to have, in principle, is a world basically without taxes—which is to say full uniformity.

We cannot do that on the export side because we need revenues, for example. We cannot play that game. So what do we want to do? I would be eclectic and say, just avoid gross differences in protection. I want to impose some tariffs on all goods to get some handle on evaders in the formal sector and to reduce the dispersion of effective protection rates among sectors.

Nevertheless, I don't want to go all the way because that will create the bias against exports discussed earlier. If I start to increase my input taxes from zero to epsilon and then on and on, the optimum will be the point where the gains in allocation from the import tax side will be offset by the penalization on the export side.

The point I want to make is that from a normative point of view a very close connection inevitably exists through these arguments, whether taken from the allocative angle or the revenue-raising perspective, between what you do with taxation and what you do with tariffs.

Discussion

RICHARD BIRD: One thing that might not have been quite as clear from your remarks, Jesus, as perhaps you meant it to be is that you are using tariffs as a sort of shorthand for the complex trade regime that John was talking about. It's quite important to understand that everything you said can be thought of with respect to a sort of "tariff equivalent" to all the other policies John mentioned.

JESUS SEADE: Yes, exactly.

CHRISTOPHE CHAMLEY: I will just make two remarks. What we understand by trade taxes in developing countries is not exactly what we understand by trade taxes in developed countries. Many trade taxes in developing countries are actually consumption taxes. It's true that for some goods there is a protective element. For lots of other goods, however, the trade tax is just the first step of a tax on consumption and might actually be the first step of a value-added tax. In a country like Tunisia, for instance, most of the value-added tax is collected at the border. We should be careful about the statistics and the interpretation of taxes on trade.

My second remark is related to what Richard Bird just mentioned on tariffs and is a point that did not come out as clearly as it might have in the paper: that is, the determination of the exchange rate, which is *the* story of quasi taxes in developing countries. A tax at 20 percent is less significant than an overvaluation of 40 percent. In Table 3.1 of the paper, however, the rationing of foreign exchange is said to have an effect on revenues of zero.

That's not how I read the evidence in countries where the government maintains a low exchange rate precisely to have an implicit tax on exports—cocoa in Ghana is a good example—and then with these resources can purchase the foreign goods that it requires. In other countries like Nigeria, it's the other way around. The government is the main exporter, and the government loses by having the wrong exchange rate. Of course, one can explain this result by political favors that can be given to the people who are lucky enough to get the import licenses, but sometimes this is not the whole story.

One should also be careful about the determination of the exchange rates. In countries like Ghana and Nigeria that have parallel rates, the parallel rate is very different. Countries where the government has tried to devalue without fiscal reform have failed, because they have forgone precisely these implicit revenues on exports. What is often done is to make the printing press work, thereby creating additional inflation. This may fix the exchange rate at a slightly better value in the short term, but, by producing additional inflation, may make the exchange rate in the longer term even worse than it was initially.

MR. SEADE: Adding to what Christophe said, the exchange rate, which is normally seen as a distortion on the trade side, is primarily a trade instrument, but it has very direct fiscal implications. Although this is not something that has been examined very carefully, it can have enormous implications because it changes the price between tradables and untradables and whom you tax.

MR. BIRD: In John's paper he mentioned that GATT gives some leeway to countries to impose certain antitrade policies and that more use is made of these by developing countries. Wouldn't it seem to be in the best interests of such countries to be constrained from using such devices?

Given our weakness of will, we'll all do things that we know are bad for us if they're there for us to do, but if we remove them from our purview as possibilities, then we don't do them—and that, of course, is what the whole multilateral free-trade agreement was about in the first place. If you don't like the effects of some of the trade policies in developing countries, it might be in the interests of developing countries, if not of all interests within those countries, to preclude themselves from being allowed to do these bad things to themselves.

JOHN WHALLEY: There's a very important issue here. If you look at what Korea did in the early 1960s and if it's true, as many people think, that duty remissions were the key to what they did, they were able to do this at that time without provoking any response from the developed countries through countervailing duties, because this was before the 1974 trade bill in the United States, before the subsidies tariff. Most trade theories would say that what Korea was doing made sense because, given that they had the tariff, it was a move toward trade neutrality.

In view of the changes we've had in the trading system in the intervening years, attempts by other countries to go down the same route have provoked strong reactions, as happened to Mexico, for example. The rules of the system have changed and currently have a very legalist notion of what's "protection" and what's "promotion" and catch cases where countries are clearly moving toward trade neutrality.

JOEL SLEMROD: I had a similar reaction to that of Jesus, that this is a valuable paper descriptively, but I wonder if there are any general rules that you can offer us about the preferability of "tax-like" fiscal policies versus nontax policies. I certainly came away with the idea that things are complicated. One simple argument, however, is that tariffs are better than quotas because they both distort trade patterns but at least tariffs raise revenue and quotas don't.

Extending this simple case, it may also be true that nontax subsidies are better than tax subsidies, because they both have the same distortion but at least the nontax subsidies don't cost revenue like tax subsidies. How generalizable are these simple principles, and are there others?

WAYNE THIRSK: I want to add to the list of questions that are being directed to you, John.

In your paper there is an eloquent plea for the application of general equilibrium analysis to these issues; so my first question is whether partial equilibrium or partial analysis of these trade issues is passé. Is it completely worthless to try to calculate the tax equivalent or the tariff equivalent of many of these policies?

The second question I have is, Even if we agree that the general equilibrium route is the way to go, how do we figure out which is the really binding constraint in many of these countries? When you've got tariffs, quotas, and foreign exchange restrictions, which one of these policies rules the roost? How can we figure out what's controlling the action?

MALCOLM GILLIS: John, you gave as an example of one of these taxlike devices the rattan business in Indonesia. I want everybody to realize that this is a perfect example of trade contagion.

Indonesian rent seekers were provided a perfect illustration in support of their case for the adoption of this policy by the Philippines' prohibition of export of raw rattan, which was thought to have worked very well. The Philippine government has announced on several occasions that this policy has been very successful, because exports rose very dramatically, about 50 percent in the space of five years. But they forgot to point out that the Philippines' share in the overall rattan export market (raw plus processed rattan) actually declined sharply. In Indonesia a particular group of rent seekers who had long sought to ban export of raw rattan were able to take the Philippines' illustration of so-called success and make it their case. Of course, it has been a disaster. The greater burden of the policy has fallen primarily on small-scale rattan gatherers in the island of Borneo.

JOHANNES LINN: John's observation that the long-term effect of tariffs under binding quotas is something to take account of is absolutely right. The World Bank adheres to the general principle that it is a good idea to reduce quotas first and then go on to the tariff side. I know we have made some mistakes—the Philippines is one case—but in principle we believe in the sequencing that you think is the right one.

On a more general note, I wonder to what extent thinking and talking in terms of taxlike effects of nontax interventions in the trade regime is helpful to the analysis of nontax trade intervention—except perhaps to the extent that it allows public finance economists to get into the act and talk about nontax measures. The static welfare effects measured by looking at taxlike effects of nontax distortions in my view are likely to be much less important than the dynamic effects that regulatory and other quantitative controls tend to have through their effects on market structure, contestability, and access.

Finally, at the very end of your paper, you talk about the difficulty of sorting out the effects of nontax interventions from the effects of tax interventions. What I have experienced in dealing with reform efforts around the globe is that your concern about the difficulty of estimating quantitatively the effects of trade reform doesn't apply only to the nontariff components. In fact, it applies across the board. My impression is that we have very few reasonably reliable quantitative estimates, ex post or ex ante, of the effects of changes in the trade regime, and your paper unfortunately doesn't add much to the evidence on what we know about the effects of liberalization as a whole or partially.

DAN USHER: Related to the comment that Johannes Linn just made, as the discussion goes on, I become increasingly confused as to what an "implicit" tax is. I know what John Whalley's paper is about, and I have no quarrel with it at all. But among the items discussed, some are pure taxes, some are trade taxes—and, in Wayne Thirsk's paper, which we'll be discussing later, we are presented with taxes on the money supply, which are essentially, and I think with as much justification, implicit transfers. A lot of what's going under the name of implicit taxes is arrangements by which some people in a country become worse off and other people in a country become better off as a result of particular government policies affecting trade, money, or anything else.

Indeed, one possibility is that this seminar—with the exception perhaps of my own paper, and that's Richard's fault—might really be about price and quantity control, because a lot of the discussion is on the effect on countries of restrictions on interest rates and other prices. Indeed, I think that price and quantity control—which is almost Wayne Thirsk's definition of a quasi tax—comes closer to the spirit of what we're talking about then any other term I can think of.

ROBERT HIGGS: I have a question, an observation, and then another question. At one point in the paper, you say, "Developing countries often have such restrictions as rationed foreign exchange and quotas in their trade regimes because, in the past, they have been directly affected by terms of trade and other external sector shocks that, if left unattended, would imply major adjustment costs for the economy."

This seems to be a testable hypothesis. There could be—may already be—measures of the extent to which altered terms of trade and other external shocks have affected various countries. So we may be in a position to test the hypothesis and determine whether the statement you make is in fact consistent with the data. That's my first question: Has such a hypothesis been tested? The hypothesis a priori strikes me as doubtful because it seems to rest on a link between the decisions made by government officials who impose foreign exchange controls or quotas and the adjustment costs for the whole economy as opposed to costs and benefits bearing on the decision makers themselves.

With that observation, I proceed to a second question. Is it feasible to test the hypothesis that some developing countries have restrictions such as rationed foreign exchange and quotas in their trade regimes because their officials have more *discretion* in the allocation of the rights to foreign exchange or the access to quotas and therefore have more to gain by creating salable political assets? If it were possible to measure the extent to which such discretion exists in the allocation of these valuable rights, then we could test my alternative hypothesis. Do you think that might be possible?

MR. CHAMLEY: To fix the exchange rate is a bit like breaking the thermometer when a person has a disease. It's true that just by maintaining the same exchange rate, some countries—at least I can think of a couple—have avoided the necessary adjustments and made the whole process much more painful at the end.

MR. SLEMROD: Is there any literature or research testing the question whether quotas per se have higher or lower deadweight losses than certain levels of tariffs? If so, has there been any effort to link these greater or lesser losses to their consequences for those economies, particularly the United States, that have clearly moved from tariffs toward quotas?

MR. BIRD: The next step will probably be to ration foreign exchange.

MAXWELL FRY: I just wanted to follow up on Professor Higgs's point on accommodative macroeconomic policies. I did some work a few years ago with my colleague David Lillien on the effects of monetary policies, specifically looking at whether countries accommodated the oil price increase. From that we extrapolated to monetary policy regimes. Our conclusion was that you can certainly smooth out short-run fluctuations. But we found that the very significant long-run effects that the uncertainty produced through accommodative or discretionary monetary policy reduced long-run growth.

MR. BIRD: It's not clear to me from this paper exactly what comparative costs are imposed on society by using one instrument rather than another to achieve a particular goal. Let me suggest, however, that as we move down this sequence from foreign exchange rationing to quotas to tariffs, there would be less rent seeking and more revenue for the government, but might there not be at least as high or perhaps even a higher marginal distortionary cost from pushing on this particular tax base? In saying this, I am assuming that I must be getting less revenue from something else or I have expanded the government sector. That's the kind of interaction that it's very hard to see in the existing presentation.

In any case, however, let me praise John Whalley for trying to put this stuff together in a table. We can all sit here and take shots at it, but it provides a substantial improvement in being able to begin to think about the way these things are hooked together. I'm just suggesting some other columns.

MR. WHALLEY: I have a comment about the numbers. The intuition I have is the following. You take this whole package of things, and you have to think of it as a combined wedge. If you talk about quotas or tariffs, you can keep that wedge unchanged. There shouldn't be any effect except that you have the rent-seeking component.

On rent seeking, there are two sets of numbers I throw out. If you look at Anne Krueger's original study, her claim was that for the 1960s in India, the cost of rent seeking just in import licensing alone was 7 percent of GDP; for Turkey it was 15 percent of GDP. In a joint paper I did in the early 1980s, we tried to pull together what was known about the value of rents in India. We finished up with a range between 30 and 45 percent of GDP for India.

That's a social cost of rent-seeking activity. If you start comparing that to some of the estimates from traditional trade models of the impact of trade liberalization, you're talking about numbers that are significantly less than 1 percent of GDP.

I echo what Johannes was saying about how little we know from the studies, but often the studies also tend to be so completely inconsistent with intuition that you just can't believe them. Some of the work done on development and growth and the role of exports in growth exemplifies this. For Korea, for instance, the estimated effect on the growth rate is something like 0.0001. No model I know of makes any sense of Korea having a fivefold or sixfold increase in real GDP per capita over a thirty-five-year period. None even comes close.

MR. BIRD: John has told us, I think correctly, that when there's a binding foreign exchange constraint, a tariff is a tax on rent. It should also be noted, however, that the people receiving these rents will try to avoid having this penalty imposed on them. Additional resource costs are involved in their trying to dodge these rent taxes.

A quite different sort of point, made by Miguel Urrutia at an earlier Sequoia seminar, is that differential exchange rates or equivalent taxes and subsidies may be necessary in a country that's in a sense too efficient in producing something for an unstable world market. A unified exchange rate at the extreme might mean that you wouldn't do anything except produce just this one product. That's fine, if you think everybody can move around the world very quickly and cease being coffee growers in Colombia and become automobile producers in Japan in thirty seconds if the price changes. But that's not the world we live in, and the adjustment costs may be so high that there is a strong argument from the point of view of development policy for having differential trade policies. John's paper calls our attention very clearly to the "nonefficiency" aspects of policy, that there are all these distributional things people are trying to do, for better or for worse. Countries (and their leaders) tend to have such long-run social goals as the continued existence of a country with a certain number of people in it.

Finally, without answering the question whether we should call all the effects of these policies taxlike, the fact that we attempt to achieve the same policy objectives through different sets of policies means that, in some sense, we always have to compare all these policies explicitly if we're to know what we're doing. Whether we want to do that in this tax-subsidy framework or some other framework is another question.

DWIGHT LEE: I think the standard view is that tariffs are less distorting. Is that not correct?

MR. WHALLEY: It's not tariffs or quotas per se, but it's tariffs versus allocated quotas with no resale.

MR. LEE: But if you compare the standard view of the quota with a tariff, one thing that might be ignored by the idea that quotas are worse is that tariffs raise revenues. Those revenues often mobilize constituent groups in favor of them. There was a statement in the paper that tariffs can reduce the value of quota rents and hence the amount of resources devoted to rent seeking, but the revenues themselves generate rent seeking. Even if there's no net increase in revenues because we reduce taxes elsewhere in the economy, there's rent seeking over whose taxes get reduced.

Tariffs may mobilize two interest groups in their favor—groups that are protected against foreign competition and groups that see

benefits from capturing those revenues. It might well be that tariffs
are more harmful than quotas, again looking at the political dimension. They might be harder to get rid of.

WARREN BROOKES: Economists estimate that we now spend $24
billion or $25 billion more on textiles in this country because of the
quota system—which is roughly equivalent to a 25 percent extra
cost imposed on our purchase of textiles. If we applied a 25 percent
tariff instead, the consumer would save $14 billion or $15 billion.
This one example suggests that the move we're making toward
quotas is imposing a decidedly greater deadweight loss on the
economy than straightforward tariffs.

CHARLES McLURE: It's important to go back to the theme of this
seminar series, which is "Including the Excluded: Extending the
Benefits of Development." I believe that a lot of bad policies have
been established in the name of creating economic development,
because there is a general inability to realize that there are no free
lunches. Let's take the case of protection, whether it is through
quotas or through tariffs. Yes, you may get some development by
protecting a certain sector, but somebody's going to pay higher
prices as a result of that protection, and somebody else is going to
benefit from it.

That somebody is likely to be a monopolist or an oligopolist. And
you're likely to have members of labor unions benefiting, unions
that might not have existed otherwise, that will grow up behind the
protective tariff. So you're going to get very concentrated benefits in
the protected sector, paid for by a lot of people who have to pay
higher prices for whatever is being protected—and those people are
not necessarily going to be wealthy. One of the better ways of
extending the benefits of development is not to engage in policies
that create concentrated benefits.

MR. BIRD: Once you start including certain groups, it's very
difficult to exclude them thereafter. They defend their turf very
fiercely. Economists seldom look at real adjustment costs, although
the politically relevant adjustment costs may be very high.

Response
John Whalley

This is meant to be basically a descriptive paper. Nonetheless, two or three prescriptions come through. One is that ultimately it is the whole package one has to consider. Monetary arrangements and monetary discipline, for example, are central. In principle, there should be duty-free treatment for capital goods and raw materials. In reality, most developing countries have low tariffs on those items but at the same time impose trade restrictions. The reason is that domestic monetary policy is not accommodating to the external regime.

If you look at the system as a whole, there are two parts to the global trading system of developed countries. On the one hand is the GATT—a contract, an agreement among countries on how they will set their trade policies—and on the other hand is the International Monetary Fund, which is an implicit contract that makes these trade policies meaningful. But when developing countries that have never signed that implicit contract and do not adhere to it talk about trying to move toward convertibility, problems are likely to emerge. A second message is that even a "successful" negotiation of tariff reductions with developing countries is likely to be insufficient to its intended purpose of gaining access to those markets. This is because there are apt to be about three other things lined up behind the tariffs that are excluded from the system of rules to which the developed, but not the developing, countries are contractually bound.

Developing countries get frustrated because they cannot get credit. Developed countries get frustrated because even if they can negotiate tariffs down, which they usually cannot, it still will not get them into developing countries' markets until they get everything else out of the way.

Wayne Thirsk raised the issue of general equilibrium analysis. I do a lot of general equilibrium work, but I would respond to his question by saying that one has to be careful because there are two different issues at stake. One is technique, and the other is the focus of the analysis. I have seen general equilibrium models of developing countries that look only at tariffs. It doesn't matter whether you use partial or general equilibrium analysis, this focus is going to mislead you. Some partial equilibrium analyses, however, at least try to add all the other bits and pieces.

The technique is conditional on the appropriate posturing of the analysis. A lot of the general equilibrium analysis I see is not very insightful because the people don't really understand the issues.

Robert Higgs asked if there were any studies of developing countries on adjustment costs. Are there any studies of developed countries? Even for the United States, to my knowledge, there are but two, by Richardson and by Klein. The numbers in these studies are very different. The whole approach and analysis are completely different. Given the potential importance of adjustment costs in trade policy, it amazes me not only how little we know about developing countries but how little we know about developed countries. There is even a gaping hole in terms of the conceptual framework used to make calculations. I have recently been working on a piece on adjustment costs, which makes the point that even in the few studies that have been done people use very simple modeling frameworks that really assume no adjustment. They calculate the number of people who move and calculate the average duration of unemployment and add the duration figure. But, if you have a model in which adjustment costs are endogenous and the costs are high enough, nobody would ever move.

Charlie McLure's comment is interesting. He said that we should emphasize that development is not advanced through protection. You would get a very strong reaction from certain economists in developing countries—an intellectual constituency that is not very strongly represented here. They will say that growth- and welfare-maximizing policies are totally different. If you are going to grow, obviously you want to import capital and capital goods and equipment, machinery, and so on. You don't want to import luxury consumption goods. You have to set priorities for your import regime. Growth maximizing is not the same as no intervention. If a volume such as this is to be read in that community and taken seriously, you have to respond to these arguments.

4

Wayne R. Thirsk

Financial Institutions and Their Quasi Taxes— A Little Bit of Craziness

Governments levy taxes to finance a wide variety of public sector activities. With the exception of head taxes, these taxes drive a wedge in the marketplace between the price paid by a purchaser and the price that a supplier of a commodity or a resource receives. The gap between what is paid and what is returned to suppliers is siphoned off as tax revenues by government.

Many government regulations that aim at controlling market prices also introduce a taxlike wedge between demand and supply prices. Regulations of this kind have frequently been referred to as quasi taxes. As will be shown below, what distinguishes quasi taxes from ordinary taxes is that the benefits they finance are targeted to particular groups in the economy. Quasi taxes do not flow into general revenues in the way that ordinary taxes that are not earmarked do. Rather, quasi taxes should be viewed as part of an overall tax and subsidy package.

Quasi taxes that exert their impact on the behavior of financial institutions in developing countries and affect the degree of financial intermediation are the focus of this paper. It begins with a brief discussion of the motives that lie behind the government use of quasi taxes applied to financial markets. That is followed by a consideration of how effective these quasi taxes are likely to be in achieving their stated objectives. The basic equivalence between financial sector quasi taxes and formal tax and transfer mechanisms is set out in the next section. After that a simple diagrammatic model is presented and used to indicate the potential range of effects that quasi taxes may have on the efficiency of resource allocation and the distribution of income. The results of some earlier empirical studies attempting to measure the size of these effects are also inserted at this juncture. Finally, some policy implications are brought out in the concluding section of the paper.

Why Quasi Taxes?

Quasi taxes appear in numerous forms, but, whatever guise they take, their ultimate aim is to control either the price or the volume of credit or sometimes both. In response to compelling political pressures governments everywhere have tried to steer more credit toward particular groups of borrowers, especially farmers, small businessmen, consumers of housing, and themselves, at terms that are more favorable than an unfettered market would provide.

Toward this end governments have typically imposed interest rate ceilings on deposits issued by formal sector financial institutions, in the expectation that cheaper costs of finance would be passed on to borrowers in the form of lower loan rates. Where lower loan rates have not occurred, the ceilings on deposit rates have often been supplemented by ceilings on loan rates for preferred borrowers. Thus the scope of quasi taxes does not include the often substantial informal financial sector or transactions with foreign financial institutions. Quasi taxes are ordinarily selective taxes on one component of a country's financial system.

Another significant type of quasi tax consists of restrictions on the portfolio composition of depository institutions. Banks and other financial lenders may be required to allocate a fixed proportion of their loans to preferred borrowers at rates below those charged on other kinds of loans. Alternatively, private commercial banks may be forced to hold a fixed percentage of their assets in the form of low-interest obligations issued by publicly owned specialized lending agencies that charge concessional rates of interest to their borrowers.[1] In either situation the effect of the regulation is to place downward pressure on the deposit rate that a competitive financial institution can afford to pay. Deposit holders are implicitly taxed by these regulations, and some will find it attractive to hold their wealth in alternative forms, such as tangible assets (real estate and jewelry, for example) or assets that arise from lending to untaxed activity in informal and foreign credit markets. In the literature on development these implicit tax policies have been referred to as the financial repression of the formal financial sector in developing countries. Conversely, financial liberalization is the term associated with the elimination of these implicit tax policies.

An additional instrument of financial repression is the imposition of high reserve requirements on commercial banks. Because central banks seldom pay interest on required reserves or, if they do, only at a relatively modest rate, high reserve requirements automatically reduce the proportion of income-earning assets held by banks and limit the amount of interest they can offer on their deposits.[2] From the government's narrow financial perspective, this state of affairs provides a number of important advantages. First, it enables governments to launch their expenditure programs without having to resort to higher explicit taxation. When the public debt arising from a government deficit is monetized by the central bank, high reserve requirements both contain the growth of credit to the private sector and enhance the size of the inflation tax base, the stock of outside money, or the magnitude of the monetary base that is diminished in real terms by inflation. Additionally, the emergence of low deposit rates makes it easier for low-yield government bonds to compete in the portfolios held by direct lenders.[3]

As noted by Fry (1988, chap. 12), credit ceilings are just as likely as credit floors to constitute a form of quasi tax on financial assets. When financial institutions are enjoined from using their excess reserves to extend credit, their incentive to compete for new deposits disappears, and deposit interest rates are likely to be depressed by the absence of competition. When the margin between lending and deposit rates increases, it is the same as if the financial institution had been subjected to a formal tax on its intermediation activities.

Most developing countries have at one point or another embraced either some or all of these forms of quasi taxation. In their analysis of the regulatory experience of ten developing countries over the period 1970–1982, Hanson and Neal (1986) found that all of them rigorously pursued directed credit programs designed to channel credit resources toward favored groups, sectors, and regions, including the public sector. Six of them—Pakistan, Morocco, Thailand, Bangladesh, and Korea—displayed modestly negative real deposit and preferential loan rates. Three of them— Nigeria, Peru, and Turkey—exhibited real deposit rates over the period that were highly negative, in the −16.5 percent to −18.6 percent range. Preferential loan rates were often lower than deposit rates. In all these countries nominal interest rates tended to be sticky, with the result that low or even negative real interest rates were primarily the byproduct of inflationary macropolicies. While noting the tendency of resources to leak away from targeted lending programs, the authors concluded from their survey that directed credit schemes and public sector borrowing act to "crowd out" nonpreferred borrowers and drive up interest rates in uncontrolled credit markets because of the heightened competition for the remaining sources of credit.

What sustains the seemingly universal appeal of quasi taxes on financial institutions? Evidently the desire by governments for relatively cheap sources of bond finance is a major part of the story. But there seems to be more to it than that, and at least two other considerations appear to be relevant. One is the stereotype, or deeply entrenched perception, that lenders, on balance, tend to be well-off while borrowers, on the whole, are either poor or not nearly as well-off as lenders. A number of directed credit programs seem to be driven by a desire to redistribute welfare from rich lender to poor borrower. Although a treatment of the probable distributive impact of financial quasi taxes is reserved for the section "The Economic Effects of Quasi Taxes" below, Adler (1965), among others, has challenged whether this popular perception bears even a remote resemblance to reality. In Colombia Adler found that the clientele of specialized lending agencies in agriculture and housing consisted primarily of the wealthy farmer and the well-off home-owner. Moreover, the implicitly taxed lender was more likely than not to be a low-income saver.

Also adding impetus to the regime of quasi taxes in many countries is the apparent desire on the part of governments to provide compensation for the handicaps that some sectors or groups are perceived to bear on account of various nonfinancial policy initiatives. Consider agriculture for instance. In many countries this sector falls victim to a battery of noncredit policies that promote the growth of nonagricultural activities at the expense of agriculture. These noncredit policies include, but are not limited to, tariff-induced import substitution and overvalued exchange rates (both of which act as an implicit tax on agricultural exports), foreign exchange restrictions and licensing schemes that grant priority to nonagricultural users, and price controls on basic foodstuffs in-tended to raise the real wage of urban workers. In the messy world of second-best political bargaining, the creation of a new distortion in resource use is often justified by the existence of earlier dis-tortions.

Another, less frequently voiced argument for quasi taxes is that they provide a useful discipline on the exercise of monopoly power in a concentrated banking system. Imperfectly competitive banks may operate with sizable spreads between loan and deposit rates, a measure of the implicit tax associated with monopolistic behavior. In such an environment regulatory restrictions on lending rates may be able to convert monopoly profits into lower lending rates and appropriate a portion of monopoly profits for the benefit of borrowers.

Finally, there is the simple-minded notion that lower interest rates will stimulate a larger volume of investment. As discussed next and as many countries have discovered the hard way, what is missing from this argument is a consideration of the supply side, or where the funds for investment will come from. Downwardly regulated interest rates may dry up some potential sources of investment finance and result in less, rather than more, investment.

Quasi Taxes—How Effective Are They?

It is one thing to establish a regime of quasi taxes on financial intermediaries. It is quite another to enforce them and have them apply as they were intended to work. Like taxes, regulations involve an element of compulsion and invite avoidance and evasion on the part of those who are coerced. Such tension is inevitable, and perverse outcomes may occur when quasi taxes attempt to rule the interplay of market forces by edict and compel financial market participants to act in ways that are inconsistent with their self-interest.[4]

Suppose banks or other intermediaries are required by regulation to lend to a group of preferred borrowers at below-market lending rates. A variety of responses from those subject to regulation would help to mitigate the repercussions of such a decree. Although regulators may have tight control over stated interest rates, they have much less influence on effective interest rates.[5] Maximum legal loan rates would be expected to induce intermediaries to charge extra fees in appraising loan applications, to collect interest in advance, and to require borrowers to hold compensating balances. To the extent that these price reactions were inadequate to offset the regulatory bite or perhaps were themselves also made subject to regulation, some further responses would be anticipated from the supply side. Lenders would have a strong incentive to curtail their supply of credit to preferred borrowers and demand substantial collateral from those who were fortunate enough to receive loans at the subsidized rates. According to Virmani (1984), such was the experience in Bangladesh, where a system of sectorally specific interest ceilings redirected credit flows away from low-interest farm and export loans toward other sectors and toward borrowers with more collateral. Alternatively, if intermediaries are sectorally specialized and deposit rates are depressed by the regulated loan rates, ultimate lenders may shift their funds to higher-yielding outlets. Either way the supply of preferred credit is diminished.

Governments have adopted a number of measures to counteract the erosion of their price controls on credit. In some cases quantity controls have been either combined with or used to replace price controls to prevent the reduction in supply of preferred credit. The credit floors described in the last section are the most common manifestation of quantity constraints. Even these lending requirements, however, can be circumvented by the simple expedient of reclassifying the purpose of a loan. For example, all acquisitions of small aircraft could be transformed into agricultural transportation loans for purposes of satisfying a credit floor on the amount of agricultural loans.

Rediscount privileges are also used to make it worthwhile for financial institutions to extend relatively low-interest loans. Providers of these loans may sell them to the central bank in exchange for low-interest central bank credit, a privilege that makes the central bank the de facto supplier of cheap credit. Nonetheless, the fungibility of funds makes it impossible to ascertain easily the effectiveness of the rediscount mechanism. Intermediaries could shift blue-chip clients who would have received loans in any event to the front of the rediscount line and thereby expand the volume of funds available for nonpreferred lending. While it introduces a financial carrot to offset the impact of the quasi tax, the rediscount mechanism may also seriously complicate the task of controlling the monetary base, as Fry (1988) has pointed out. Moreover, by contributing to an elaborate pattern of financial layering, rediscounting may raise the resource cost of shifting funds from ultimate lenders to ultimate borrowers, as also noted by Fry (1988).

Another technique for diverting credit into lower-paying employments is a system of obligatory investment or forced lending that is sometimes imposed on private financial intermediaries. Adler (1965) gives a detailed description of how such a system works in Colombia. A network of obligatory investments for private intermediaries sustains a system of less than average interest rates on loans made by a raft of public lending institutions catering mainly to agriculture, housing, and small business. The Agricultural Bank (Caja Agraria), for example, is the primary agricultural lender; it receives its loanable funds from sales of its low-yielding bonds to the central bank and to savings institutions and commercial banks, which are obliged to purchase them. Similarly, the major mortgage lender, Banco Central Hipotecario, issues a twenty-year bond that insurance companies, capitalization companies, and all issuers of savings deposits are required to purchase. Because of the unprofitability of savings deposits, commercial banks issue few of them, and most savings accounts are collected by the public lending institutions, which pay only a modest return on them. Adler estimates that the obligatory investments generate yields that are on average only about half, and sometimes even less than that, of the market-determined return on a corporate bond.

Both the lessons of experience and the insights of economic theory suggest that the successful application of financial quasi taxes depends critically on the compartmentalization of a country's capital markets. Just as a discriminating monopolist must prevent opportunities for resale in higher-priced markets, a government relying on quasi taxation must continuously combat profit-seeking pressures to break down capital market barriers. Suppliers of credit have to be prevented or discouraged from shifting their funds to higher-yield activities, and users of credit must be deterred from profitable relending. Otherwise, arbitrage behavior will render quasi taxes ineffective.[6]

As Hanson and Neal (1986) concluded from their examination of ten developing countries, there is an inevitable leakage of resources from targeted sectors. Relending is particularly difficult to control. If, for example, lending rates are below deposit rates, those fortunate enough to have access to funds effectively have the keys to a virtually riskless money machine.[7] With rationing of loans some forms of relending may be disguised as mergers. As described by Fry (1988), some large firms that receive rationed credit may use those resources to buy out profitable smaller firms that have been excluded from the loan market.

The Equivalence of Taxes and Quasi Taxes

Figure 4.1 can be used to illustrate some of the similarities and differences that exist between quasi taxes on financial intermediaries and formal tax policies. The supply and demand curves for loanable funds shown in Figure 4.1 represent behavioral relationships in the formal financial sector of a typical developing country. As interest rates increase, savers are willing to hold a larger fraction of their wealth in the form of deposits issued by this sector. Demand, however, diminishes at higher rates either because borrowers can turn to other sources of credit or because it becomes unprofitable to use borrowed funds.

In the absence of taxes of any kind, a competitive financial sector would establish a uniform interest rate, risk factors aside, of i_0 and furnish credit on the scale of L_0 to borrowers.[8] If an explicit tax on financial transactions were introduced at this point, it could be viewed as either adding to the cost of supplying deposits or subtracting from the return to lending. Either way a wedge would be driven between the interest rate paid by borrowers and that received by depositors. In Figure 4.1 such a wedge is portrayed by the distance *AF*. With a wedge of this size borrowers pay the now higher interest rate i_2, and depositors receive the now lower interest rate i_1. Tax

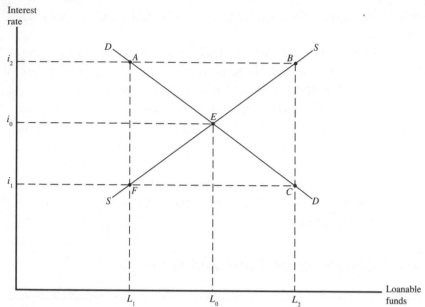

Figure 4.1. Quasi taxes and transfers.

revenues in the amount depicted by the rectangle AFi_1i_2 are collected. Taxes of this kind exist in Turkey and the Philippines, where ad valorem taxes are assessed on the gross receipts of the banking system.[9]

Quasi taxes replicate many of the effects of a formal tax. For example, a ceiling on deposit rates of i_1 would curtail the supply of deposits and loans to L_1 just as an explicit tax of AF would. If loan rates were free to adjust, the competition for a diminished credit pool would drive interest rates to i_2 and equilibrate the demand for and the supply of credit.[10] If loan rates as well as deposit rates were restricted to i_1, loans would have to be rationed on a nonprice basis. Exactly how this might be done, efficiently or otherwise, is discussed in the next section. If it were done efficiently, borrowers who would be willing to pay interest at i_2 on the margin would instead receive loans at the reduced rate of i_1. The combination of the interest ceilings and efficient rationing would be equivalent to imposing an explicit tax of *AF* on financial institutions and earmarking the entire proceeds of the tax to provide an interest rate subsidy to borrowers. Thus although an explicit tax would generate positive tax revenues, the equivalent quasi tax has no direct revenue implications because it is coupled with a subsidy or transfer of equal value. Indirect revenue losses could arise, for example, if interest rate ceilings spur demands for savings-related tax incentives.

In the case in which loan, but not deposit, rates are regulated at the level i_1, there are several possibilities concerning who pays the cost of the subsidy provided to borrowers. Most likely the lower return from lending will bring downward pressure to bear on deposit rates, and depositors will finance the subsidy. Some cross-subsidization among borrowers may also occur, however, if financial institutions can extract higher lending rates from nonpreferred borrowers. Finally, if the regulated institutions earned some monopoly rents before being regulated, it is probable that a portion of the subsidy cost will be paid for by a reduction in these rents. The last possibility is the most favorable regulatory outcome since it, and it alone, would not provoke any resource misallocation.

The quasi tax can also be usefully compared with a formal subsidy scheme for borrowers, for example, the practices of some public lending agencies in which the loan rate is held below the deposit rate. The losses entailed by these lending practices are recovered from government revenue transfers intended to help pay for current expenditures or received as part of a capital transfer agreement. In Colombia Bird (1984) has outlined how the central government has made budgetary transfers to the Land Credit Institute (ICT) on a regular basis and also, on an occasional basis, to the Agricultural Bank. In 1979, for example, slightly less than 1 percent of central government expenditures was allocated as a capital transfer to the ICT.[11]

In Figure 4.1 the vertical distance *BC* represents a formal subsidy to lenders. With a subsidy of that size it would be possible to charge lenders a low rate of i_1 while paying depositors the higher rate of i_2. The revenue cost of financing this subsidy is shown as the rectangular area BCi_1i_2. Whether these subsidies are implicit or explicit, the World Bank (1989, pp.60–61) has found that they can be sizable, ranging from 4 to 8 percent of gross domestic product in Brazil, Mexico, and Costa Rica.

The Economic Effects of Quasi Taxes

Since quasi taxes are capable of duplicating the effects of explicit, earmarked taxes, it is natural to evaluate the impact of quasi taxation according to the normal criteria of efficiency, equity, and administrative ease. Enforcement complications and issues were dealt with earlier; this section concentrates on the efficiency and equity aspects of quasi taxation.

The efficiency features are most easily appreciated with the aid of the simple diagrammatic model shown in Figure 4.2. The model is adapted from Chamley (1987) and is an interesting extension of Harberger's (1962) two-sector tax incidence model.

The model rests on a number of critical assumptions, which are spelled out and discussed below.

1) The supply of real capital to the economy is fixed—as shown by the length of axis $O_F O_I$ in Figure 4.2—and is allocated according to the supply of funds between the formal financial sector (F) and the informal financial sector (I). Foreign exchange controls insulate the economy from activities in the world capital market. Wealth owners hold indirect claims to the economy's capital stock by holding the indirect liabilities issued by firms or moneylenders in both sectors.

2) Savers can switch their assets easily between the formal and informal credit markets, so that the deposit rate paid in the formal sector matches the (risk-adjusted) rate of return on investment in the informal market.

3) Borrowers, however, cannot move between sectors and are therefore prevented from borrowing in one market and lending in the other.

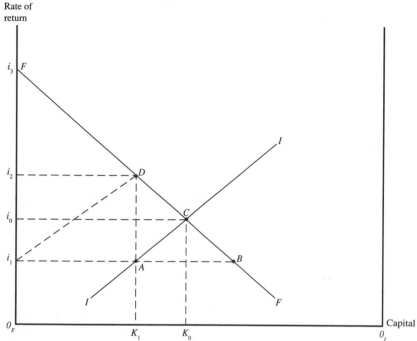

Figure 4.2. The inefficiency of quasi taxes.

4) To simplify matters, there is no uncertainty with respect to investment returns or the ability or willingness to repay loans and therefore no risk premiums. Intermediation costs are also assumed to be zero.

5) When interest ceilings are imposed on formal sector loan rates, firms in that sector are unable to offset their effect by a policy of requiring compensating balances or other behavior that raises effective loan rates.

6) The economy enjoys macrostability such that nominal interest rate changes correspond to real interest rate variations and any indirect revenue effects attributable to quasi taxation do not create fiscal deficits.

7) Efficient relative prices prevail in the rest of the economy and produce a convergence between private and social rates of return on investment.

8) In the absence of regulation the formal financial sector behaves in a competitive fashion.

Given these assumptions, an initial capital market equilibrium is featured in Figure 4.2 where the interest rate i_0 is received by owners of wealth in both sectors and supplies of deposits and credit in the amount $O_F K_O$ emanate from the formal sector. The functions FF and II indicate the returns on investment financed by loans extended from the formal and informal sectors respectively. By assumption, the function II also represents the supply of deposits to the formal sector.

When interest rate ceilings on loans (and hence deposits) are introduced into the formal sector, the interest rate in that sector declines to i_1, and deposits (and loans) issued by it contract to $O_F K_1$ at the lower deposit rate. Credit in the amount of $K_1 K_O$ transfers to the informal sector, where the larger supply depresses interest rates on loans to i_1 as well.[12] At the regulated loan rate there is an excess demand for formal sector loans of AB, and the amount of loanable funds on hand must be rationed out in some manner among potential borrowers.

How the rationing is carried out has an important bearing on the determination of efficiency costs. There are several possibilities. If lenders in the formal sector ration funds efficiently, they will make funds available only to their highest rate-of-return borrowers. In that case the marginal borrower would earn a rate of return of i_2 on his investment. Since the marginal borrower in the informal sector earns only i_1 on his investment, there is a misallocation of investment resources and a loss of capital productivity on the marginal investment equal to the difference between i_2 and i_1. Using similar reasoning, it can be seen that the size of the inefficiency resulting from the quasi tax is represented by the area of the triangle ACD.

That is not all there is to it, however. At the margin borrowers lucky enough to receive a loan will reap an economic rent of DA, which also represents the maximum amount that they would be willing to pay to enjoy that rent. If other prospective borrowers have to incur similar rent-seeking costs to compete successfully for access to funds, there is an additional social cost associated with the area of the rent-seeking rectangle DAi_2i_1. In that case the total inefficiency cost of the quasi tax would consist of the trapezoidal area $DCAi_1i_2$.

If, however, formal sector lenders are unable or unwilling to ration funds efficiently, the social costs of the quasi tax are elevated. Consider the extreme case, for example, where the most efficient borrowers are replaced by those who are least efficient. Assume, for simplicity, that these two groups are of equal size, represented respectively by the equal distances i_1A and AB in Figure 4.2. If the most efficient borrower were pushed aside for the least efficient, the loss in investment efficiency would be measured by the difference between the rates of return i_3 and i_1. As the next most efficient borrower was replaced by the next most inefficient borrower, a slightly smaller efficiency cost would be incurred until, as the process continued, point D on FF was reached, where no further efficiency loss occurs. By then the total cost of inefficient rationing would correspond to the triangular area i_3Di_1.

In the case of inefficient rationing the costs of quasi taxation consist of the triangle i_3Di_1 plus the triangle ACD. The former triangle represents the cost of investment misallocation within the formal sector; the latter triangle indicates the cost of the distortion in the distribution of investment between the formal and informal sectors. In addition, if potential borrowers consider their selection for loan eligibility part of a random decision-making process, they will also be willing to incur some rent-seeking expenditures.

Without detailed empirical inquiry it is difficult to determine which of the two rationing scenarios is more realistic.[13] The empirical work currently available has tended to opt for the efficient rationing paradigm. Table 4.1 presents some recent estimates by Chamley and Hussain (1988) of efficiency costs for Indonesia and

Table 4.1

Efficiency Impact of Financial Liberalization in Thailand and Indonesia

Variable	Indonesia	Thailand
Increase in real deposit rates (points)	0.1	0.09
Initial level of M_2/GDP	0.2	0.38
Final level of M_2/GDP	0.3	0.68
Allocative gain (percentage of GDP)	0.5	1.4
Savings in rent-seeking costs (percentage of GDP)	2.0	3.4
Total benefit (percentage of GDP)	2.5	4.8

SOURCE: Chamley and Hussain 1988.

Thailand. The allocative cost, corresponding to the triangle *ACD* in Figure 4.2, is measured according to the formula $\frac{1}{2}\Delta i(\Delta M_2/GDP)$, where Δi is the increase in real deposit rates resulting from financial liberalization and $\Delta M_2/GDP$ is the growth in savings deposits, relative to GDP, issued by formal sector financial institutions. Rent-seeking expenditures, corresponding to the rectangle $i_2 DAi_1$ in Figure 4.2, are estimated from the formula $\Delta i(M_2^o/GDP)$, where M_2^o/GDP is the ratio of savings deposits to GDP before liberalization.

As shown in Table 4.1, the allocative gains of financial liberalization range from 0.5 percent of GDP in Indonesia to 1.4 percent in Thailand. In both countries the estimated reduction in rent-seeking expenditures is larger, varying between 2.0 percent of GDP in Indonesia and 3.4 percent in Thailand. Summing these benefits, the total gain from liberalization is estimated as 2.5 percent of GDP in Indonesia and 4.8 percent in Thailand.

How robust are these estimates? Apart from measurement errors, which plague every empirical effort, they are sensitive to the accuracy of the numerous assumptions on the basis of which they are constructed. Two of these assumptions, in particular, are likely to give cause for concern and have enjoyed a controversial history. There is a noticeable lack of agreement in the literature on the nature of the opportunity cost of new deposits issued in the formal sector after a liberalization policy. Much of the early literature on this topic assumed extremely limited savings choices and characterized savers as holding the bulk of their wealth in unproductive forms such as land and precious metals. McKinnon (1973), for instance, viewed the alternative to holding a deposit as a much lower yielding direct investment in traditional technologies. In their appraisal of the liberalization experience, Brown (1973) for Korea and Ranis (1977) for Taiwan both argue for a dramatic shift in wealth holding from unproductive real assets and a consequently large increase in the degree of financial intermediation in the economy.[14] In both countries there was a spectacular growth in the recorded savings rate. Ranis claims that, when real deposit rates rose in Taiwan from 10 percent in 1958–1960 to about 15 percent in 1963–1965, the gross saving rate doubled from 10 to 20 percent of GDP, 70 percent of which derived from households and more than 80 percent of which flowed through formal financial channels. In terms of Figure 4.2, the impact of this alternative view is to assert a much larger gain stemming from financial intermediation, a gain associated with the trapezoid DCK_1K_O rather than the triangle ACD.

The more recent literature on this subject is less sanguine and pays more attention to the role of curb or informal markets than the earlier literature did. In their study of Indonesia and Thailand Chamley and Hussain (1988) found that liberalization was not associated with a higher savings rate.[15] Other recent work reviewed by Fry (1988) reaches a similar conclusion. Van Wijnbergen (1983), meanwhile, has questioned the conventional wisdom by suggesting that the informal sector, because of its relatively low reserve requirements, is a more efficient intermediator than the formal sector. According to this view, the supply of credit would decline in the economy if savers switched their claims to formal sector deposits.

The other key assumption imbedded in Figure 4.2 is the supposition that relative price structures in the economy's commodity and factor markets are efficient. Given what we know, or think we know, about the plethora of distortions that exist in developing economies, this is a doubtful assumption. Without it, however, there is a strong likelihood that the financial sector will efficiently allocate funds to socially wasteful investments. Thus the efficiency payoff to financial liberalization may very well depend on the success of prior reforms of prices and policies in other sectors of the economy, especially the trade sector.

A precise determination of the income distribution consequences of eliminating financial quasi taxes is no easier to pin down. There is a theoretical presumption, however, that if banks and other intermediaries are prevented from charging higher loan rates for riskier investments, they are apt to resort to nonprice methods of reducing their exposure to risk. As Virmani (1982) has argued, one way to do this is to insist on higher collateral requirements in rationing loans. If access to loans is tied to initial ownership of assets, it seems probable that such a lending scheme would skew the distribution of loans in favor of the rich. As McKinnon (1973, p.73) puts it, "cheap credit . . . may not benefit the little man at all" if he is thrown into the arms of informal sector moneylenders.

If poor borrowers tend to be concentrated in the informal sector, however, the model implicit in Figure 4.2 unambiguously predicts that quasi taxes in the formal sector will depress loan rates in the informal sector and therefore improve the welfare of the poor. Conversely, a financial liberalization, although it might allow the poor greater access in the formal market, would also raise informal sector loan rates and harm the poor. Using a more complicated three-sector model consisting of two informal ("old" and "new") sectors as well as a formal sector, Roemer (1986) arrives at the same conclusion. In his model liberalization works to attract funds out of the informal markets and harm poor borrowers with no access to the formal market.

A complete picture of the income changes resulting from liberalization would also have to consider the income profile of depositors in the formal sector and moneylenders in the informal sector.[16] If the former are poor and the latter are rich on balance, liberalization would have a mixed effect on income distribution, helping both one group of poor and another group of rich households. Unfortunately, there is a dearth of empirical studies that have tried to sort this matter out. It is interesting to note, however, that Ranis (1977, p. 38) reports results for Taiwan that contradict the normal predictions of how interest rates respond to liberalization. When real interest rates in the formal sector rose from 10 percent in 1958–1960 to 15 percent in 1963–1965, it is alleged that interest rates in unofficial markets— "deprived of some of their monopoly content"—actually fell from about 50 percent in the late 1950s to about 25 percent in the early 1960s. Under this scenario it is much more likely that the poor borrower and depositor would gain at the expense of the rich moneylender.

A more complete picture would also need to examine the indirect effects of liberalization on the labor market. If quasi taxes and cheap credit induce excessive capital intensity in production, the elimination of quasi taxes would contribute to the welfare of low-income groups through higher wages and more employment opportunities.

Although there is something of an empirical void on the subject, it is difficult to disagree with Fry's overall assessment (1988) of quasi taxes: that they are likely to reduce both the quantity and the quality of investment, encourage capital intensity, worsen income distribution, and increase the degree of industrial concentration.

In Korea, Costa Rica, Brazil, and Colombia there is some, but hardly overwhelming, evidence to support the view that financial liberalization contributes to a more even distribution of income, both directly in the capital market and indirectly in the labor market. On the basis of a wider sample of developing countries' experience, Fry (1988, p. 153) concludes that "the bulk of the empirical evidence . . . is consistent with the McKinnon-Shaw view that financial liberalization increases saving, improves the efficiency with which resources are allocated among alternative investment projects and therefore raises the rate of economic growth." Asian countries, for example, that relied most heavily on selective credit policies experienced the lowest rates of economic growth.

Policy Implications

In their design and operation quasi taxes generally correspond closely to the notion of a negative tax expenditure. A tax expenditure, on the one hand, is a form of preferential tax treatment that reduces demand prices relative to supply prices and encourages greater output of a particular item. There is an implicit grant from taxpayers in general to the users of that item. A quasi tax, on the other hand, raises demand relative to supply prices and discourages the supply of some product. In this case there is an implicit transfer from the suppliers to the users of that product.

Whether tax expenditure or quasi tax, all instruments of public policy should be judged by their ability to meet the goals set out for them, assuming that these goals are in some sense worthy. Quasi taxes imposed on financial institutions have been defended on grounds of stimulating investment, improving income distribution, channeling credit to neglected sectors, and correcting for the distortions created by other government policies. It has been argued here that directed credit programs are not very well suited to serve any of these purposes. These programs are far too blunt an instrument to redistribute income effectively. Because they are poorly targeted, any redistribution associated with them is likely to be inefficient or even perverse. Because of their supply-inhibiting effects, these programs also cannot be reasonably expected to stimulate investment. Less investment and investment misallocation are more likely. Redirecting sectoral credit flows is also likely to fail to the extent that it relies on forcing institutions to do the unprofitable. Finally, while financial quasi taxes may help partially to neutralize other distortions in the economy, they also introduce fresh distortions, such as the promotion of greater capital intensity.

The essential reason that quasi taxes fail as a policy measure is that they do not tackle economic problems directly but approach them indirectly in ways that are guaranteed to cause inefficient outcomes. If more investment is sought, it is better to adopt measures that stimulate various kinds of saving, private, public, and foreign. Similarly, if more equal distribution of income is desired, tightly targeted expenditure programs are likely to work better than any tax-related measure. And an explicit subsidy, which rewards lenders for redirecting credit, is apt to be crowned with greater success than compelling lenders to make unprofitable loans.

Although quasi taxes on the transactions of financial institutions may be unattractive, it would be a mistake to conclude that explicit taxes on these institutions would be much better. While an explicit transaction tax would at least generate some revenue and eliminate price rationing and some amount of rent seeking, it can be argued that there are better ways of raising revenue than taxing the gross receipts, and perhaps even the income, of financial intermediaries. Invariably these explicit taxes end up as taxes on the business use of inputs and provoke serious inefficiencies in the intertemporal and intersectoral use of resources.[17]

If financial quasi taxes have very little to recommend them, it would also be a mistake to reach for the implication that their immediate elimination is called for. As the experience of the Southern Cone countries (Chile, Uruguay, and Argentina) has vividly taught us, successful financial liberalization must be seen as part of a wider reform effort involving a carefully planned sequence of policy reforms. The object lesson coming from the Southern Cone is that macrostability, realistic exchange rate policies, and trade liberalization are logical prerequisites to a satisfactory financial liberalization. Otherwise, if the appropriate macro, exchange rate, and trade policies are not already in place, financial liberalization could exacerbate instability and reinforce inefficient resource use. After the domestic financial system has had sufficient time to adjust to a new competitive environment, the final step in the sequence of reform initiatives is to link with the world capital market by freeing up the economy's capital account and accepting free trade in financial services.

Comment

Maxwell J. Fry

I find being a discussant somewhat more difficult than presenting my own paper. My biggest worry is that I won't find anything to say or to quarrel with in the paper I have been asked to discuss. I did, however, find a few things to quarrel with.

First of all, the subtitle "A Little Bit of Craziness" could be changed to "Total Insanity." There should be some differentiation between misguided policy and stupid policy. We have quite a variety of policies here. Some, I believe, fall into the first category; others most definitely fall into the second category.

Perhaps one saving grace in this whole area is the inability of less-developed countries to raise tax revenue. If they could raise it, they would probably be doing much more damage than they do to their financial sectors.

Fungibility is another saving grace. Indeed, Korea is certainly guilty of most of the stupid policies in the financial sector that we see around the world. Fortunately, it has an extremely vigorous curb market, which reallocates the funds in a more appropriate way.

It is with Figure 4.2 that I start more specific criticism. We have here two market diagrams, the informal market and the formal market. We are shown that if you repress the formal market, the interest rates in the curb market fall because resources are moved into the curb market away from the repressed formal banking system. Deposits go down, the supply in the curb market goes up, and the interest rate in the curb market falls.

I disagree with that. From the nontax literature the expectation is precisely the opposite: namely, financial liberalization, not financial repression, will lower curb market rates because the two assets in the portfolio presented in Figure 4.2 are not the dominant assets being reallocated.

In the paper the point is made that the welfare costs could be bigger if substitution is from unproductive, tangible assets—jewelry and so on—into productive, tangible capital. Yet this diagram doesn't allow for that. You need to have at least a three-asset model in which there are unproductive inflation hedges, deposits in the formal banking system, and curb market loans. Then financial liberalization, which allows deposit rates to rise, could produce either effect on the interest rate in the curb market.

If the substitution is mainly out of tangible assets held as inflation hedges, then the total supply of credit increases, and the curb market rate will fall. The evidence that we have, which is very limited and mainly from Asia, on the effects of financial liberalization on the curb rate is entirely consistent with the view that substitution in this three-asset model is predominantly from inflation hedges, not from curb market loans into bank deposits, when deposit rates are allowed to rise as a result of financial liberalization.

A second specific point I want to make is on the incidence of the tax. Wayne mentions three possibilities for the incidence of a quasi tax in the form of a loan rate ceiling for preferred borrowers. One, depositors could receive a lower return on their savings because the banks have to supply preferred borrowers at a lower rate of interest. Two, nonpreferred borrowers may be subject to this tax because the supply of loans to nonpreferred borrowers is reduced and therefore the equilibrium rate goes up. Three, bank stockholders may be paying part of the tax.

In this situation, however, if the loan demand of nonpreferred borrowers is inelastic enough, the deposit rate of interest could actually rise. Suppose you require banks to make 20 percent of their portfolio available to preferred borrowers who otherwise would not be borrowing because their projects require huge subsidies to make them financially viable. If you had a completely inelastic demand by nonpreferred borrowers, they would then bid up the loan rate so that the competitive deposit rate would rise sufficiently to finance not only the total original stock of unpreferred lending but also the required 20 percent of preferred lending. In this extreme case, with a completely inelastic demand for loans, depositors actually benefit from this portfolio restriction. So it can go either way.

I came across this possibility when I was working on managing deficit finance, where exactly the same analysis applied. Managing deficit finance is about the particular form of taxation of the financial system called the inflation tax. It is clearly a stupid policy to impose loan rate ceilings on nonpreferred borrowers, because there is tremendous advantage in allowing the loan rate to go up to attract more deposits into the banking system whether you're using that 20 percent for government finance (as in the inflation tax) or for preferred borrowers (as in Wayne's paper).

Another point concerns the statement that empirical work has tended to opt for the efficient rationing paradigm. That is, if you have demand and supply curves and you ration, you hold the price down so that you are not at the equilibrium but on the supply curve down to the southeast of the equilibrium, then your market-clearing price is way up on the downward sloping demand curve, and you finance all the stuff, left and upward, on your demand curve.

Of course, if you have loan rate ceilings as well, you don't clear the market that way: you use rationing. My own work and work recently done by Alan Gelb of the World Bank suggest that the qualitative effects on the allocation of funds rather than the quantitative effects are the primary costs of financial repression. The big cost is the inefficiency of the rationing process that in fact supplants the market pricing. Because you don't let the loan rate clear the market, all kinds of games are played to reallocate resources.

Finally, I am bothered by the paper's lack of attention to the dynamic aspects. If in fact your rationing was inefficient and you are moving to an efficient allocation, then the dynamics are the real issue. Distorting investment is clearly very much a dynamic process. The dynamic costs are first order, with everything else, including the triangles, of second-order importance.

Discussion

DWIGHT LEE: I would like to question a comment in the paper to the effect that we need to be cautious in getting rid of bad policies. You mention that to liberalize the financial situation we need macrostability and realistic exchange rates. You could probably make the same argument with respect to liberalizing trade. Should we liberalize trade? Well, let's be cautious about that because we have the wrong exchange rates and the wrong macropolicies and so forth.

No doubt some costs would be associated with liberalizing these policies, but my guess is that they'd be largely transitory. What you have here is, at least from the political point of view, a prescription for paralysis. People are going to latch onto this argument and say, "Oh, you're right, but let's wait until we get all these other policies corrected." It reminds me of arguments I've had with people who say, yes, I'm in favor of the market, but we've got to get the distribution of income correct before we turn the market loose.

But the distribution of income never gets correct from their point of view. It's always out of kilter. It's always unfair; so there's always an excuse not to open up the market. It seems to me that you have a somewhat analogous situation with this argument.

CHRISTOPHE CHAMLEY: I would like to make three comments. On the issue of sequencing, I would certainly emphasize the fiscal issue. After all, many countries resort to seignorage—a quasi tax that is so commonly understood as taxation of the financial sector that the two should be considered together. Why? Precisely because their fiscal affairs are not in order.

Let's compare the excess burden of an inflation tax with taxation of financial institutions, with the standard excess burden of regular taxes, just considering the first of the distortions that Dan Usher discussed. It's clear that inflation has a much higher excess burden in these terms. But countries do not carry out such a cost-benefit analysis, precisely because there are other costs than price distortions: these are administrative costs, and the fiscal administration is weak. Therefore, in my view fiscal affairs have to be restored before anything can be done about the quasi taxation of financial institutions.

My second comment concerns interpretation of Figure 4.2 and the effect of liberalizing interest rates on the informal market. Max Fry said that we should introduce three assets. Actually, we can consider the model just as it is.

The trick is that the demands for loans in the informal market and the formal market may not be independent. If there is some link between the two, then liberalization of interest rates in the formal market will make the whole loan system (formal and informal together) more efficient. We might then observe a reduction of the demand for loans in the informal market and therefore a decrease of interest rates in the informal markets.

To make the point clear, assume that the informal sector has an upward-sloping supply curve for loans and that the total demand for loans (for the informal and formal sector together) is fixed. When the tax on the formal sector is reduced, that sector makes more loans. The demand for loans in the informal sector is then reduced, and the interest rate in the informal sector is reduced.

Finally, in the new models of growth of Lucas and others, the rate of return is not very indicative of the effect of increased capital accumulation on growth, and it is possible that the financial liberalization leads to huge effects, although with the standard tools we have, we don't see the result.

JOHN WHALLEY: I have three comments, two of which are references to recent literature. The first is that I have been involved with a thesis done by Hassan Imam—a dynamic sequence general equilibrium analysis of interest rate ceilings in India. What come across are very large welfare effects of eliminating these ceilings. He has numbers on a present-value basis of about 10 percent to 15 percent of GDP per year. His interpretation is that the savings rate in India in the base period is high and, on top of that, the implicit wedge that he has is very large. If you take that at face value, it indicates that these interventions for certain countries may be very important.

The second comment concerns the issue of whether banks should be taxed. You use intermediation services as a way of acquiring commodities. If you buy a car, whether you borrow or pay cash, you get the car; but when you borrow, real resources are used by the financial intermediation industries, for which there is no direct welfare payoff. You have to use those resources, however, to get the gains from trade.

There is no presumption in favor of neutral tax treatment of banks or financial intermediation in this framework. Typically, there is an optimal tax structure, which trades off the gains from trade against the resources sinking into the black hole of intermediation services.

The final comment is on market structure issues. My impression is that in the literature on rural credit markets there is a presumption of concentration, which means you need to intervene. Many of the regulations you are talking about might be argued to be an offset to some of this market structure.

JOHANNES LINN: To the extent that we want to tax banks like other corporations on their corporate income, we know that it is very difficult to tax banks effectively. Are we dealing, perhaps, in part here with an argument of second-best taxation, that when taxing banking services, we are aiming to tax the profits of banking institutions rather than services themselves? The question then becomes whether you are actually reaching the banking sector profits through taxing the services they provide and at what cost in inefficiency.

ROBERT HIGGS: I have a question in several parts, which has to do with the question raised early in the paper. The paper asked what sustains the seemingly universal appeal of quasi taxes on financial institutions. Most striking is that they *are* seemingly universal; that in itself is worth noting. You then consider several possible answers to the question. The first is that governments are looking for cheap sources of finance for themselves, and you believe that to be a major part of this story but not the whole story.

The second possibility you identify is that there is a desire to redistribute welfare from rich lender to poor borrower, but you dismiss that because it does not seem plausible. I agree. It does seem implausible. The third consideration is the apparent desire of governments to provide compensation for handicaps that some sectors or groups are perceived to bear on account of various nonfinancial policy initiatives.

You continue that line of thought by way of an observation on the messy world of second-best political bargaining in which the creation of a new distortion in resource use is often justified by the existence of earlier distortions. The problem here is that these are not new distortions; they are usually distortions of very long standing; so I am not sure whether we could ever find them being created *de novo* to compensate for other government measures.

Finally, the possibility is raised that the artificially lower interest rates will stimulate a larger volume of investment, but you dismiss that as a simple-minded notion, which it is. These credit market interventions only distort the *structure* of investment.

If we consider all your possible answers to the question, it appears that none of them holds up very well or seems very plausible except the first one, which is that government is looking for a cheap source of finance for itself, for its own purposes. If so, I would add just one observation. In public finance, when people get down to talking about actual administration of taxes as opposed to taxes on the blackboard, one of the important ideas is the concept of "tax handles." Can the government grab hold of something and squeeze tax out of it? We might want to consider the same concern when we are talking about quasi taxes. It may be that these kinds of regulations on financial institutions are simply a very easily grasped handle for quasi taxes.

RICHARD BIRD: A related point is that we tend as economists, quite properly, to argue that it is always better to do things directly and explicitly. Then we find that out there in the world there are enormous political advantages to being obscure. I call this "the political economy of underhandedness." The importance of this point is greatly underplayed as a rule.

WARREN BROOKES: To what degree is deposit insurance present in LDCs? That is certainly one of the most explicit financial subsidies, which has a tendency to promote money flows to high risk and away from low risk and money flows to losers as opposed to users.

MR. BIRD: It is not very prevalent. A lot of this applies very nicely to the United States, doesn't it? Wayne made the point that segmented markets are important; yet he also stresses the great importance of fungibility, so that the informal market corrects the problems of the formal market.

MR. BROOKES: In a certain sense what we are seeing here is the flow of funds out of the formal market into the curb market—the curb market being the money market mutual funds, which are uninsured—out of the insured formal market.

JERRY JENKINS: The analogy Warren offers has merit. Combining it with Richard's extrapolation from the paper suggests that, in the absence of formal (explicit) deposit insurance, banks would increase deposit interest rates or suffer an increased flow of funds from banks to money market mutual funds and other alternatives. Thus might government deposit insurance allow lower rates of interest to be paid to depositors for attracting any given volume of deposits with insured banks.

Although Richard is quite correct that deposit insurance is not prevalent in developing countries, in many of these countries the perceptions of depositors may be no different from what they would be if a formal insurance system existed. Wherever and to the extent that this is the case, the effective role of the informal or curb market might be very similar to that of money market mutual funds in the United States—the flow of funds to either serving to communicate something about the magnitude of problems in formal banking systems but otherwise providing no correction of those problems.

Putting all of this together leads me to a conclusion, for the moment, that both segmented markets and fungibility are necessary but insufficient conditions for informal markets to contribute to corrections of formal market problems; for sufficiency another condition is necessary—that depositors not expect government to prevent bank failures in the formal system. Accordingly, for curb markets to contribute to corrections of formal market problems, depositors must believe that government will not bail out failing banks.

By this conclusion curb markets might be expected to contribute to corrections of formal market problems in Taiwan and Korea but not in Peru—although without deposit insurance as such, the Central Bank of Peru is required by law to prevent banks from failing. Short of such explicit assurance, depositors in many other developing countries can have a reasonable belief that government will bail out bankrupt banks. If a government has previously done exactly that (especially if it had said it would not), that history provides encouragement for perceptions of depositors that implicit guarantees exist. Thus the government of Chile, with its new banking law, is going to great lengths to persuade depositors that it will not repeat the bailouts of its past.

MR. WHALLEY: I am curious about a feature of the diagrams in the paper. Most of the discussion is focused on a single closed-economy situation in which you are looking at the effects of integrating the internal financial market.

Consider a country that has complete freedom of access to the international capital market. Might it not be the case that one of the biggest quasi taxes is what is going on in the external sector and what is going on through exchange controls? The controls separate the national capital market from the international market, and many of the measures of gains and losses are going to be dramatically amplified if the slope of the supply curve becomes completely elastic.

MAXWELL FRY: I want to get back to the point about whether you need a three-asset model or a two-asset model. Christophe was saying that you can do it with a two-asset model but you need different assets. Go back to the famous Tobin paper in 1965, where you have households holding outside money backed by government bonds financing government consumption and productive physical capital.

Tobin shows that if you tax money holdings, you will have a portfolio redistribution in favor of productive tangible capital, and incomes will rise as the capital-labor ratio increases. You can easily turn that on its head and have the household sector holding either inside money intermediated through the banking system to business firms holding productive capital or unproductive inflation hedges. Now you tax money: there are less funds in the banking system to finance the productive capital stock, households switch into unproductive inflation hedges, and the capital-labor ratio falls. This sort of financial utilization analysis can be within a two-asset model, but you can't then talk about curb rates of interest, which really do require a three-asset model.

My second point is on what is perhaps misleadingly called the sequencing of financial liberalization. We should call it prerequisites for successful financial liberalization, and two are absolutely essential. One, as Christophe has mentioned, financial repression is primarily to obtain finance for the government. If you're going to liberalize, you've got to think either where the money is coming from to finance the same amount of government expenditure or where can you cut government expenditure. Otherwise liberalization doesn't work.

Second, the financial liberalizationists have been guilty of ignoring microinstitutional issues and in particular the need for prudential supervision for exactly the reason already brought out, that we have implicit deposit insurance all over the world, in every country—even in Chile, which said that it was laissez-faire until 1977, when it took over one of the banks and began down the path of complete renationalization because everybody knew the banks were insured. Prudential supervision and sorting out fiscal policy are prerequisites to successful financial liberalization.

MR. BIRD: I got involved in this subject to some extent because after thirty years of sad experience with fiscal reform, I decided one had to look somewhere else to start the process. It's bad news to hear you've got to get the fiscal side straight first.

WAYNE THIRSK: Michael McKee just slipped me a note that I'd like to share with you. He says the prohibition on usury is biblical in origin. Therefore, God has ordained financial repression.

[Laughter]

MR. BIRD: That was indeed the last word.

Response

Wayne R. Thirsk

Maxwell Fry suggests retitling the paper so that it refers to enormous insanity. I guess I would agree; it is just typical Canadian understatement to do otherwise.

More substantively, I accept his criticism of Figure 4.2 that I have oversimplified the world in putting out a particular story of how quasi taxes work in a streamlined two-asset model. Ideally, one should work in the third dimension and look at a three-asset model. Once you do that, you can obtain a richer variety of potential results.

I was certainly aware of the limitations surrounding Figure 4.2; so I did mention how one would interpret some of these efficiency cost calculations if, in fact, that third asset consisting of tangible assets were to exist. That aside, I certainly accept the basis for that criticism.

I also think there is some merit in Fry's other incidence possibility, where we could conceivably think of a situation in which depositors become better off rather than worse off as a result of these quasi taxes. It may only be a special case. It certainly relies on making the assumption that the demands exerted by nonpreferred borrowers for finance are highly, if not totally, inelastic. I would certainly like to be in the banking business if my customers were completely price insensitive. One wonders why banks didn't sock it to these nonpreferred borrowers to begin with.

I also accept the argument that the costs of financial repression will be greater if the inefficient rationing paradigm is the most likely scenario. I agree as well that the dynamic costs of quasi taxes in the form of lower growth rates are omitted from the analysis. Basically, in Figure 4.2 we are looking at the intersectoral misallocation of resources. The intertemporal misallocation of resources requires a more sophisticated framework to be adequately dealt with; but I didn't want to get into that level of complexity, and the paper therefore neglects this aspect of cost.

On Dwight Lee's comment, I have some sympathy for what he says. We have to be sure we don't let the best become the enemy of the good. All of us are a bit chastened, however, by the experience of the Southern Cone countries, which experimented with financial liberalization without having a lot of experience to guide them. It is clear that the experiment failed, and the consensus among economists who looked at the pieces that were left over is that they didn't get these other policies correct to begin with, and in a sense that doomed the attempts to liberalize the financial side of the economy. As a result, it has given financial liberalization in at least that part of the world a bad name. Having not quite got it right, it is not clear that we are going to have another chance to get it right again in the future. I certainly agreed with most of what Christophe Chamley had to say. I would just reemphasize his point about the understatement of the efficiency costs when you do not explicitly take into consideration the intertemporal distortions that these quasi taxes are responsible for.

On John Whalley's mention of the international capital market, I wanted to deal with an economy that implicitly had foreign exchange controls. If one wanted to extend the scope of the analysis, one could take into account the implicit quasi tax associated with these foreign exchange controls.

Going back to the issue of whether we should tax financial institutions, I am in basic sympathy with the proposition Christophe has put forward about banking being an intermediate input and therefore an undesirable tax base. Another part of me, however, says that if you were cunning enough to figure out how to apply a value-added tax properly for financial institutions, you should do it. My concern here is that in the countries of which I am aware that tax their banks and financial institutions, those taxes have had bad results. I think particularly of Turkey, which applied a hefty transactions tax, something on the order of 25 percent, imposing a very sizable barrier to the growth of financial intermediation activities in that country.

Robert Higgs's question of why we do it is a good one. Traditionally, many developing countries have had governments that have tried to intervene actively in promoting certain sectors or activities. Agriculture and small businessmen and exporters have been viewed as being subject to some kind of competitive handicap—often a handicap imposed by other parts of government policy. The financial quasi taxes in part are an attempt by governments to appear to be dealing evenhandedly with these so-called neglected sectors or activities. Obviously though, there is some truth in his suggestion that these quasi taxes may be fairly easy tax handles to employ.

On Warren Brookes's question of deposit insurance, I am not aware of any developing country that has a full-fledged deposit insurance scheme, but the problem here is one of moral hazard. If depositors are insured, they don't care how their money is lent out. If it is squandered or wasted, so what? They are going to be covered by the insurance. This reassurance relaxes the discipline that the depositors might otherwise force on financial institutions and makes it that much more imperative that governments supervise these financial institutions very carefully in the absence of depositor awareness.

5   *Malcolm Gillis*

Tacit Taxes and Sub Rosa Subsidies through State-owned Enterprises

Four decades ago state-owned enterprises (SOEs) were not numerous in less-developed countries (LDCs) and were, with a few notable exceptions (Turkey, Mexico), typically confined to a few sectors of their economies.[1] Commonly, SOEs in LDCs were limited to the so-called natural monopolies (decreasing-cost public utilities), monopoly production of such sumptuary products as liquor, beer, and tobacco, and so-called basic necessities, such as salt and matches. The relatively small role of SOEs in national economies meant, of course, that the scope for using them as vehicles for explicit as well as implicit subsidization and taxation was narrow.

After independence was achieved for dozens of LDCs in the two decades after World War II, the number as well as the relative importance of SOEs in LDC economies expanded rapidly. This was particularly so in Africa: more than half of Africa's SOEs were established between 1967 and 1980. In Tanzania alone the number of SOEs increased tenfold from 1965 through 1985 (World Bank 1988). By 1980 SOEs were common and often dominant in manufacturing, construction, banking services, natural resources, and agriculture. And although SOEs before 1950 were typically small-scale undertakings in most LDCs, many are now among the largest firms in their countries, and some are among the largest enterprises in their fields anywhere in the world (Gillis and Peprah 1981).

The relative economic importance of SOEs in LDCs is apparent from Table 5.1, which shows for the periods 1974–1977 and 1984 the percentage share of such firms not only in gross domestic product but in gross investment. While the weighted average share of the LDC enterprises in GDP was, for 1974–1977, only slightly higher than for SOEs in industrial nations (8.0 percent), the average share in LDCs almost doubled during the 1970s while that for industrial countries showed little change (Short 1983, p. 1). The average share of SOEs in total investment in 1974–1977, however, was nearly three times that in industrial countries. And while the share of SOEs in

Table 5.1

SOE Shares in Value Added and Investment, 1974–1977 (weighted average) and 1984 (weighted average)

	SOE value added as percentage of GDP (at market prices)	SOE fixed investment as percentage of gross fixed capital formation
Developing countries (1974–77)[a]	8.6	27.0
Developing countries (1984)[b]	10.9	28.2
Developing countries, by region (1974–77)[a]		
Africa (17 nations)	17.5	32.4
Asia (10 nations)	8.0	27.7
Latin America (19 nations)	6.6	22.5
Industrial countries (1975–79)[b]	8.0	9.9

NOTE: 1984 sample for LDCs covers twenty-eight countries for value added and thirty-seven countries for investment averages.
SOURCES: a. Short 1983, Table 1. b. Gouindon Nair and Anastasios Filippedes, "How Much Do State-owned Enterprises Contribute to Public-Sector Deficits in Developing Countries, and Why?" (World Bank Working Paper Series 45, 1988).

GDP was markedly higher in Africa than in Asia or Latin America, there was, in 1974–1977, much less difference between regions in the enterprises' share in gross investment: the relative share of developing country SOEs in gross investment approached or exceeded one quarter of GDP in virtually all regions. Roughly similar overall patterns prevailed also in 1984. The share of LDC SOEs in value added rose to 10.9 percent, on the average, while the share of the enterprises in total fixed investment was 28.2 percent.

Such figures, however, must be interpreted with care. Cross-national comparisons of the quantitative importance of SOEs in LDCs probably understate the enterprises' share in GDP, since such comparisons generally include only SOEs owned by central governments. A case in point is Colombia. There central government SOEs in the early 1980s accounted for between four percent and seven percent of GDP, well below the average for all LDCs. But when all government-owned firms at all levels of government are included, the SOE share in GDP was between 10 percent and 13 percent, well above the average (Bird 1984).

In any case, growth in the relative importance of these enterprises has meant that the latitude for channeling explicit subsidies through SOEs has become very substantial in many LDCs, even as the overwhelming majority of them, as we shall see, are not subject to the same explicit tax regime that applies to their private sector counterparts. Beyond that, the notable growth in the quantitative importance of these enterprises has greatly expanded the scope for using them both as channels for implicit, and also largely hidden, subsidies and as instruments not only for extracting resources from the private sector through tacit taxes but also for burdening the private sector with taxlike costs that yield no revenues for government. Moreover, the available evidence suggests that governments have found their state enterprise sectors more suited for awarding implicit subsidies than as means of imposing hidden taxes on the private sector, a state of affairs quite consistent with usual interpretations of rent-seeking behavior.

Finally, we will see that explicit subsidies for particular activities are often accompanied by implicit subsidies (for the same purpose) that often escape detection by analysts.

The next section offers a typology of implicit subsidies and taxes commonly implemented through SOEs in developing nations. The following section presents a discussion of the rationales, both stated and apparent, that have been used to justify these practices. Common and uncommon methods of effectuating implicit subsidies and taxes are described in this section, which also examines the efficacy of such subsidies and taxes, in light of the objectives that they have sought to achieve and of other economic considerations.

A Typology of Subsidies and Taxes Implicit in SOE Operations

Implicit subsidies and taxes through public enterprise sectors have come to assume so many different forms as to defy attempts to place them in categories manageable for analysis. For example, any typology of subsidies must recognize the essential differences between implicit subsidies channeled through SOEs and intended for the benefit of producers or consumers (largely in the private sector) and those not targeted to achieve specific social or economic purposes but rather intended to favor public over private enterprises generally, or at least within a particular sector. For taxes the typology must also distinguish between implicit taxes that provide a wedge between flows among the state enterprise sector, other state enterprises, and the private sector on the one hand and flows between the state enterprise sector and the government on the other.

The typologies offered in this paper have the merit of recognizing these distinctions but are not by any means to be viewed as airtight or fully comprehensive. Moreover, since tax and subsidy aspects of state-owned financial enterprises are covered in Chapter 4, by Wayne R. Thirsk, they are treated only peripherally here.

Implicit subsidies. Several important conceptual distinctions are useful in the analysis of subsidies, be they explicit or implicit. These distinctions are often blurred or, even worse, ignored. The first important distinction concerns the difference between explicit and implicit subsidies channeled through SOEs. For present purposes an explicit subsidy is one that is clearly and fully recorded in governmental budgets or, if an "off-budget" item, is reported as a line item in publicly accessible financial reports of a decentralized agency and is expressly labeled as an outlay supporting a targeted activity. For example, the Indonesian central government budget annually presents estimated amounts of expenditure for payments to SOEs to support subsidies on fertilizer and on domestic consumption of petroleum products. These are obviously explicit subsidies.

Associated with these explicit subsidies, however, are additional subsidy costs not reported in any budget document or any easily accessible report of decentralized agencies. These subsidies arise from pricing policies governing the supply of natural gas to state-owned fertilizer plants and from delivery of special allocations of low-cost crude oil to government refineries. These additional subsidies are hidden not only from the view of the general public but often from the view of decision makers in government as well.

It turns out that, particularly where SOEs are concerned, such hidden or implicit subsidies are often associated with explicit subsidies and also often interact with explicit subsidies in quite complex fashion. For this reason it is often neither possible nor advisable to discuss implicit subsidies without specific and detailed reference to explicit subsidies for the same activity. Several examples of such joint subsidies are examined in subsequent sections.

A second set of important distinctions in the analysis of subsidies concerns differences among financial costs, economic costs, marginal and average subsidy costs, welfare costs, and the administrative and compliance costs of implementing subsidies. Costs of the last type are truly implicit and indeed are rarely recognized as a cost of subsidy programs. They are akin to those treated by Dan Usher in Chapter 2 and are therefore not discussed further here.

Financial costs are ordinarily easier to define and identify for explicit than for implicit subsidies. In many cases financial costs of explicit subsidies are reported as the amounts of actual or planned outlays in budget documents. Even for explicit subsidies, however, the presence of cross-subsidization may mask very large costs. For example, a state-owned electricity company may confer heavy subsidies on one class of users, recouping some or all of the costs by setting tariffs for other users at prices well above marginal costs.

Even without cross-subsidization financial costs of implicit subsidies are usually fully or partially hidden, sometimes in more than one relatively inaccessible set of SOE or government accounts. Financial costs of implicit subsidies may take the form of actual outlays incurred by SOEs on behalf of the subsidized activity; or they may take the form of receipts forgone, intentionally or not, by either SOEs or the parent government in the process of subsidizing an activity or undertaking. Therefore, implicit financial costs of a given subsidy may show up as reduced SOE profits, taxes not paid to government, or in other guises even more difficult to detect. For example, financial costs of implicit subsidies are sometimes hidden under the cloak of so-called equity injections from governments to SOEs. Equity injections into SOEs to cover all or a part of the cost of subsidy programs have virtually nothing to do with the financial structure of the enterprises and everything to do with covering the enterprise losses in operating subsidy programs.

The economic costs of subsidies, whether explicit or implicit, may be larger or smaller than the financial costs but more often are larger. Cases will be presented wherein the economic costs of a subsidy are a large multiple of the financial cost. Simply put, the economic cost of a subsidy is the difference between the sale price of the subsidized good or service and its economic value at the point at which the sale price is charged. For a traded consumer good, for example, the economic subsidy is the difference between actual retail prices and border prices.

For some purposes analysis of subsidies necessarily must focus on marginal cost, while for other purposes average cost is the appropriate concept (see McLure, this volume). Where questions of economic efficiency are concerned, subsidies must be measured in relation to marginal costs. Where the focus is on implications of subsidies for income distribution, average cost is the relevant concept.

The welfare cost of a subsidy is merely the deadweight loss, or excess burden, associated with a subsidy program. Welfare costs of subsidy programs are ordinarily a small fraction of financial or economic costs but can nevertheless amount to a nontrivial share of GDP, as in the cases of many kinds of implicit and explicit petroleum product subsidies in LDCs.

A quarter-century of dealing with explicit and implicit governmental subsidies in several nations has caused the present author to be somewhat skeptical regarding figures reported for subsidy costs and even more skeptical about the prospects for accurate computation of the financial, much less the economic and welfare, costs of subsidies. After all, many subsidy programs have evolved as an outgrowth of rent-seeking behavior by powerful interest groups, resourceful in devising methods of concealment.

For these and other reasons, it is generally useful to attempt to compute both the full financial costs and the economic costs and welfare costs of subsidy programs. Subsequent sections present estimates, where available, of all three kinds of costs. Where economic costs of subsidies exceed financial costs, this is ordinarily a clear signal that implicit subsidies are being used to supplement (sometimes unintentionally) the usually somewhat more transparent financial subsidies. The excess of economic subsidies over financial subsidies for a given subsidy program is, as we shall see, usually due to hidden or even unrecognized subsidies on inputs used to produce the targeted item.

There are also cases, however, in which the financial costs of subsidies exceed their economic costs. This state of affairs is usually a clear sign of truly massive waste or rampant corruption in the operation of the subsidy program.

Recent Indonesian experience with pesticide subsidies presents just such a case. The financial subsidy to pesticide use was very large from 1976 through 1986. Even after pesticide prices were increased by 100 percent in 1986, the subsidy per liter was nearly twice as high as the retail price. Overall the financial cost of the subsidy, as reported in the government budget, was about US$129 million in 1986–1987. But the economic cost of the subsidy for this traded good was only $31 million (World Bank 1987). Therefore, to achieve an economic subsidy of $31 million, the government spent more than four times as much. Viewed another way, if the entire $129 million spent by the government for the subsidy had been used to import and subsidize ready-to-use pesticides, not only could the same amount of pesticides as used that year have been provided free of charge, but farmers could have been paid $3.85 for each liter used. Inasmuch as pesticides in Indonesia are "manufactured" (actually mixed) by several local firms using largely imported chemicals and distributed by the government through local agencies such as cooperatives, it can only be concluded that either the domestic manufacturers or the distributing agencies reaped very large gains at the expense of the government, the farmers, and the environment.

The present discussion divides implicit subsidies into two basic types: those designed to bestow specific benefits on particular groups of producers and consumers and those that generally favor public enterprises over private enterprises.

The use of SOEs as vehicles to provide both explicit and implicit subsidies has contributed materially to large deficits in the state enterprise sector in several nations. For developing countries generally, the overall deficit for the state enterprise sector (after receipt of current government transfers by the SOEs) averaged 3.9 percent of GDP in the late 1970s, with a range of 0.1 percent (Dominican Republic) to 23.4 percent (Guinea). A large but unknown fraction of such deficits may be attributable to implicit subsidies, since presumably a portion of current government transfers (an average of 1.6 percent of GDP) was supplied to cover costs of explicit subsidies included in budgets. Taking these current transfers into account, the overall deficit of public enterprise sectors averaged 5.5 percent of GDP. We will see later that by the early 1980s, SOE deficits increased still further, reaching as much as 10 to 12 percent of GDP in some nations.

Subsidies intended for domestic producers and consumers.
Governments have used numerous types of implicit subsidies channeled to producers and consumers outside the normal budgetary
framework but through SOEs. Among the more common of these
subsidies are those involving energy and energy products, transportation, and foodstuffs.

1. Petroleum products, coal, and charcoal. Governments have
chosen to bestow implicit subsidies on domestic consumption of
several kinds of petroleum products, for a wide variety of reasons.
These subsidies have been most common in oil-producing (not
necessarily oil-exporting) nations but have occasionally been used
by oil-importing nations as well. In oil-producing LDCs the implicit
subsidies on energy use are typically effectuated by setting retail
prices of refined products sold domestically by the government-
owned oil enterprises at levels below border prices for the fuels.
The resulting losses on domestic operations of the SOEs have
usually been financed by drawing down of SOE profits arising
from oil exports.

In some countries subsidization of the consumption of oil
products through SOEs has extended across virtually the entire
range of distilled products, from gasoline and diesel fuel through
kerosene, fuel oil, and, in a few instances, aviation fuel. This group
of countries has included Bolivia, Colombia, Ecuador, Egypt, Indonesia, and Venezuela. Other governments have sought to confine
subsidies to one or two kinds of refined products, including kerosene and fuel oil (Pakistan). In still other instances governments
have implicitly subsidized motor fuels only, not by underpricing of
fuel per se but by setting fuel taxes well below those required to
cover the marginal cost of road use, as in Jamaica (Bird and Miller
1989).

In addition, some coal-producing nations, such as Indonesia and
the Philippines, have conferred implicit subsidies on coal users by
setting domestic prices below border prices, without reimbursing
the national coal SOE for its losses. Others have effectuated large
implicit subsidies to charcoal users (including, in Bolivia, tin

smelters) through artificially cheap sales of government-owned timber used in charcoal making.

The budgetary costs of many of these energy subsidies have been very substantial in a number of LDCs. Until 1987, for example, Indonesia long subsidized consumption of refined petroleum products, both explicitly and implicitly. The explicit subsidy was effectuated by holding the domestic delivered price of these products well below the costs of production reported by Pertamina, the state oil enterprise. The resulting deficits in Pertamina's domestic operations were covered by transfers from the national treasury and were listed each year as a current expenditure in the national budget. The financial cost of the explicit subsidies reached 9.2 percent of total government tax revenues in 1980–1981. The implicit subsidy stemmed from the fact that Pertamina was able to secure a large portion of the crude it refined for the domestic market at prices as low as one-third to one-fifth the f.o.b. export price. This crude ("pro rata crude") was supplied by foreign oil companies to Pertamina, as provided in Indonesia's production-sharing contracts in oil.

Explicit and implicit subsidies together amounted to two-thirds of the opportunity cost per barrel of refined petroleum products in 1980–1981, the height of the second oil boom (Gillis 1980a). Significantly, the implicit subsidy in 1980–1981 was $11.83 per barrel, or 119 percent of the explicit subsidy. The economic cost of both subsidies together amounted to nearly 5 percent of GDP, and the implicit subsidy alone was 2.7 percent of GDP (Gillis 1980a, pp. 53–56).

Other countries with histories of petroleum product subsidies channeled through SOEs include Bolivia, Colombia, Ecuador, and Pakistan. In Pakistan the economic costs of subsidies in 1979 reached 31 percent of the opportunity costs of kerosene and 28 percent of those of fuel oil (de Kuijper and Erickson 1979).

In the mid-1970s Bolivia constrained prices of refined petroleum products to levels only 57 percent as high as their opportunity costs (McLure 1981).[2] This was a clear case of an implicit subsidy, since the state-owned oil company, YPFB (Yaciemientos Petroleferias Boliviana), suffered lower profits as a result.

Colombia has long experience with tacit petroleum subsidies implemented through the state oil enterprise, ECOPETROL (Empresa Colombiana de Petroléos). Throughout the 1960s and 1970s, the subsidies were effectuated by a combination of exchange rate manipulations and ceilings on prices of crude oil purchased by ECOPETROL for use in its refineries (Gillis and McLure 1978). A preferential exchange rate as much as one-third below the prevailing exchange rate applied to crude sales by private oil companies to ECOPETROL. By itself this special petroleum exchange rate resulted in implicit subsidies to refiners equivalent to 27 percent of the ex-refinery price in 1975. This subsidy was passed on to consumers. In addition, ceilings were established on crude prices paid to all companies at levels well below the opportunity cost of crude at the wellhead. Together the preferential exchange rate and the ceilings on prices paid for crude purchases caused gasoline and diesel fuel prices ex-refinery to be about one-third those that would have prevailed without both implicit subsidies (Gillis and McLure 1978).

2. Fertilizer subsidies. Fertilizer subsidies are widely used in LDCs, particularly those that are also producers of natural gas. Often, as in Indonesia (see below), farm-gate prices are set below border prices. But sometimes, as in Turkey, fertilizer is subsidized vis-à-vis the domestic cost of production but taxed relative to the border price.[3] In any case, rates of subsidy for fertilizers in the early 1980s were rarely below 30 percent of delivered costs. Subsidy rates of 50 percent to 70 percent are not uncommon, however, and rates in some cases have reached 90 percent, as in Nigeria (World Bank 1986, p. 98). Here again we find cases where implicit subsidies on state enterprise operations strongly supplement explicit subsidies. In several instances the explicit subsidies have been financed directly by budgetary allocations to publicly owned fertilizer distribution systems or state-owned fertilizer plants.

Explicit subsidies, for example, apply on a portion of the Indonesian fertilizer subsidy, which appear as a line item in that nation's budget. But a sizable share of the overall subsidy is truly implicit; it has been a consequence of underpricing of government-owned natural gas in sales to government-owned fertilizer firms. In Indonesia, natural gas supplied to P. T. Pusri (one of the largest producers of urea in the world) and two other fertilizer SOEs has been sold by Pertamina at a price low enough to yield an implicit subsidy of as much as $20 per barrel of oil equivalent at the height of the energy boom (World Bank 1981, p. 42) to as little as $4 per barrel of oil equivalent in years of depressed energy prices in the mid-1980s.[4] Fertilizer subsidies of both types grew rapidly until 1986 but were curtailed thereafter. The explicit fertilizer subsidy was reduced in that year through an increase in fertilizer prices, and the size of the implicit subsidy had diminished because of the decline in energy prices. Still, even as late as 1987, both subsidies together were 29 percent of the farm-gate price, or 42 percent of all government development spending on agriculture (World Bank 1987, pp. 10–12).

3. Iron and steel subsidies. Implicit subsidies provided to state-owned iron and steel mills have assumed a variety of forms. These include subsidies arising from import monopolies and concessional finance, discussed under other categories in this taxonomy, and, in at least one case, cross-subsidies from private to public steel firms. In India a large steel-making firm was taxed, and the revenues were transferred to public steel plants.[5] Enterprises in this sector often benefit from implicit subsidies on materials and fuel used in iron and steel fabrication. A good example is the large Indonesian SOE Krakatau Steel. Through 1986, for all natural gas supplied by the state oil enterprise to Krakatau Steel and used as a raw material in the production process, the enterprise paid a price that was only 21 percent that charged to other domestic industrial users and only 14 percent of the price of gas exported as liquefied natural gas.

4. Electricity. In virtually all LDCs, electric power is supplied by state-owned monopolies subject to government regulation. Governments have generally been loath to allow the enterprises to raise electricity rates as costs of generation and distribution increase. Consequently, use of power by several classes of customers tends to be subsidized, with particularly large subsidies for residential users. In one sample of seventeen LDCs, for example, tariffs for industrial

users exceeded those for residential users by roughly 4 percent to 145 percent, even though differences in the underlying marginal costs of production tend to go in the opposite direction (Linn and Wetzel 1989).

Apparent subsidies for power consumption have been growing, not declining, over the past two decades: whereas average rates of return to LDC power companies averaged 11 percent in 1970, they declined steadily thereafter, to between 5 percent and 6 percent in the first half of the 1980s, while the enterprises' self-financing ratio (internal funds as a proportion of investment requirements) fell from 25 percent to 17 percent (World Bank 1988, p. 142). Electric power firms in many LDCs provide yet another example of the combination of explicit and implicit subsidies often found in SOE operations.

The Colombian and Indonesian cases are illustrative. In Colombia, where an ambitious investment program raised power's share in total public investment by 50 percent (to 38 percent) by 1985, the combined deficits of the nation's power utilities amounted to fully 1 percent of GDP by 1986 (World Bank 1988, p. 143). This occurred despite large explicit and implicit subsidies from the state oil company ECOPETROL, both on the sale of natural gas for power generation and on preferential loans to the electricity sector (Bird 1984, p. 342).

In Indonesia operations of the state-owned power company Perum Listrik Negra (PLN) have long been heavily subsidized by deep underpricing of fuel used in power generation.[6] Oil supplied 86 percent of the energy used in electric power generation in the late 1970s (Gillis 1980a, p. 14) and about 68 percent of that produced in the mid-1980s.

5. Urban transportation. Where it is subsidized in LDCs, urban transportation tends to be supported by two principal types of subsidies: (1) those on motor fuel, whether by underpricing of refinery products as in Indonesia, Colombia, Bolivia, and several other oil producers or by maintenance of very low fuel taxes (road user charges) as in Jamaica (Bird and Miller 1989); (2) subsidies for

public bus transport, as in Ankara, Bangkok, Calcutta, Istanbul, Jakarta, Karachi, Khartoum, and dozens of other cities, especially capital cities. Perhaps the heaviest subsidies have occurred in new, capital-intensive metros in such cities as Caracas and São Paulo. These systems cost $1.4 billion and $2.3 billion respectively but serve a much smaller proportion of the urban population than bus services (World Bank 1988, p. 145).

Even heavy subsidies, however, have in many cases not yielded an adequate quality of bus services (Bird and Miller 1989, p. 59). Calcutta provides an interesting example. There the publicly owned bus company generates revenues that cover only half the system's *operating* costs, so that it requires a subsidy of $1 million per month. Yet the public bus company has a lower fleet utilization ratio and a higher staffing ratio than unsubsidized private competitors. In addition, the public company has costs per passenger-kilometer that are 2.7 times higher than those of private sector competitors (World Bank 1988, p. 145).

6. Water. Water supplies are heavily subsidized all over the world, not least in parts of the United States and in the Soviet Union (Gillis 1989). Subsidies apply both to agricultural water and to potable water. Public irrigation systems operated by government-owned enterprises and by governmental departments in developing countries had already absorbed $250 billion in public funds by 1984, with recent annual rates of investment running between $10 billion and $15 billion. It has been estimated that over half of all investments in agriculture in LDCs in the 1980s will go into water resource development; in Mexico fully 80 percent of all public investment in agriculture since 1940 has been in irrigation projects (Repetto 1986, p. 3). There charges for irrigation water average only 11 percent of total costs. And in a sample of World Bank irrigation projects in LDCs, revenues cover only 7 percent of project costs, on average, while in most other countries revenue from farmers covers less than 20 percent of capital and operating costs (Repetto 1986, p. 1).

The situation for potable water supplies is somewhat different: subsidized consumption is prevalent but tends to be less expensive than for agricultural water. Attempts are often made to target lower-income households through "lifeline" tariffs involving very low rates for an initial small block of consumption, as in Colombia (Bird and Miller 1989), or rising block rates, as in Belo Horizonte, Brazil, or Bujumbura, Burundi, or provision of public standpipes in densely populated urban areas, as in Indonesia. Even so, high water connection charges, as in both Indonesia and Colombia, as well as other factors, mean that one quarter of the developing world's urban population has no access to safe water; many buy water from private vendors at rates from four to fifty times as high as paid by more affluent households for piped water (World Bank 1988, p. 145).

7. Foodstuffs. Food subsidy programs intended for the benefit of low-income consumers are common throughout the developing world, particularly for such commodities as rice, wheat, sugar, cassava, and, increasingly in the poorest nations, sorghum. In a few nations some or even all outlays for food subsidies are explicitly included in governmental budgets. But in many cases the costs of the subsidy programs have been borne by farmers, often poor farmers, through legal marketing monopolies that pay farm-gate prices well below world prices or even below prevailing domestic prices (Horton 1989, p. 146). In such situations the subsidies are of course implicit. In still other cases state-owned monopolists in food importing buy at world prices or at concessional terms from aid donors and resell to consumers at lower prices. In these instances the costs of the subsidy program may be hidden in government subventions to the importing agency.

Explicit or implicit, the costs of food subsidy programs loom large in total government spending in dozens of LDCs, although the relative share of such subsidies in government budgets has been declining in the past fifteen years, particularly in Sri Lanka, Bangladesh, and Pakistan (World Bank 1986), Indonesia (Gillis 1985), and Tanzania, where a maize subsidy was abolished in 1982. Even so, food subsidies in the 1980s have taken between 5 percent and 10 percent of total government expenditure in all five countries and have amounted to as much as 40 percent of total government expenditure in Egypt (World Bank 1986, p. 91). Moreover, in several countries surveyed by Horton (1989, p. 146) the direct costs of food subsidy programs equaled or exceeded 3 percent of GDP (China, Egypt, and Sri Lanka).

Implicit, nontargeted subsidies from governments to SOEs. Implicit subsidies included in this category involve those that are not necessarily provided to achieve specific income distribution or developmental goals but rather are intended to favor, or have the effect of favoring, public over private enterprises generally. Certain of the subsidy types included in this classification, however, may in fact support subsidies for a particular purpose. For example, preferential loans or income tax exemptions for electric power companies may be motivated by governmental intentions to subsidize electricity generation or may be consequences of generally available concessional loans and tax exemptions for all state-owned enterprises. Indeed, concessional loan terms and income tax exemption are two of the most important and longstanding of this group of subsidies. Another type, however, has become increasingly important in more recent years and is discussed first.

1. Governmental guarantees on SOE debt. All borrowing by state-owned enterprises is backed by the parent government. This guarantee may be formally stated or may be implicit; in either case the guarantee amounts to an implicit subsidy, since the costs of guarantees tend not to show up in government budgets or accounts. This holds whether SOEs are exempt from income taxation or fully taxable.

The implicit subsidy arises because SOE debt is viewed by lenders as sovereign debt. Lenders are therefore willing to provide more debt to an SOE than to a private enterprise with assets of the same value. Consequently, SOEs benefit from preferential access to domestic as well as foreign loan finance (commercial or otherwise). Further, SOEs with formal or implicit debt guarantees can secure artificially cheap credit; ordinarily SOEs do not pay risk premiums on capital that are nearly as high as those paid by private firms (Gillis, Jenkins, and Lessard 1982).

Moreover, where SOEs are subject to the same income tax treatment as private firms, the foregoing implicit subsidy on SOE borrowing is supplemented by another subsidy. This subsidy arises from the fact that in virtually all nations interest on debt is fully deductible from the income of the firm. Since debt guarantees allow state enterprises to become more highly levered than private firms, which must finance their new investments with a higher proportion of equity finance, SOEs end up with a smaller stream of taxable income than would a private firm with an identical stream of income measured gross of interest expenses and taxes (Jenkins 1985). Hence, even when fully taxable, SOEs tend to have tax advantages over private firms.

The costs of the implicit subsidy from debt guarantees can be staggering. For example, when a state-owned marketing board was liquidated in Senegal in 1980, the government assumed bank debts equivalent to 15 percent of GDP (World Bank 1988, p. 170).

In any case, implicit subsidies of this type are now widespread. Direct foreign borrowings of SOEs accounted for more than one-fifth of total foreign debt in ninety-nine LDCs. In Brazil, Mexico, the Philippines, Portugal, Zambia, and other heavily indebted countries, SOEs have accounted for more than half of outstanding external debt (World Bank 1988, p. 170). As countries have veered into financial crisis from the debt excesses of SOEs, the costs of the implicit subsidy from debt guarantees have become more evident.

In fact, this subsidy has become in many countries a very large tax, in the form of the inflationary consequences of budget deficits (discussed below) further bloated by debt service difficulties. In several of the more notable recent cases, responses by LDC governments to financial crises have led to large losses for central banks, losses that are not accounted for in conventional measures of public deficits but that have similar implications for economic stability. To illustrate, the conventional measure of public deficits placed the Chilean deficit in 1983 at only 3 percent of GDP, when in fact the deficit including central bank losses was 9 percent of GDP. Argentina's fiscal deficit in 1986 as conventionally measured was only 2 percent; counting losses of the central bank it was 7 percent. In Costa Rica the conventional fiscal deficit in 1985 was an apparently manageable 1.8 percent; properly measured to include central bank losses it was an unmanageable 7.1 percent of GDP (World Bank 1988, p. 66).

2. Preferential access to domestic credit. The implicit subsidy flowing from formal or informal government guarantees on SOE debt applies both to foreign and to domestic borrowing by the firms. But in many countries there is in addition another type of subsidy on SOE borrowing. This subsidy arises when SOEs in banking are important in the domestic financial system. In these circumstances SOEs often enjoy not only preferential access to credit, relative to private firms, but often highly concessional credit terms.

This type of subsidy has been particularly significant in a number of African nations and in Indonesia, Brazil, Korea, and Turkey, among others. In Indonesia SOEs clearly enjoyed both preferential access to credit and concessional borrowing rates on most loans until a major financial reform in June 1983. So-called command loans from state-owned banks to nonfinancial SOEs in the very large Indonesian SOE sector (Gillis 1982) were common, as were arrears on such loans (30 percent to 40 percent of loans outstanding).

Even without direct governmental instruction requiring government-owned banks to lend to SOEs, this kind of lending entails sizable risks of the sort present anywhere where a financial institution lending to borrowers is also connected with its owners. In such cases standard lending practices may not be followed, with the result that SOEs contract debt for uneconomic projects. This problem occurred on a sizable scale in Benin, Cameroon, Madagascar, and Mali, where heavy losses by government banks on loans to SOEs led to decapitalization of the banking system. In Benin matters became particularly serious by 1986. Borrowing by nonfinancial SOEs reached 13 percent of GDP, most of which was nonperforming debt (World Bank 1988, p. 171).

Preferential access by SOEs to domestic loans not only serves to crowd private firms out of the domestic credit market but in many countries (including the four African nations cited above) has resulted in virtual paralysis of the entire financial system and heavy demands on future budgets, when governments (as in Senegal) have had to assume SOE debts that are a large fraction of GDP.

3. Tax exemption. Many LDCs, unlike the United States, do (nominally at least) subject SOEs to much the same taxes, especially income taxes, applicable to private firms. Examples include Colombia (since 1974), India, Pakistan, Indonesia, Sri Lanka, Tanzania, the Philippines, Syria, and (since 1984) China. In Indonesia SOEs typically accounted for three-quarters of nonoil corporate tax revenues through the 1970s, and slightly over half after 1980 (Gillis 1989). But a larger group of countries grant SOEs full or partial tax exemption from virtually all taxes, especially income taxes. Among countries where SOEs are wholly or largely exempt from income taxes are Brazil, Bolivia, El Salvador, Iran, and Colombia before 1974 (Floyd 1977).

Practice on taxation of SOEs therefore varies substantially. In general, however, public enterprises in LDCs pay considerably lower taxes than comparable private firms. While in a few cases this is due to explicit tax exemption for SOEs as a group, in many other cases SOEs are nominally subject to all taxes but are de facto exempt, owing to extralegal accommodations (based partly on tradition) between SOE managers on the one hand and the government and the tax administration on the other. For example, even though Colombian SOEs were nominally subject to income taxes after 1974, virtually no income taxes were paid by such firms over the next five years. Lower effective tax rates may also occur in SOEs because of the high proportion of their investment financed by debt: since interest payments are almost everywhere allowed as a tax deduction, the effective tax rate on total income from capital will be lower than for private firms, which for reasons discussed earlier have lower debt-equity ratios.

The implicit subsidy arising from income tax exemption is obvious enough, but one feature of this particular subsidy merits additional discussion. Income tax exemption allows SOEs great latitude for using cash flows from operations in reinvestment in the enterprise. This source of finance has at times been significant in several countries that exempt SOEs from taxes, including Korea from 1961 to 1972, Brazil from 1966 to 1975, Uruguay from 1975 to 1976, and Taiwan from 1960 to 1974 (Gillis, Jenkins, and Lessard 1982). Seen in this way, tax exemption for SOEs constitutes another form of concessional finance for the enterprises.

Implicit taxes. Implicit taxes imposed through SOE operations may assume several forms. Some are true taxes, in that they produce revenues for governments. Others are not true taxes, in that they yield no current government revenues, but have taxlike effects on the private sector or other government-owned enterprises. These taxlike effects include not only those that increase the costs of affected private or public firms but also those that impose costs on the general taxpaying public, including inflation exacerbated by SOE deficits.

Both types of implicit taxes may be split into two categories: first, taxes and taxlike devices implicit in flows between public enterprises and the private sector; second, those implicit in arrangements between the state enterprise sector and the owner.

Implicit taxes on flows between SOEs and the private sector. This category includes two of the most venerable forms of revenue-producing implicit taxation as well as two that have only recently been widely recognized as taxlike devices.

1. Fiscal monopolies. Fiscal monopolies have been used as methods of garnering revenues for the state for at least two millenniums, dating back to the salt monopolies of biblical times. This form of implicit taxation survives today not only in LDCs but in the United States, particularly at subnational levels of government, and was phased out for tobacco in Japan only in 1983 (Shoup 1989). In modern times state-owned fiscal monopolies in LDCs tend to be confined to such sumptuary products and services as tobacco, beer, spirits, gambling (lotteries), and pawn shops. The island province of Zanzibar in Tanzania, however, still relies heavily on revenues

gained from its monopoly on export sales of cloves to cigarette manufacturers in LDCs and food-processing firms in industrial countries. Moreover, fiscal monopolies do not always result in governmental revenues: for several years during the 1960s and early 1970s the state-owned beer monopoly in Ghana sold beer at a loss because of a presumption within the government that price increases to compensate for inflation would have costly political repercussions among urban elites.

Revenues from fiscal monopolies have tended to decline in relative importance in most LDCs since 1945. In Colombia, where departmental governments have been entrusted with the collection of taxes (but not the setting of rates) on liquor produced in the departments since 1923, taxes from this source grew more slowly than income in all but four of Colombia's twenty-two departments from 1967 to 1975 (Bird 1984, p. 245). Nevertheless, liquor tax collections remained an appreciable source of revenue in ten departments, where they equaled or exceeded 1 percent of regional GDP, a sizable tax ratio in a nation where that of the central government rarely exceeds 10 percent.

Elsewhere fiscal monopolies have tended to fare less well. The central government of Indonesia maintains a monopoly on all pawn shop operations. An important revenue source for the Dutch in colonial times, this monopoly produced virtually no proceeds by 1980.

Casual observation in any case suggests that LDCs are increasingly shifting away from the use of fiscal monopolies in the taxation of sumptuary and other goods toward explicit ad valorem or specific excise taxes on these items. Several reasons lie behind this trend, but revenue needs provide the principal explanation: inefficient operations in the monopolies may mean low or negative profits. And while explicit excises on beer, liquor, and tobacco may be evaded to some degree, many LDCs have been more successful in limiting evasion of these taxes (particularly when imposed at specific rates) than of broad-based sales and income taxes.

2. Marketing boards. Government-established marketing boards

have been used in a large number of LDCs ranging from Colombia and Peru in Latin America to the Philippines and Thailand in Asia and in numerous African nations, where they have been most common. Marketing boards have been awarded monopoly status in the buying and selling of commodities for domestic consumption, especially foodstuffs for export. In Mexico a large state monopoly controls imports, domestic procurement, and distribution of a wide range of agricultural goods (World Bank 1988). Governments have also conferred monopoly status on state marketing boards in Ghana (for cocoa and timber), in Senegal (peanuts) (Gillis et al. 1987), in Kenya (tropical timber before 1960, export of gems), and in much of the rest of sub-Saharan Africa (World Bank 1988). In many other countries marketing boards have lacked de jure monopoly status but have attained de facto monopoly positions as private traders in the affected commodities have been crowded out, as in Colombia, Peru, and the Philippines (World Bank 1986). Finally, in several countries government marketing boards and similar agencies coexist with private sector firms, as in Indonesia (rice), Sri Lanka (rice), India (grains), and Kenya (maize and beans).

Rather obvious implicit taxes have been imposed on farmers by monopoly marketing boards. Such taxes are merely the difference between the sale price in national or world markets and both the often inflated costs of the marketing board and the price paid by the board on purchases from farmers. Not all marketing boards, however, have channeled such taxes to the national treasury. In Ghana, for example, in the 1960s and early 1970s, inefficiencies and patronage costs in the state Timber Marketing Board were great enough to offset virtually all the margin between revenue from export sales and costs of procurement. As a result, loggers were taxed fairly heavily, but no tax revenues accrued to the government (Gillis 1969, unpublished).

The Ghanaian experience with cocoa and the history of marketing boards generally in Tanzania are illustrative of the difficulties often involved in the attempt to collect implicit taxes through marketing boards. The Cocoa Marketing Board in Ghana was established under British colonial administration. Implicit taxes were high from the beginning and from 1955 to 1960 ranged from 13 percent to 50 percent of the f.o.b. value of exports. The implicit tax rate varied because farmers were paid a fixed price regardless of world prices; in effect the short-term marginal tax rate was 100 percent (Roemer 1984, p. 208). Just before and just after independence in 1957, the proceeds of the implicit tax constituted more than a tenth of government revenue, much of which was converted into sizable foreign exchange reserves, equivalent to seventeen months of imports. By 1960 Ghana's share in world cocoa exports was still nearly one-third. Over the next five years cocoa taxes declined steadily owing to depressed world prices. Prices paid to producers also declined in real terms, by almost two-thirds.

From 1967 to 1970 the world cocoa market was buoyant, implicit taxes on farmers were again very high, but implicit tax revenues from cocoa grew slowly. One reason was that potential profits were reduced as a result of high operating costs. But the marketing policies followed by the board also accounted for a large part of the problem. From 1967 through 1969 the board received export prices that were only 85 percent of the prevailing world price for cocoa. The managers, pressed for cash flow to support many activities unrelated to cocoa, consistently sold cocoa short during the rising market of those years (Anderson 1970). For the period 1977–1982 cocoa revenues continued to decline even as the implicit tax on farmers remained high but largely uncollected. This was a consequence of rampant smuggling of cocoa to the Ivory Coast, where producers' prices were more than ten times those available in Ghana (Ansu 1984, p. 228).

The Tanzanian experience of the 1970s and early 1980s is also instructive. The government maintained a monopoly in marketing of all major food and export crops. Although farmers suffered very substantial implicit taxes, through establishment of low producer prices, implicit tax revenues received by the government were insubstantial, owing to the high costs of the marketing parastatals, which had losses equal to nearly 20 percent of their combined turnover, requiring both heavy subventions from the government and large overdrafts from the banking system (Lele 1984, p. 182).

In both Ghana and Tanzania, then, sizable implicit taxes were imposed on farmers, but a very large share of the revenues so gained was dissipated through inefficiencies or inappropriate marketing strategies.

3. Nonrevenue implicit taxes. We have seen how the quest for government revenue through some forms of implicit taxes may be throttled by mismanagement. But some taxlike levies implicit in SOE operations are imposed on the private sector and other SOEs but by their nature do not yield government revenues. Two of these are discussed here.

Arrears in satisfying accounts payable of SOEs have clear taxlike effects on creditors. This state of affairs has been common in a number of countries, including Egypt, Morocco, Portugal, many sub-Saharan African nations (World Bank 1988, p. 169), and Indonesia. Arrears of this kind have been particularly serious in economies experiencing rapid inflation.

This taxlike levy has been particularly common in accounts payable *within* state enterprise sectors. In the early 1970s, the Indonesian state oil company, Pertamina, owed millions of dollars in arrears to the State Food Marketing Board (BULOG), which supplied rice rations to 40,000 Pertamina employees. In other cases chain reactions in arrears have occurred that have seriously eroded financial discipline within the entire public sector. Painful cases in point occurred in Gambia and in Egypt (World Bank 1988, p. 170). In Egypt the railroad SOE refused to pay SOEs in engineering because of mounting arrears owed by the central government. Consequently, the engineering SOEs refused to pay arrears to SOEs in steel. In turn the steel SOEs refused to pay the state-owned power company.

A second type of implicit tax that yields no governmental revenue occurs when governments award monopoly (and often duty-free) import privileges to SOEs. One particularly costly case occurred in Indonesia. In the early 1980s, the state-owned firm Krakatau Steel was appointed sole importer of steel products (Gillis and Dapice 1988, p. 326). In subsequent months and years private and public sector firms paid a substantial premium on steel purchased from Krakatau Steel and used in downstream manufacturing. Higher profits on steel importing in Krakatau Steel did not even result in higher income taxes paid to the treasury, since the enterprise was still carrying forward tens of millions of dollars in losses from earlier years.

Taxes implicit in flows between SOEs and the government. Of this particular group of implicit taxes, only the first received much attention before the 1980s.

1. Inflation. Operations of SOEs have in many countries resulted in a significant implicit tax that does not reach government coffers but does serve as a form of government finance: higher taxes on money balances caused by large deficits in the operation of SOEs.

Deficits in the state enterprise sectors of LDCs as conventionally measured (that is, deficits not including central bank losses associated with financial crises) in the mid-1970s averaged, as we have seen, 4 percent of GDP. The problem worsened in the period 1981–1984, particularly in such countries as Brazil, Costa Rica, the Dominican Republic, Ecuador, Egypt, the Philippines, Turkey, and Venezuela, where SOE deficits have been between 3 percent and 12 percent of GDP. In all these nations the rest of the public sector would have generated a fiscal surplus without the net transfers to the SOEs (World Bank 1988, p. 171).

Countries with shallow financial systems are particularly vulnerable to inflationary consequences of large budget deficits (Gillis et al. 1987). In virtually none of the countries listed above is the ratio of liquid assets to GDP high enough to allow deficits of these magnitudes without substantial inflation.[7] In both Brazil and the Philippines, for example, the liquid asset ratio is about 30 percent, about half as high as the ratio typically found in developed nations. Where the ratio is 30 percent, a deficit of 5 percent of GDP would (if financed by the central bank) itself cause the money supply to grow by 17 percent; a deficit of 8 percent would cause the money supply to grow by 27 percent.[8] In fact, in both cases the money supply would have to grow by much more than the amounts required to finance SOE deficits if the private sector were not to be completely crowded out of credit markets.

SOE deficits of 5 percent and 8 percent of GDP are clearly inflationary under these circumstances. The implicit taxes on money balances resulting from inflation induced by such deficits have been sizable in dozens of countries, where annual inflation rates of 25 percent have been common since 1982.

2. Reserve requirements on SOEs in banking. All central banks require commercial banks to immobilize a portion of their deposits in the form of legal reserves that may not be lent to prospective customers. Generally among LDCs legal reserve requirements fall in a range of 20 percent to 30 percent, but at times they have been as high as 50 percent in Chile and a few other nations. Because central banks generally do not pay interest on required reserves held with the bank (Gillis et al. 1987), the legal reserve requirement amounts to an implicit tax on all banks, including the state-owned banks found in many LDCs.

Given financial intermediation costs equal to 3 percent to 4 percent of deposits in many LDCs, this implicit tax inevitably means either artificially low real interest rates for depositors or deficits in bank operations or both. The result is either an implicit tax on money balances, where interest rates for depositors are thereby depressed, or higher borrowing costs for firms.

3. Governmental arrears to SOEs. Arrears in SOE accounts receivables from the government as owner constitute an implicit tax on the enterprises. In several LDCs unpaid bills owed by the government as owner to state-owned utilities producing power, water, and telecommunication services have been as large as the value of one year of the governments' consumption of such goods and services. In Gambia the treasury owed the state power company an amount equal to 4 percent of government revenues in 1984 (but the state power company owed the government four times that amount) (World Bank 1988, p. 170).

Arrears owed by governments to SOEs take other forms. Governments often renege on promises to fund grants and subsidies to SOEs; these become obligations for future years. Arrears of this kind in Morocco amounted to 2.5 percent of GDP in 1984 (World Bank 1988, p. 171).

Implicit Subsidies and Taxes: Rationales and Efficacy

In some cases governments have articulated, sometimes clearly, the justifications for the use of particular implicit subsidies or tacit taxes. Many subsidies, as well as a few taxes, have been adopted for such announced reasons as to improve income distribution and public health, to further economic development and stabilization goals, to protect the environment, or, particularly in the case of tacit taxes, to alleviate administrative exigencies, that is, difficulties in collecting explicit taxes from large numbers of small agriculturists.

In other cases, however, rationales for using tacit taxes and subsidies have been unacknowledged by governments. Often this has been because the subsidy or tax was either unintended or beyond the control of poorly staffed government agencies. But there are instances in which governments have become well aware of the subsidy or tax but have strong political reasons for masking its existence.

This section presents the rationales most often used in support of such subsidy or tax programs and examines the efficacy of such programs in light of the putative objectives.

Income distribution and public health rationales. A wide array of implicit subsidies channeled through SOEs, as well as the explicit subsidies with which many of them are often associated, have been justified on grounds of their effects in reducing poverty, income inequality, and threats to public health. Certain types of implicit taxes have also been promoted in the name of promoting public health.

Explicit as well as implicit subsidies on domestic consumption of refined petroleum products have often been justified by the claim that such subsidies are redistributive: specifically, that they are required to make affordable the purchase of gasoline, fuel oil, and especially kerosene by low-income families. This argument has been explicitly employed in Bolivia, Colombia, Indonesia, and Pakistan.

Wherever used, this type of subsidy has generally not achieved the desired results and has been costly in efficiency losses to the economy. Gasoline and diesel fuel subsidies in Bolivia, Colombia, Ecuador, and Indonesia have been much more effective in benefiting the 5 percent to 10 percent of the income distribution wealthy enough to own vehicles. Subsidization of motor fuel could, however, redound primarily to the benefit of poorer households if confined to the use of fuel for urban bus transport. But urban transportation, if subsidized at all (see below), is best supported not by motor fuel subsidies but by explicit subsidies to urban transport enterprises, whether public or private. Such a subsidy program can be targeted to the urban poor in ways impossible to achieve with motor fuel subsidies.

Many nations subsidizing motor fuel also subsidize kerosene consumption, primarily to benefit low-income households; a few, such as Pakistan, have focused petroleum product subsidies on kerosene alone. This subsidy program suffers from two major problems. First, subsidies on kerosene necessitate similar subsidies on automotive diesel fuel. Otherwise kerosene may be used as a fuel in diesel engines, with attendant problems of fouling both the air and ultimately automotive engines, as has occurred in both Pakistan and Indonesia (when kerosene was, for a period of one month, much more heavily subsidized than diesel fuel). But subsidizing both kerosene and automotive diesel fuel is an expensive proposition: in Indonesia, the *economic* costs of subsidies on these two items alone amounted to 4.5 percent of GDP in 1979–1980 (Gillis 1980a, p. 57).

Second, available studies on the income distribution effects of kerosene subsidies suggest that only a small proportion of the benefits are received by the poor. To illustrate, in Indonesia in the early 1980s the poorest 40 percent of the population consumed only 20 percent of total kerosene. This means that for every one rupiah of subsidy benefiting the poor, four rupiahs of that subsidy benefited the relatively well-off. Thus the heavy subsidy helps the poor, but it helps the relatively well-off (the upper 60 percent) considerably more. Moreover, subsidies on domestic consumption of petroleum products have involved significant welfare costs for most nations that have used them. In Bolivia deadweight losses from energy subsidies in the mid-1970s were between 0.3 percent and 0.6 percent of GDP, depending on assumed elasticities of demand (McLure 1981). In Indonesia the economic waste associated with petroleum product subsidies has been estimated at about 0.5 percent of GDP, given a price elasticity of demand of 0.5 percent (Summers 1979).

We have seen that implicit and explicit foodstuff subsidies channeled through SOEs are widely used. While these subsidies are often intended to help overcome temporary food insecurity by stabilizing food prices, consumer subsidies on basic foodstuffs have most commonly been justified as means for overcoming the long-term inadequacies of the diets of the poorest people. Seen this way, food subsidy programs represent an investment in improved nutrition and health and therefore an investment in human capital. As a redistributive device such programs may be particularly essential in LDCs lacking a large and varied spectrum of income transfer programs that can be deliberately manipulated to achieve any desired distributive outcome (Bird and Horton 1989, p. 13). Indeed, in some countries food subsidies may be the only way to get any help to the rural poor, even if not very efficiently (Gillis 1985; Bird and Horton 1989, p. 14).

Implicit food subsidy programs, rather than explicit programs supported through budgetary outlays, turn out to be decidedly inferior, especially in income redistribution effects. Implicit implementation of food subsidies is accomplished through a variety of devices, including export taxes in food-exporting nations, statutory monopolies that pay low prices for domestically produced food, artificially low prices of imported food, and sometimes heavy subsidies on fertilizer and pesticides. All these implementation methods except subsidies on agricultural inputs serve to shift the costs of the subsidy programs back to farmers. Inasmuch as the rural poor are often among the poorest in most nations and inasmuch as most rural households are farm households, implicit subsidies tend not to yield intended effects on income distribution and also tend to have a strong urban bias: in Bangladesh in 1973–1974 the poorest rural households consumed only twenty-three pounds of rationed grain, while comparable groups in urban areas consumed ten times as much (World Bank 1986, p. 93). Finally, the fertilizer subsidies that do help insulate farmers from the effects of artificially low food procurement prices often accrue largely to better-off farmers in better-irrigated areas (World Bank 1986, p. 96).

Food subsidy programs around the world suffer from a variety of other problems, including very high costs contributing to already large budgetary deficits (see preceding section) and therefore to inflation (which probably affects the poor more severely than the rich) and the failure to target subsidies to nutritionally vulnerable groups (use of subsidies on bread rather than on cassava, as in Brazil and Indonesia). Further, where costs of the subsidy program are shifted back to farmers or imported foodstuffs are heavily subsidized, subsidies lead to depressed food production. The problems inherent in the operation of some food programs, including the program used in Tanzania in the early 1980s, have caused some analysts to conclude that such subsidies are probably not a good policy instrument, at least in African nations (Horton 1989).

Subsidized consumption of potable water can be justified on grounds of both income redistribution and public health, given the very high incidence of waterborne diseases in many LDCs. Delivery of low-cost drinking water is particularly vital in areas where the poorest households buy water from inefficiently small private water carriers. These charges are often three (Nairobi), four (Lome and Lagos), eight (Indonesia), or even twenty-eight (Karachi) times the costs of publicly provided piped water (World Bank 1988, p. 145).

Governments have provided several forms of explicit and implicit subsidies for urban, but not often rural, drinking water consumption. Installation of strategically placed and subsidized water stand-pipes has been an effective means of delivering water to the urban poor in Jakarta (Berry 1979). Elsewhere connection charges have been subsidized, but even with heavy subsidies the charges are often beyond the reach of the poorest, as in Indonesia. Lifeline rates and rising block rates for water consumption have become common. If water demand is more sensitive to income than to household size, such schemes could involve substantial redistribution in favor of the poor. Perverse distributional results, however, have been found in many water subsidy programs (World Bank 1988) even when water charges are related to property values in progressive fashion (Bird and Miller 1989, p. 58).

Finally, subsidized water is of little benefit to the poor who have no access to public water supplies. This includes about 25% of the urban poor in the largest cities in Colombia (Bird and Miller 1989, p. 59) and the overwhelming majority of poor rural dwellers in dozens of LDCs.

Implicit subsidies for electric power provided by SOEs were earlier shown to be common among LDCs. While this subsidy is often justified on grounds of income redistribution, the effects of the subsidy suggest otherwise. Except perhaps for subsidies to rural electrification in a few countries such as Malaysia (Gillis 1982), subsidization of electric power entirely misses the poorest households without access. Moreover, even the poor who do have access have far fewer electrical appliances than wealthier consumers. Moreover, large subsidies on electric power consumption have generally led to wasteful levels of consumption (World Bank 1988, p. 143), a phenomenon well documented in several countries, including Colombia (Bird 1984), Indonesia (Gillis 1980a), and Bolivia (Gillis 1977).

The usual justification offered for subsidies to urban transport is that of assisting the poor. It does seem clear that the urban people in many LDCs spend a high fraction of their income (sometimes as much as 10 percent, as in Kingston, Jamaica) on travel, but often the poor forsake travel on publicly owned and subsidized buses for private carriers, which often provide better service (Heraty 1980). Middle-income groups, not the poorest, derive the greatest benefits from metro systems such as those recently installed in Caracas and São Paulo (World Bank 1988, p. 145). Therefore, it is not at all clear that subsidies to public transport always reach those who would most benefit.

Subsidies to urban transport SOEs tend to encourage urban sprawl and low-density development (Urrutia 1980) and have also served to squeeze out more efficient private carriers, whose costs per passenger-kilometer are often less than half those of public carriers (World Bank 1988, p. 144).

One rationale that has been offered, usually ex post, for the collection of explicit as well as implicit taxes through fiscal monopolies on tobacco, beer, and spirits is that such levies reduce both consumption of harmful products and the external costs to societies not realized by consumers of these items. Such taxes may be consistent with improving public health but are virtually everywhere quite regressive (McLure and Thirsk 1978), except apparently for some taxes on alcohol in such countries as Papua New Guinea (Bird 1983). Tacit taxes on sumptuary items, like explicit taxes imposed on them, are also consistent with the dictates of the literature on optimal taxation, since demand for these goods tends to be relatively price-inelastic. But it has also been argued that sumptuary taxes are inferior means of curbing social costs from consumption of beer, spirits, and tobacco. McLure (1988) contends that better means of reducing these costs are available, including prohibition or taxation of advertising expenditures.

Economic development and stabilization rationales. Some of the subsidies and tacit taxes discussed above have also been based on the rationale that they would foster economic development and economic stabilization as well as improve income distribution. This has often been the case for subsidies on motor fuels and electric power consumption. Quite apart from the often heavy financial and welfare costs cited earlier for these types of subsidies, they can also introduce long-term inefficiencies in the economic structure through their effects on choice of technology, particularly in energy-intensive undertakings both in SOEs themselves and in private firms.

Deep energy subsidies have in fact had significant effects on public and private investment decisions in several countries, including Indonesia (Gillis 1980a), Bolivia (Gillis and McLure 1981) and Venezuela, particularly in such highly energy-intensive activities as production of ferronickel (four times as energy-intensive as nickel produced from sulfide ores), cement plants, zinc, aluminum, and copper smelters, tungsten refining, and alumina plants. Such investment projects typically show very high net present values at subsidized energy prices but often involve negative domestic value added if border prices for energy are used instead (Gillis 1977).

Attempts have also been made to justify SOE subsidies on grounds that they help in restraining inflation. This argument has been used for subsidies generally in many countries (Tait 1977) and in support of energy subsidies in particular in Bolivia, Indonesia, and other oil-producing nations. A common view is that any given increase in energy prices required to reduce subsidies will be associated with an equivalent or nearly equivalent increase in costs and inflation rates. This view not only confuses onetime price level increases with inflation but ignores the fact that in most LDCs energy costs as a proportion of total costs are very small, except of course in the obvious cases of power generation, some transport, cement, and minerals processing. In Indonesia, for example, fuel costs in the early 1980s were less than 15 percent of total costs even in such activities as interisland shipping and urban bus transport. For virtually all other sectors of the economy, fuel costs were considerably less than 2 percent of total costs (Gillis and Dapice 1979). Thus an increase of 50 percent in subsidized fuel prices would not be expected to raise total costs by much more than 1 percent, even when the full effects of the increase are passed through.

Subsidies on fertilizer, pesticides, herbicides, and agricultural credit are often expected to yield development benefits in agriculture as well as stabilization benefits in the form of greater national food security, in addition to promoting the welfare of poor rural farmers. There is not much doubt that these subsidies, particularly when offered together, can result in very substantial increases in agricultural production over the short to medium term, especially when the subsidies are large (and expensive) as has been the case for food grains in Indonesia (Timmer and Falcon 1984) and cattle ranching in Brazil (Repetto and Gillis 1988). The sustainability of the higher agricultural productivity induced by these subsidies is, however, another question, as is the environmental soundness of heavy encouragement of fertilizer and pesticide use.

Further, large implicit and explicit subsidies on fertilizer have led to substantial waste in Indonesia, where fertilizer use increased by 77 percent from 1980 to 1985 alone, resulting in triple the allocation of fertilizer per hectare in Indonesia as in Thailand and the Philippines (World Bank 1987, p. 102).

Finally, certain agricultural subsidies have been not only expensive but counterproductive. This was the case for pesticide subsidies also in Indonesia through 1987, where it was discovered that several of the heavily subsidized pesticides were elsewhere actually used in experimental plots to *increase* the numbers of pests, because of the greater effects of the pesticides on their natural predators.

Taxes and subsidies, primarily the former, implicit in the operations of many kinds of state-owned marketing boards, particularly those handling agricultural exports, have often been based on the rationale that they provide important support for maintenance of economic stability in several ways: first, by restraining income growth of farmers during periods of high prices, thereby presumably moderating domestic inflationary pressures; second, by placing a floor on farm income during periods of depressed export prices, thereby relieving rural economic distress; third, where domestic consumption of the commodity in question is significant, by protecting consumers from sudden, large price increases.

For these stabilization benefits to materialize, the marketing boards must sterilize a large portion of the taxes they collect during boom periods, in order to finance price supports for farmers when prices are low. We have seen, however, that many marketing boards have not accumulated the necessary surpluses during booms to finance subsidies during busts. In some cases this has been due to capture of surpluses by governments for general budgetary use. In others, failure to accumulate sufficient reserves has been due to mismanagement, as in the Cocoa Marketing Board in Ghana, or mismanagement and political patronage, as in the Timber Marketing Board in the same country.

Environmental rationales. An increasingly common rationale offered for some of the subsidies discussed in this chapter has been based on environmental considerations. This rationale has usually been offered ex post rather than ex ante.

Implicit subsidies on kerosene, for example, have been justified not only for reasons of income distribution but on grounds that they help to restrain deforestation and therefore erosion through their effects in reducing firewood consumption. Most of the rural poor, however, use kerosene almost exclusively for lighting, not for cooking. Where that is the case, subsidies on kerosene do not help to curb firewood gathering or deforestation or erosion. When viewed as an environmental program, a kerosene subsidy may be not only ineffective but vastly more expensive than other programs of erosion control.[9]

Attempts have also been made to justify fertilizer subsidies on grounds that they serve soil enrichment and conservation purposes. These arguments rarely stand up to close analysis, particularly in semiarid tropical countries where what is most needed is better adapted, but rarely subsidized, organic fertilizers and the use of moisture-retaining methods. In addition, there is some evidence that sustained use of chemical fertilizers can actually reduce fertility (World Bank 1986, p. 96). Moreover, subsidies to chemical pesticides and herbicides leading to overuse can lead and have led to significant environmental damages, rather than environmental protection (World Bank 1988, p. 118).

Unacknowledged rationales. The rationales for some types of implicit taxes and subsidies are rarely, if ever, made explicit and must usually be deduced from other, often difficult to find, evidence.

Inertia or ideological predisposition may account for the existence and persistence of one of the most important implicit subsidies for SOEs: tax exemption. Or it may have been thought that SOEs serve so many distributional, developmental, stabilization, and environmental goals that this form of subsidization is advisable on general principles. The costs of this type of implicit subsidy can be very substantial, in terms not only of forgone tax revenues but of the competitive advantages (Gillis and McLure 1981) provided to SOEs over their often more efficient, lower-cost private sector counterparts (Gillis 1977, Gillis et al. 1987, World Bank 1988).[10] In addition, failure to subject SOEs to income taxation runs the risk that the thereby much larger reinvestable earnings of nontaxable SOEs may not be used for socially profitable investments.

Here the U.S. experience is illustrative. Taxation of the income of the Tennessee Valley Authority might not have prevented TVA from undertaking massive investments in uneconomic nuclear power generation plants in the 1960s and 1970s. But taxation would certainly have severely curtailed the enterprise's capacity to do so. Similarly, taxation of the earnings of the Mexican oil enterprise PEMEX (Petroleos Mexicanos) might not have prevented much of Mexico's oil rents from finding their way to condominiums in Aspen or bank accounts abroad but would surely have reduced the scope for these rent-skimming activities.

Implicit subsidies arising from government guarantees on SOE debt and from preferential access to loan finance for SOEs also do not appear to be based on any acknowledged rationale, other than the view that the enterprise progeny of the government should as a matter of course be able to secure loan finance more easily and cheaply than private sector firms, if for no other reason than to promote objectives sought by governments through the enterprises they control.

Debt guarantees furnished to SOEs can also result in significantly higher borrowing costs not only for the parent government but for private sector borrowers as well. This is because no LDC faces perfectly elastic supplies of external credit; country risk is not entirely a figment of bankers' imaginations. Unbridled borrowing by SOEs in some heavily indebted countries, as noted earlier, has ended by imposing very high costs on their economies, particularly in the form of debt service strain and inflation.

Implicit subsidies and taxes due to arrears owed by SOEs to other firms and to SOEs by governments cannot be based on any remotely credible rationale. But we have seen how these forms of tacit taxes and sub rosa subsidies can wreak havoc within the entire public sector, not just the public enterprise sector.

Rationales based on administrative or political exigencies.
Several types of tacit taxes have been based on administrative, if not overtly political, rationales. One possible reason, other than traditions inherited from colonial times, for continued use of fiscal monopolies to tax sumptuary items such as tobacco was the belief that implicit taxes inherent in monopoly profits are less easily evaded than explicit taxes on the same items. This contention is doubtful in countries where tax stamps could be used to collect explicit taxes on cigarettes. Even in countries where tax evasion is rife, such as Indonesia and Colombia, excise tax administrations using stamps and relatively minimal enforcement mechanisms have proved reasonably effective in combating evasion of cigarette and beer taxes. In addition, monopolies of all stripes face less pressure for cost minimization than firms facing at least some competition, so that any benefits from control of evasion through fiscal monopolies may be dissipated in inefficient operations.

Marketing boards are often established not only for stabilization purposes but also because of the inability of tax administrations to collect explicit taxes from large numbers of small agriculturists. By monopolizing export trade in agricultural commodities, marketing boards can presumably obtain a "tax handle" on the agricultural tax base that would otherwise be unavailable. Many marketing boards with monopoly status have in fact garnered large amounts of implicit taxes on agricultural exports, as in Senegal, Malawi, and Ghana on occasion. The search for such revenues, however, is sometimes carried too far. The role of the Cocoa Marketing Board in the demise of the cocoa sector in Ghana is well documented (Ansu 1984, Roemer 1984).

Conclusion

Implicit or tacit taxes and subsidies through SOEs, particularly subsidies, are ubiquitous in LDCs. They are often associated with, or found alongside, explicit taxes and subsidies. Jointly, and often even separately, they often involve substantial financial, economic, and welfare costs. Some of the implicit subsidies have yielded notable benefits for targeted groups and unfortunately for putatively non-targeted rent seekers as well. A few of the implicit taxes have generated substantial revenues. But a much larger number of implicit taxes and subsidies have encountered little success in attaining desired results. Most, even the successful ones, are associated with costs largely unintended by governments.

Implicit subsidies and taxes in any case have little to recommend them over explicit taxes and subsidies unless one believes that lack of transparency in government operations achieves some high social purpose. In the case of implicit subsidies channeled through SOEs, the presence of the subsidies can be, and often is, used to explain or justify all manner of poor performance by the enterprises in their other operations having nothing to do with implementation of the subsidies. Where subsidies through SOEs are explicit, as in rural electrification efforts in Malaysia or in former subsidies to the Pakistan state-owned airline for trips between East and West Pakistan, the owner may justifiably insist on healthy operations in other, nonsubsidized activities of the enterprise.

The use of implicit rather than explicit taxes is difficult to justify on any economic grounds. Governments, knowing that implicit taxes are economically inefficient, may nevertheless find that they are politically efficient: they constitute a way of making some people worse off without their knowing it.

Comment
Charles E. McLure, Jr.

Malcolm Gillis has provided us with his usual exhaustive survey of practices around the world, this time focusing on the use of state-owned enterprises (SOEs) to implement explicit and implicit tax and subsidy policies. I learned a great deal from his paper and will have relatively little to say about it directly. Thus I want to take part of the time allocated to my discussion to present some of my own musing on the subject.

Costs and Benefits

I would have liked to see Malcolm make two further distinctions in his discussion of various types of costs of taxes and subsidies. In this discussion I am going to focus primarily on subsidies, but most of what I say is equally relevant for taxes.

First, I find it useful to distinguish between average and marginal costs as the basis for measuring subsidies, since these are the same only if costs are constant. It may be appropriate to measure subsidies relative to average costs if one is interested in distributional effects; but for efficiency purposes it is marginal costs that should provide the base line in calculating subsidies. Suppose, for example, that average costs are rising. In such a case prices that fully cover average costs nonetheless entail a subsidy, in the sense of not covering marginal costs.

The second distinction, that between financial and opportunity costs, is related to the first. I recall vividly a meeting at the Ministry of Mines of a petroleum-exporting country during the early 1980s in which I was advocating the use of marginal cost pricing principles in determining whether there was a subsidy to the domestic use of petroleum products. I was assured that domestic prices covered marginal costs, even though gasoline was then selling for only about U.S. fifteen cents per gallon, because the country was a low-cost producer; they apparently had no idea that the relevant concept of cost was the opportunity cost at which oil could be sold. (Of course, OPEC limitations on exports change the nature of the argument somewhat, but the basic point remains valid; the relevant concept of cost is generally not the cost of production.) At various points Malcolm's paper makes it clear that, like all good economists, he fully understands this distinction. But the point needs to be made explicitly, repeatedly, and in bold letters, given the proclivity of noneconomists not to realize the pivotal role played by opportunity costs in so many areas.

In focusing on marginal opportunity costs one must be careful not to focus exclusively on private costs and benefits. Thus, for example, the pricing of gasoline used in motor vehicles would ideally take into account the marginal social cost of road use, and in appraising the benefits of subsidies to urban transportation one should not ignore the benefits of reduced congestion and pollution. But at the same time one must be wary of those who would wrap all sorts of ill-conceived policies in the flag of external social benefits. There is little doubt that well-designed incentive policies can contribute to economic development. But it is equally clear that nations throughout the world have adopted unwise and uneconomic incentive policies in the professed pursuit of such high-sounding goals as encouraging "industries that are fundamental to the development of the country."

Why SOEs?

Malcolm's paper provides further evidence that state enterprises have amassed a generally dismal record around the world, even if one leaves aside the experience of avowedly socialist countries. It is difficult for any market-oriented economist to understand how and why so many governments have fallen into the trap of believing that state enterprises can and will do so many good things and will not do bad ones. (I am dealing here only with the misguided but honest belief that state enterprises are desirable. I do not address the "kleptocracy model," in which those in power are simply using various high-sounding arguments to hide their real objective, the satisfaction of their own greed—for money, power, or whatever. This is not to say that this model does not describe much of the actual use of state enterprises; presumably it does.) One can hardly understand how, as Malcolm describes the problem, they may have "thought that SOEs serve so many distributional, developmental, stabilization, and environmental goals that this form of subsidization is advisable on general principles." It is worthwhile to speculate on the answer.

Is the problem merely ideological, as the quotation above might suggest? Or is it based on bad economics? Do they really fail to understand the importance of "getting the prices right"? This explanation is suggested by the example I just gave of basing the pricing of petroleum products on costs of production. Do they realize that prices are hardly ever right when SOEs are involved?

Do they not see that the managers and employees of state enterprises generally do not have adequate incentives to operate in the true public interest? Experience throughout the world (not to mention introspection) shows anyone willing to see that incentives are largely lacking in state enterprises and that enterprises often serve the interests of their managers and employees, but not the public. Can anyone honestly believe that it is appropriate to give SOEs monopoly powers, either by prohibiting private competition or by rendering competition not viable because subsidies are available only to SOEs?

How can anyone fail to realize that the most important issue in achieving distributional objectives is often *access* to public services (including those provided by SOEs) by low-income households, not the price charged for service? Are they just engaged in intellectual sloppiness when they argue that subsidies for the consumption of gasoline and electricity improve the distribution of income when the poor are not major consumers of either (either directly or indirectly) and do not work for anyone who is? Or is it intellectual dishonesty? Is it the fundamental failure to understand that there are no free lunches?

My view on the matter is that well-meaning advocates of state enterprise (that is, those to whom the kleptocracy model does not apply) have fallen prey to an age-old delusion, that man is perfectible. If man were perfectible, economic plans would be constructed with wisdom and intelligence and implemented with honesty and efficiency. One would not need to worry about the kinds of problems that Malcolm and I have mentioned, including lack of incentives, corruption, the use of SOEs for political payoffs, the risk that SOE debt will drag an entire nation into financial difficulties, or arrears of payments to (and from) SOEs that threaten the financial stability of the enterprises (or governments and other enterprises). Indeed, we would not even need to worry about poorly conceived policies, including those that masquerade as populist while in fact squeezing the lowest classes in society, for such policies would presumably not be adopted by perfect men.

A more realistic view, however, would recognize that, alas, man is far from perfect and does not appear to be getting better very fast— certainly not fast enough to form the predicate for fundamental economic policies. This might lead to recognition of three crucial derivative conclusions: that men do not do so well as markets in determining resource allocation; that SOEs offer ample opportunity for the exercise of the imperfections to which man is subject; and that efforts to use SOEs to achieve even worthwhile goals are therefore likely to be dashed on the rocks of ignorance, incompetence, and self-interest, producing the problems listed above—and others.

Discussion

ALVIN RABUSHKA: My comments are collectively on what I'll call the Gillis-McLure paper. Only a handful of countries have managed to run highly profitable and efficient statutory boards or state-owned enterprises (SOEs). Singapore, for example, is one in which virtually every one of these enterprises is very profitable, so much so that they've been bullied into lowering prices in the services they supply. In Hong Kong the post office annually turns over hundreds of millions of dollars in profit to the government treasury. The government-owned railway in Hong Kong is immensely profitable, and most of the other services provided directly by government, except for the purely social services such as health care, tend to be profitable, beneficial, and efficiently run.

It is difficult to expand this list by leaps and bounds, but it would be an interesting exercise to enumerate the handful of exceptions to the general thrust of the paper and try to find out why these few work well. Since we are not likely to dismantle all these institutions overnight, perhaps we can learn some lessons on how to sell them and how to minimize the waste, fraud, and abuse found in these institutions all over the world.

A second comment is that I'm inclined by the Gillis thesis to draw the conclusion that one ought just to sell them all off regardless of price—even give them away if need be. Perhaps it is possible to design some kind of a share system, so that every citizen acquires a pro rata share of the ownership, or just give them to any foreigner who wants them, even if you can't sell them off for some positive price.

The last point I want to make concerns social philosophy. Economists are guilty of thinking in terms of market efficiency, market failure, public efficiency, and public failure. A different framework would be more helpful in advancing understanding. It is not simply that political leaders followed socialism and got into economic trouble, or the public choice paradigm of concentrated benefits and diffuse costs in democracies, or that the leadership wasn't educated in basic economics. The prevailing model for many of these third world countries is the "kleptocracy" model. If you assume kleptocracy is a more accurate model for a good part of the third world, it instantly provides an answer as to why SOEs exist everywhere. The answer is that they are a very effective way to steal.

SOEs also allow government leaders to staff them with people who are going to be loyal. The provision of public services at a reasonable price for reaching the poor is simply not a consideration at all. If it occurs, it's an accidental consequence of good luck and good fortune.

I think this approach gives you a better orientation. The political problem is how to convert kleptocracy into something that would be more responsive either to efficiency considerations or at least to some broader democratic notion that when leaders fail over long periods of time, the public can ultimately throw the bad guys out.

JOHN WHALLEY: After Malcolm's presentation of an aerial bombardment of subsidies around the world and percentages of this and percentages of that, it's very hard to defend these things, but I have two methodological qualifications.

The first is the marginal issue. As soon as you get into the marginal cost pricing debate, you can't conclude anything about the social costs of these things from their revenue costs. Just because there are large budget costs associated with these things per se, there's absolutely nothing we can conclude on straight analytical grounds.

The second thing is that even if there is some inefficiency associated with pricing arrangements, it can be offset by quantity constraints. With respect to many of the things you discuss, there's a lot of quantity rationing. Let's suppose we start with the fertilizer and pesticide subsidy. In many countries import licensing affects many of the inputs, and we can come up with stories that suggest on efficiency grounds that there's a rationale for some kind of offset.

JOHANNES LINN: I am concerned about the definition of subsidy and tax. The starting point has to be the definition of an efficiency price for a particular service, which is a very complex issue. It depends very much on the service, and we may have different costs for different uses of a particular service and for different times of day or year. Therefore, we have different efficiency prices depending on the cost structure of a particular service.

Not only do costs differ among users, but also subsidies and taxes tend to differ among users for the same service—water and power are common examples. Therefore, it's very important to think about cross-subsidization for a particular service (or for that matter cross-taxation, since subsidies are being matched by taxes even though in the aggregate no financial subsidy may flow into a service). You may have major inefficiencies within the service, which could be a serious concern, even though in the aggregate a particular public utility enterprise is financially sound and does not require budgetary subsidies.

ROBERT HIGGS: In Table 5.1 the shares of capital formation for the SOEs are much greater than their shares in GDP. I assume that at least some of the difference arises from the relatively great omission of investment in the sector of the economy outside the SOEs, much of which is agricultural or other rural activity where investment may be more difficult to estimate than it is within the SOEs.

Even if that's correct, however, I suspect we would still find that SOEs are producing a greater proportion of the economy's investment than of the economy's output. Only very large measurement errors would offset the differences you show in the table, which are twofold to threefold on average, depending on the continent.

Given that the difference is real and not purely an artifact of measurement error, we then observe what you say about why the subsidies to the SOEs occur. That is—to make a long story short— that the subsidies are good politics for the people in a position to decide on such things and not that they are actually correcting for misallocations arising from externalities.

A disconcerting implication of the relatively high share the SOEs have in capital formation would then be that with the passage of time a greater and greater proportion of the output of these countries is going to be produced in the SOE sector, where you've already concluded there's tremendous inefficiency and waste. The implication is that we're going to see an even worse inefficiency of resource allocation in the future of these countries than we see at the moment.

CHRISTOPHE CHAMLEY: Just a small comment on fertilizers to concur with John Whalley. Subsidies have to be considered in the broader context, and they depend very much on the taxation of the agricultural sector. It's easy to construct a case where you have a tax on output and a subsidy at the same rate, where the whole tax is falling on other factors.

DWIGHT LEE: I'd like to pose a general question regarding our topic of hidden taxes. From whom are they hidden? Are they hidden from those paying them, those imposing them, or perhaps both?

It's true that the people paying these taxes might not know what the cost of any particular program is and, depending on how the people respond to these costs, those who are imposing the taxes might not have a very good indication of what those costs really are either. But there might be hope, maybe long-run hope, maybe naive hope, but at least hope in the increasing integration of the world economy with increased flow of goods, increased flow of capital, increased flow of financial assets, and increased flow of information. The hope is that people will recognize that they are being taxed relatively more heavily than other countries and will be able to respond by moving capital.

Capital will be able to flee some of these taxes, and to that extent the cost of this taxation will be more readily apparent to politicians who lose their tax bases. So there may be more discipline on this process in the future, at least at the margin, as a result of a kind of Tiebout effect and increasing competition between governments.

CHARLES McLURE: I have just a couple of minor points. One, picking up on what has been said about pricing and costs, simply using a pricing policy that's uniform nationwide will often cause taxes and subsidies to the extent that costs aren't the same nationwide. We saw that particularly in Bolivia with its high costs of transportation to the hinterlands. Uniform pricing is popular politically, but it's economic nonsense.

The second point is that often these public enterprises create enormous private costs for individuals that are unconscionable. I remember a particular instance in Nairobi. Water from standpipes used by poor households was provided by a public enterprise or by part of the government. But since public employees were charged with turning the standpipe valves on and off, it was only possible to get water during working hours. Of course, that meant that if you had a job you had either to take off work to get water or to hire somebody else to go get the water for you.

You don't have to be very bright to arrange to turn the water on when people aren't at work, rather than only when they are at work. Coming back to what Dwight said, I would argue that you can rely on competition to achieve many things. But competition is not necessarily going to get the standpipes turned on at the right times.

RICHARD BIRD: The first point I want to raise concerns viewing SOEs as part of the big policy system that's used to deliver hidden taxes and subsidies. They may be very inefficient instruments for this purpose precisely because they are not really under the control of the state. Many years ago Paul Streeten said somewhere that if a country really wished to control its goods-producing sector, it should leave it in private hands, because (drawing on the British experience) public enterprises once created are out of the control of the state.

Let me give you two contradictory examples on another point. The first is very much along Alvin Rabushka's line on kleptocracy. There is part of a Caribbean island, which shall remain nameless, in which the tobacco monopoly was a main source of finance for the secret police, who kept the dictator in power. That's a very good example of a country that's run exactly the way he said it was.

A contradictory example from another Caribbean island illustrates that an SOE might have been a better instrument than anything that they had. In this case the lack of an SOE allowed serious problems to emerge that an SOE could have obviated. The government had closed the public urban transport system. The immediate result was the development of an efficient private sector system that delivered better service than they had before. Unfortunately, governments tend to get upset when everybody comes out in the street and starts burning tires and stoning ministers' cars and so on every time the gas price is changed; so they tend to be very reluctant to change fuel prices.

Previously, changes in the world oil price had been passed through to the final price to some extent, but the urban transport system was subsidized through the budget. Now, however, the state bus system had been abolished. In its place a large community of very articulate, very active small entrepreneurs called minibus drivers had developed. These people could pack twenty people in each bus and deliver them at any point in the capital city at a minute's notice, which made it very, very difficult to pass through increased world prices. In fact, since the fuel tax was a major component of the explicit tax revenues of this country, it was easy to calculate that they were losing far more by not being able to raise fuel taxes than they had lost before in the form of the subsidies that the World Bank and everybody else had told them were so terrible.

Another point concerns the effect of public enterprises on deficits. It's clear that in any one year SOEs add to the deficits of developing countries. If you look at it over a period of time, however, it's easy to show that the variance of SOE and government budget deficits do not directly correspond. In fact, in the LDCs for which information was available in the 1970s, the variance in the official (without SOE) government deficit was only about half what it would have been as a consolidated (with SOE) deficit because of the offsetting movements of enterprise deficits. Indeed, one can understand a risk-averse government preferring a portfolio, so to speak, of entities that it would expect to lose money in different years and hypothesizing that over time and in combination it would be in a better-off position.

Finally, I have been glad to hear so much discussion of distributional issues because, in my view as a policy economist, transition and distribution are what make life difficult.

With just efficiency and stable equilibrium to worry about, we'd have no great problems. But we live in a world where distribution matters, especially perceived distribution. Many years ago I wrote somewhere that you cannot understand much of the discussion one hears about the fiscal system in Latin America unless you understand that the rich consider themselves to be middle class, the middle class to be poor, and the poor to be nonexistent. That's really what a lot of this is about. External analysts are concerned with access and the bottom 40 percent, but these aren't necessarily concerns that shaped these policies in the first place.

Response
Malcolm Gillis

Charlie makes the point that I need to be much clearer about distinguishing between marginal and average subsidy costs. He is correct.

John suggested that I didn't get to the point about why implicit taxes and subsidies are worse than explicit ones. One reason is that I don't think you can recommend implicit taxes or subsidies over explicit ones unless you believe that lack of transparency in government operations achieves some high social purpose.

There are some subsidies that I didn't talk about and some taxes that I didn't talk about. In the case of subsidies channeled through state-owned enterprises, I find that when they're explicit, they can generally be kept under control and cannot easily be used to justify all manner of failure in SOEs. There are two outstanding examples. One was Pakistan International Airways (PIA) in the days when there were an East and a West Pakistan. For a few years all flights between East and West Pakistan were subsidized, largely because India wouldn't let PIA fly over the continent. They had to go way around, and so the government paid a subsidy for each passenger flown and gave it to PIA every quarter. That way PIA could not claim that any losses it was making were due to the fact that it had a social function to perform for the government, and it kept things on pretty much an even keel.

In Malaysia for a long time the government provided an explicit subsidy for rural electrification directly to the state electricity enterprise, usually based on numbers of kilometers of power lines extended in the rural areas. Therefore, if the enterprise showed losses at the end of the year, it couldn't claim that it was due to the fact that it had expensive rural development goals to fulfill.

Alvin Rabushka noted that a handful of countries have run highly profitable SOEs—Singapore, for example. Singapore is an interesting case. Some of my students were involved in selecting the aircraft purchased by Singapore Airlines. Instead of doing as is done in some countries I could mention, where the type of aircraft chosen depends on the amount of money paid under the table, they actually went out and did a classic cost-benefit analysis. They were very careful, and they knew that if they weren't very careful, they would answer to Lee Kwan Yew.

Alvin also said that perhaps we ought to give SOEs away. We tried that in Indonesia with a printing company, and nobody wanted it. Nobody came to the giveaway. That was partly because of other labor policies that the government was going to enforce, such as a prohibition against firing anybody. You've got to look at other policies when you're looking at how you dispose of these enterprises.

John Whalley said you can't conclude anything from financial cost. I agree with him, but financial costs are important to compute, first of all, because that's what first gets the attention of a decision maker. Second, the relationship between financial costs and economic costs is often very revealing. We really did not know much about the extent of the tragedy of the Indonesian pesticide subsidies until we noticed that the financial costs were far in excess of the economic costs.

Is Indonesia an extreme case? No. Actually not. There are about 200 major SOEs in Indonesia, and in general they're not so bad. They pay taxes. A lot of them pay dividends to the state. Garuda is a good example, as is the state tin mining enterprise. I could tell you stories about golf courses and jets and so forth, but I've since discovered that we find a lot of that in the private sector too that the stockholders don't know about. I employ mainly Indonesian examples because practically every case I've given is one that I have calculated myself, and I am much more comfortable giving those numbers than those derived by the methodology of others.

There was a point about offsetting taxes. That was a good point, but I don't know many sectors, except for Thai rice, where taxes on foodstuffs in developing countries are very substantial. Dwight Lee asks from whom subsidies are hidden, from the public or from the decision makers. My answer is, often both. I can't tell you how many hours I've spent trying to convince this or that person that the failure to charge border prices for natural gas sold to fertilizer companies was really a subsidy and wasn't a figment of my imagination.

Richard suggested that SOEs are not really under the control of the state. I can readily agree with that. He also noted that sometimes an SOE can be a better instrument for some policy purposes than anything else. One could add a lot of things to this paper, but I don't want it to become a book.

6 *Richard M. Bird*

Conclusion

To a considerable extent this volume constitutes a taxonomic exercise. To say this is not in any way to denigrate the effort represented here: defining and classifying any phenomenon is invariably one of the first and most important steps in understanding and analyzing it. What this book does is to bring out some of the important connections between a number of subjects—financial regulation, trade policy, public enterprise pricing, and the excess burden of taxation—that are usually considered quite separately. These disparate policies all have in common the fact that they effect implicit taxes (and subsidies) and act exactly like budgetary taxes and subsidies in the sense that they reduce the purchasing power of some segments of society—and generally the economic well-being of society as a whole.

The first European explorers to search for the New World usually started with some kind of map before them. As a rule, however, these maps represented more imagination than reality, indicating little more than a general direction in which to go and perhaps some kind of wavy coastline, with an island here and there. Invariably the interior behind the coast was left blank, occasionally with some such legend as "Here there be Monsters!" This book suggests that the Monster of Implicit Taxation not only exists but is important and, perhaps, proliferating in many developing countries.

The task of tracking down and counting the precise number of such monsters and quantifying how important their existence is for those concerned with sound development policy for the most part remains to be done by later explorers in this new world. At this point all that can be done is to conclude with two last observations, one bearing on the question of why implicit taxes exist and the other on the even more pressing problem of what might be done about them, once their existence is recognized.

To understand why implicit taxes not only exist but are often the instrument of choice for many governments, it is important to understand that the very vices deplored throughout this book—the opacity and deviousness of implicit taxation—may confer important political advantages. The very prevalence of indirect ways of doing things surely suggests that there is considerable political mileage in operating in this way. As Machiavelli might have said, the prince who can tax his subjects without their being aware of it is clearly one up on the poor soul who has to deal with conscious, and complaining, taxpayers. The very clarity of regulatory action compared with the obscurity of the effects of such measures makes them attractive to politicians who want to make some constituents happy while leaving others in blissful ignorance of the fact that they are paying for such happiness. Why politicians prefer so often to use the back door rather than the front door may perhaps not need further discussion in Washington or any other national capital.

What does need further discussion, however, is how they can so often and for so long get away with, in effect, fooling substantial numbers of people into believing that the hidden tax approach is beneficial when, as the papers in this book demonstrate, it is in fact generally disadvantageous to most people most of the time.

It is hard to believe that even the cleverest dictator or the most naive populace can exist forever on illusion alone. The American showman P. T. Barnum once said that a sucker was born every minute. A corollary may be that if you can catch them young enough and get them on your side, you may be able to stay in power for a long time. Another prominent American, Abraham Lincoln, had a different idea, however. He said that you can fool all the people some of the time and some of the people all of the time but not all the people all of the time. If Lincoln's view—which is really the philosophical underpinning of popular democracy—is valid, one cannot sustain an illusion-driven economy forever. The Barnums of this world may make money (or stay in office) for years, even decades. In the end, however, it is likely to be the Lincolns that make history. In particular, as recent events in Eastern Europe suggest, in the long run even the most predatory state is constrained by the reality that bad policies, explicit or implicit, produce bad results.

Humanity's record in designing and implementing institutions is of course far from perfect, and it is unlikely that any country, whether in the first, second, or third world, is about to bring all its hidden ways of doing things into the chill light of day. Nonetheless, academics and analysts must clearly support openness rather than secrecy since the entire scholarly world is in a sense erected on the basic belief that it is always better to know than not to know. In this spirit, improvements in our knowledge about the effects of hidden policies should, eventually, lead to improvements in policy outcomes. The best way to deal with implicit taxes is thus to bring them as much into the open as possible through such devices as regulatory budgets, increased accountability of state-owned enterprises, and so on. The question that should always be asked is, What explicit tax (and expenditure) policies would accomplish the same results as this or that implicit policy? The answer to this question, imperfect as it will inevitably be, should reveal a great deal about the effects of tl e implicit taxes now found throughout the developing world.

The authors and discussants represented in this volume have given us some idea of the relative magnitudes of the policies they have considered and the methods that might be used to learn more about them. Clearly, however, much more work needs to be done to determine the additivity of these magnitudes, the interdependence of implicit and explicit taxes and expenditures, and so on and on. In the present state of knowledge, we cannot say with certainty how important implicit taxes are relative to explicit taxes or whether they work in the same ways or at cross-purposes. The map of Implicit Taxland largely remains to be filled in, but at least now its existence and importance should be indisputable. Few tasks are more important for those concerned with improving public policy than further explorations in the "new" world of implicit taxation. Making the facts about implicit taxes—or as good an approximation of the facts as can be obtained—more transparent should, if nothing else, make it more difficult for governments to conceal the full implications of their actions. This would be no small accomplishment.

Notes and References

1. Richard M. Bird, More Taxing Than Taxes?: An Introduction

Notes

1. Prest 1985, p. 11.
2. Ibid., p. 15.
3. See, in particular, Surrey 1973.
4. Prest 1985, p. 15.
5. See, for example, Surrey and McDaniel 1985, and OECD 1984.
6. McLure 1988, pp. 27–30.
7. World Bank 1988, pp. 43, 61, 80, and chap. 8. The only quantification attempted was of inflation taxes, which were estimated to be as high as 4 percent of GNP in countries such as Argentina, although such figures were said to be unsustainable over time.
8. World Bank 1983.
9. Mohammed and Whalley 1984. A later study (Acharya et al. 1985) calls the basis for this estimate weak but itself goes on to emphasize the importance of controls over industry in India, the similarity of these controls to a system of "private taxation" (p. 237), and the close link between the growing importance of such hidden taxes and the growth of the "black" economy.
10. Newbery and Stern 1987, pp. 194 (Newbery) and 237 (Tanzi). As Newbery (p. 194) says, "nontax instruments that lower the market price of factors (such as overvalued exchange rates) will lower the apparent cost of government

> expenditure and may be equivalent to higher levels of taxation and expenditure in a less distorted economy."

11.   Gray 1984.
12.   Fry 1988; see also Chamley and Hussain 1988 for an explicit analysis of such "indirect" taxes on financial assets as reserve requirements, interest rate and credit ceilings, and selective loan requirements.
13.   Krueger, Schiff, and Valdes 1988, for example, find that the "indirect" effects of government policies (such as protection) on agricultural incentives generally outweigh the effects of such more direct policies as export taxes and import subsidies. Many others have of course treated trade issues in what may be called a tax framework: for a particularly interesting early example, see Shoup et al. 1959; for a recent explicit analysis of exchange rate management as a tax policy, see Frenkel and Razin 1988.
14.   Rabushka and Bartlett 1985, pp. 51–52.

References

Acharya, Shankar N., et al. 1985. *Aspects of the Black Economy in India*. New Delhi: National Institute of Public Finance and Policy.

Chamley, Christophe, and Qaizar Hussain. 1988. "The Removal of Taxes on Financial Assets in Thailand, Indonesia, and the Philippines—A Quantitative Evaluation." Unpublished paper, World Bank. Washington D.C., June.

Frenkel, Jacob A., and Assaf Razin. 1988. "Exchange-rate Management Viewed as Tax Policies." Working Paper no. 2653, National Bureau of Economic Research. Cambridge, Mass., July.

Fry, Maxwell J. 1988. *Money, Interest, and Banking in Economic Development*. Baltimore: Johns Hopkins University Press.

Gray, Clive S. 1984. "Toward a Conceptual Framework for Macroeconomic Evaluation of Public Enterprise Performance in Mixed Economies." In *Public Enterprise in Mixed Economies: Some Macroeconomic Aspects* by Robert H. Floyd, Clive S. Gray, and R. P. Short. Washington, D.C.: International Monetary Fund.

Krueger, Anne O., Maurice Schiff, and Alberto Valdes. 1988. "Agricultural Incentives in Developing Countries: Measuring the Effect of Sectoral and Economywide Policies." *World Bank Economic Review* 2: 255–71.

McLure, Charles E., Jr. 1988. "Fiscal Policy and Equity in Developing Countries." In *Policy Reform and Equity: Extending the Benefits of Development*, ed. Elliot Berg. San Francisco: ICS Press.

Mohammed, Sharif, and John Whalley. 1984. "Rent Seeking in India: Its Costs and Policy Significance." *Kyklos* 37: 387–413.

Newbery, David, and Nicholas Stern, eds. 1987. *The Theory of Taxation for Developing Countries*. New York: Oxford University Press for the World Bank.

OECD. 1984. *Tax Expenditures: A Review of the Issues and Country Practices*. Paris: Organisation for Economic Co-operation and Development.

Prest, A. R. 1985. "Implicit Taxes: Are We Taxed More Than We Think?" *Royal Bank of Scotland Review* no. 147 (September): 10–26.

Rabushka, Alvin, and Bruce Bartlett. 1985. "Tax Policy and Economic Growth in Developing Nations." Unpublished paper, Agency for International Development. Washington, D.C., November.

Shoup, Carl S., et al. 1959. *The Fiscal System of Venezuela*. Baltimore: Johns Hopkins University Press.

Surrey, Stanley S. 1973. *Pathways to Tax Reform*. Cambridge, Mass.: Harvard University Press.

Surrey, Stanley S., and Paul R. McDaniel. 1985. *Tax Expenditures*. Cambridge, Mass.: Harvard University Press.

World Bank. 1983. *World Development Report 1983*. New York: Oxford University Press for the World Bank.

————. 1988. *World Development Report 1988*. New York: Oxford University Press for the World Bank.

2. Dan Usher, The Hidden Costs of Public Expenditure

1. Adam Smith, *The Wealth of Nations*, Stigler-Cannan ed. (Chicago: University of Chicago Press, 1976), book 4, chap. 9, p. 208 of vol. 2.

2. By the community's marginal valuation, I mean the sum of the valuations of all citizens, on the assumption that guns are a pure public good.

3. There is not a great deal of literature on the overhead cost of public expenditure. See, for instance, M. Mendelson, *The Administrative Cost of Income Security Programs, Ontario and Canada*, Occasional Paper no. 9, Ontario Economic Council, 1979.

4. The concept of deadweight loss in taxation is central to modern public finance. See, for example, Robin Boadway and David Wildasin, *Public Sector Economics* (Boston: Little, Brown, 1984).

5. Equation 4 abstracts from the effect of the provision of the public expenditure on the taxpayer's purchase of the taxed good. The cost-benefit rule when this is taken into account becomes

$$\sum_{i=1}^{n} MRS_i = S\left[MRT - t\sum_{i=1}^{n} \frac{\partial x_i}{\partial G}\right]$$

where $S \equiv 1/(1 + \epsilon_{xt})$. In this equation i refers to one of the n people in the community, MRS_i is his marginal valuation of the public good, MRT is the marginal cost of the public good, G, and the derivatives $\partial x_i/\partial G$ are the effects on consumption of the taxed goods x_i of a small increase in the supply of the public good. See A. B. Atkinson and N. Stern, "Pigou, Taxation, and Public Goods," *Review of Economic Studies* (1974): 119–28; and David Wildasin, "On Public Good Provision with Distortionary Taxation," *Economic Inquiry* (April 1984).

6.   There is a wide variation among estimates of marginal cost of public funds
       because such estimates are very sensitive to assumptions about the magni-
       tudes of the underlying elasticities of demand and supply. In the earliest
       empirical paper on the subject, Harry Campbell ("Deadweight Loss and
       Commodity Taxation in Canada," *Canadian Journal of Economics* (1975):
       441–77) estimates marginal social costs of taxation to be about $1.25 per
       dollar of public expenditure. Edgar Browning ("The Marginal Cost of Public
       Funds," *Journal of Political Economy* (1976): 283–98) estimates the compa-
       rable figure for the United States to be between $1.09 and $1.16. The papers
       differ in that Campbell estimates the loss from the reorientation of consump-
       tion brought about by excise taxation while Browning is concerned with the
       labor-leisure choice as affected by the income tax. Charles Stuart ("Welfare
       Cost per Dollar of Additional Revenue in the United States," *American
       Economic Review* (1985): 352–62) derives a series of estimates varying,
       according to the assumptions about elasticities of labor supply and other
       aspects of the economy, between $1.07 and $2.33.

7.   For a community with *n* people, this consideration is accounted for in the
       general formula, in note 5, connecting costs and benefits of public expendi-
       ture. The marginal benefit of the extra tax resulting from the provision of a
       unit of the public good is

$$\sum_{i=1}^{n} t \frac{\partial x_i}{\partial G}$$

8.   To the taxpayer, an income tax is the equivalent in certain simple models to
       an excise tax on all consumption goods. In an economy with identical
       consumers, and with one type of consumption good that requires *P* hours of
       labor to produce, an income tax levied at a rate *t* is equivalent to an excise tax
       at a rate τ when

$$PX = Y(1 - t)$$

and

$$PX(1 + \tau) = Y$$

where *Y* is gross income measured with hours of labor as the numeraire and
X is the corresponding net income. Suppose the number of hours of work is
invariant with regard to changes in the tax rate. With the excise tax, the
elasticity of the tax base to the tax rate becomes $\tau/1 + \tau$, and $\Delta W/\Delta R$ in
accordance with equation 4 becomes $1 + \tau$. With the income tax, the
elasticity of the tax base to the tax rate is necessarily 0 since *Y* is invariant, and
the value of $\Delta W/\Delta R$ in accordance with equation 4 is 1. The resolution of the
apparent conundrum gets to the heart of the meaning of the marginal cost of
public revenue. Although the two taxes are identical from the point of view
of the taxpayer, they are not so from the point of view of the accounting of the
public sector. As long as the labor supply is invariant, the optimal supply

of public goods is that for which the relative valuation of private goods and public goods are just equal at the margin to the ratio of their costs of production. This condition holds when public revenue is raised by an income tax and G is produced up to the point where marginal valuation equals marginal cost. It does not hold when public revenue is raised by an excise tax on private goods because the tax raises their marginal valuation above their marginal cost without raising the marginal valuation of public goods at all. Optimality is only achieved when the balance between the valuations of private goods and public goods is restored. This can be achieved either by taxing public goods at a rate τ or by a cost-benefit rule such that the marginal valuation of public goods exceeds marginal cost by a factor $1 + \tau$.

9. A burgeoning literature on the social cost of tax evasion is surveyed by F. A. Cowell in *Cheating the Government* (Cambridge, Mass.: MIT Press, 1990).

10. For empirical work on the cost of transfers, see Edgar K. Browning and William R. Johnson, "The Trade-off between Equality and Efficiency," *Journal of Political Economy* (1984): 175–203; and Charles L. Ballard, "The Marginal Efficiency Cost of Redistribution," *American Economic Review* (1988): 1019–33. Both papers present ratios of losses to the top four quintiles of the American population to gains to the bottom quintiles. Their estimates depend critically on assumed elasticities of the tax base to the tax rate. Browning and Johnson's "preferred" estimate is 3.49. Ballard's preferred estimate is between 1.5 and 2.5.

11. A person's expected utility, W, is

$$W = \pi u(C^P, E) + (1 - \pi)u(C^U, E)$$

which is a function of π, E, C^P, and C^U in the first instance. However, equations 13, 14, and 15 allow C^P and C^U to be expressed as functions of y^P, y^U, and T. This allows W to be expressed as a function of π and E, with y^P, y^U, and T as parameters.

12. For given t and T, expected utility can be written as

$$W = \pi (E)u((1 - t)y^P, E) + (1 - \pi(E))u((1 - t)u^U + T, E)$$

where the utility function covering consumption and effort, $u(C,E)$, has the properties $u_C > 0$, $u_{cc} < 0$, $u_E < 0$, and $u_{EE} < 0$. Effort, E, is chosen to maximize W, so that

$$\pi'(u^P - u^U) + \pi u_E^P + (1 - \pi)u_E^U = 0$$

where u^P and u^U are the values of utility if one is prosperous and if one is unprosperous. Since $\pi' > 0$ and the difference $(u^P - u^U)$ gets smaller as T increases, the absolute value of the expression $\pi u_E^P + (1 - \pi)u_E^U$ must get smaller too. This can only happen when E is reduced; diminishing marginal disutility of labor implies that E and the absolute value of u_E must increase or decrease together.

13.   On the effect of unemployment insurance on the incidence of unemploy-
       ment, see Dale T. Mortensen, "Unemployment Insurance and Job Search
       Decisions," *Industrial and Labor Relations Review* (1977): 505–17; and
       Robert H. Topel, "On Layoffs and Unemployment Insurance," *American
       Economic Review* (1983): 541–59. The effect of provision of welfare for
       unmarried mothers on the incidence of illegitimacy is discussed in Charles
       Murray, *Losing Ground: American Social Policy 1950–80* (New York: Basic
       Books, 1984); and Victor R. Fuchs, *How We Live* (Cambridge, Mass.: Harvard
       University Press, 1983), chap. 4.

14.   Two seminal articles on the effects of public indebtedness and saving are
       Martin Feldstein, "Social Security, Induced Retirement, and Aggregate Capi-
       tal Accumulation," *Journal of Political Economy* (1974): 905–26; and Robert
       Barro, "Are Government Bonds Net Wealth?" *Journal of Political Economy*
       (1974): 1095–1117. Both papers apply equally well to public indebtedness
       financed by bonds and to public indebtedness in the form of promises to pay
       old-age pensions. Feldstein argues that public indebtedness substitutes for
       private capital formation when one's motivation for saving is to provide for
       one's old age. Barro argues that public indebtedness has no effect on private
       capital formation when people expect to make bequests to their children.

15.   The subject is surveyed in Robert Bish, "Improving Productivity in the
       Government Sector," in David Laidler, ed., *Responses to Economic Change*
       (vol. 27 of background studies for the MacDonald Commission) (Toronto:
       University of Toronto Press, 1986).

16.   The concept of rent seeking was introduced by Gordon Tullock in "The
       Welfare Costs of Tariffs, Monopolies, and Theft," *Western Economic Journal*
       (1967): 224–32. The name "rent seeking" first appeared in Anne Krueger,
       "The Political Economy of a Rent-seeking Society," *American Economic
       Review* (1974): 291–303. Somehow the name stuck. This is a pity, for, in my
       opinion, the term "rent seeking" is one of the least expressive terms in the
       entire lexicon of economics. If rents mean anything at all, firms always seek
       rents, in ordinary commercial transactions and in their dealings with
       government; there is nothing in the term "rent seeking" to suggest the
       wasteful competition for public favor that the term has recently come to
       mean. A number of important papers on rent seeking, including the two
       cited above, are included in James Buchanan et al., *Toward a Theory of the
       Rent-seeking Society* (College Station: Texas A&M University Press, 1980).

17.   The possibility of socially advantageous rent seeking has been discussed by
       Robert J. Michaels, "The Design of Rent-seeking Competitions," *Public
       Choice* (1988): 17–29.

18.   On the economics of corruption, see Susan Rose-Akerman, *Corruption: A
       Study in Political Economy* (Academic Press, 1978). For a nice collection of
       examples, see Arnold J. Heidenheimer, ed., *Political Corruption: Readings in
       Comparative Analysis* (New York: Holt, Rinehart and Winston, 1970). See also
       F. T. Lui, "A Dynamic Model of Corruption Deterrence," *Journal of Public
       Economics* (1986), 215–36.

19. The connection between rent seeking and corruption is discussed in Elie Appelbaum and Eliakim Katz, "Seeking Rents by Setting Rents: The Political Economy of Rent-Seeking," *Economic Journal* (1987): 685–99.

3. John Whalley, Taxlike Features of Developing Country Trade Regimes

Notes

1. See Whalley 1989a and the two volumes of research studies from this project (Whalley, 1989b and 1989c). Earlier papers from the project are contained in three research monographs published by the Centre for the Study of International Economic Relations, University of Western Ontario (see Whalley 1987, 1988a, and 1988b).
2. See Bhagwati and Srinivasan 1983 for an extensive discussion of the effects of tariffs. This, one of the leading advanced texts on the subject, devotes six chapters out of twenty-four to the effects of tariffs, and only two to other trade policy instruments. Other leading texts such as Caves and Jones 1985 give little more (if any more) coverage to non-tariff trade barriers.
3. See Young 1987, Chang 1989, and Bucay and Perez Motta 1989.
4. Destler 1986, page 12, states that "the tariff supplied about half of federal revenues as recently as 1910."
5. This is under GATT Article 11.
6. See Anjaria 1987, Eglin 1987, and Roessler 1988.
7. In Mexico, for instance, quantitative restrictions in 1986 only apply to around 35 percent of imports, sharply down from figures (100 percent) for the early 1980s. See Bucay and Perez Motta 1987, page 228.
8. See also the discussion in Clarete and Whalley 1988a, 1989.
9. But foreign currency black markets are common and, in most countries with these controls, endemic. See Azam and Bestey 1988, Culbertson 1988, Glen 1988, Harris 1988, and Pinto 1988. See also Nguyen and Whalley 1989.
10. These require deposit of purchased foreign exchange for a specified period (between six months and two years) before importation is authorized. Such schemes were widely employed in Africa before the recent move of liberalization (see Leith 1974, for instance, for discussion of the Ghanaian case in the 1960s and early 1970s) and are still used in some Latin American countries (Whalley 1989c notes their current use in Argentina).
11. According to Bird 1974, between the years 1962 and 1971, export taxes ranged from 1 percent to 18 percent of total tax receipts in Latin America and between 2 and 12 percent in the Pacific.
12. See the discussion of the Philippine situation with coconut and copra export taxes in Clarete and Roumasset 1983, for instance.
13. See the discussion in Todaro 1985, for instance.

14.   See the discussion in Cohen 1977. He states (p. 600): "until late 1961 the central government set annual maximum export quotas for tea in order both to stabilize domestic tea prices and to subsidize the smaller tea estates."

15.   India also uses such schemes, but these have resulted in countervailing duty cases against Indian exports in the U.S. market. Korea's scheme adopted in the 1960s and 1970s has since been phased out, in part because of U.S. countervailing actions.

16.   See Kim and Westphal 1977 and Hong 1979.

17.   See Guo 1989 for a brief description of how the special economic zones in China operate.

18.   Wadhva 1977 describes how the (Indian) "government has directly supported development of 'new non-traditional' exports such as setting up 100 percent export-oriented ventures in free-trade zones like the Kandla Free Trade Zones and the Santa Cruz Electronic Export Processing Zone."

19.   One claim sometimes heard is that existing exporters, already trading abroad, move into the free-trade zones and continue their existing operations but, in addition, receive duty remissions on intermediate inputs. These claims suggest that free-trade zones may, in part, simply confer lump-sum benefits on existing exporters as much as they create new export activity.

20.   See the discussion of financial institutions in developing countries in Shaw 1973 and McKinnon 1973.

21.   See Hong 1979.

22.   Although the use of these registration schemes has not been given a high profile in the literature that seeks to explain how Korea managed to grow so quickly both in GDP and in trade terms, these instruments may have been one of the more important.

23.   Interactions between policy elements and the ways in which the effects of one depend on the form others take are also a theme stressed in a recent modeling piece by Clarete and Whalley 1988b.

24.   See Bhagwati and Srinivasan 1983, p. 117.

25.   See also the discussion in Oyejide 1989.

26.   See Whalley 1989a and Clarete and Whalley 1988a.

27.   See further discussion of this characterization in Alburo and Shepherd 1986 and Clarete 1989.

28.   See Clarete's 1984 analysis of the effects of tariff protection on manufacturing in the Philippines.

29.   Thus when Clarete and Whalley (1989) include Harris-Todaro urban-rural effects in their model of tariff liberalization in the Philippines, much larger effects occur than when Harris-Todaro effects are excluded. See also the analysis of incidence of effects of sector-specific minimum wages in a Harris-Todaro framework in Imam and Whalley 1985.

30.   See Kim and Westphal 1977 and Lee and Naya 1988.

31.   See Kwack 1989.

32.   See Krueger 1974, which suggests that for India about 7 percent of GNP

could be dissipated in rent seeking for import quotas and about 15 percent of GNP for Turkey. Mohammed and Whalley 1984 put rent-seeking costs of all controls (not just trade controls) in India at around 30 to 45 percent of GNP.

33. See also Clarete and Whalley 1988a.
34. See the discussion of China, for instance, in Guo 1987.
35. See the discussion of developing country tax systems in Bird 1987, Dewulf 1974, Greenaway 1981, and Shoup 1966.
36. See the discussion of recent liberalization in Whalley 1989a and World Bank 1989.
37. See the discussion of Table 3.2 in the text.
38. See Mohammed and Whalley 1985 on Indian literature on the intersectoral terms of trade.
39. See the discussion of tax evasion in India in Goswami 1988 and black market–official market links in Nguyen and Whalley 1989.
40. See the discussion of experience in Southern Cone countries in Corbo and de Melo 1987.
41. See Whalley 1989a.
42. See the discussion in Whalley 1989a.
43. See Prebisch 1962, Lewis 1954, Chenery 1960, Myint 1958, and Myrdal 1957.
44. See the discussion of conditionality in Williamson 1983 and Helleiner 1986.
45. See also the discussion of timing and sequencing of trade liberalization in developing countries in Edwards 1984 and Wolf 1986.

References

Alburo, F., and G. Shepherd. 1986. "Trade Liberalization Experience in the Philippines, 1960–84." Working Paper 8601, Philippine Institute for Development Studies, Manila.

Anjaria, S. J. 1987. "Balance of Payments and Related Issues in the Uruguay Round of Trade Negotiations." *World Bank Economic Review* 1: 669–88.

Azam, J. P., and T. Bestey. 1988. "Parallel Markets in Ghana: Theory and Evidence." Paper presented at the Harvard Institute for International Development Workshop on Parallel Markets, November 10–12, 1988, Cambridge, Massachusetts.

Bautista, R. M., J. H. Power, and Associates. 1979. *Industrial Promotion Policies in the Philippines*. Manila: Philippine Institute for Development Studies.

Bhagwati, J., and T. N. Srinivasan. 1983. *Lectures on International Trade*. Cambridge, Mass.: MIT Press.

Bird, R. M. 1974. *Taxing Agricultural Land in Developing Countries*. Cambridge, Mass.: Harvard University Press.

———. 1983. "Income Tax Reform in Developing Countries: The Administrative Dimension." *Bulletin for International Fiscal Documentation* 37 January: 3–14.

———. 1987. "A New Look at Indirect Taxation in Developing Countries." *World Development* 15, no. 9: 1151–61.

Bucay, N., and E. Perez Motta. 1987. "Mexico." In *Dealing with the North*, ed. J. Whalley. Research Monograph, Centre for the Study of International Economic Relations, University of Western Ontario, London, Ontario.

———. 1989. "Trade Negotiation Strategy in Mexico." In *Developing Countries and the Global Trading System, vol. 2, Country Studies from a Ford Foundation Project*, ed. J. Whalley. London: Macmillan Press.

Caves and Jones. 1985. *World Trade and Payments, An Introduction*, 4th ed. Toronto: Little, Brown & Company.

Chang, E. T. 1989. "Barriers to Korea's Manufactured Exports and Negotiation Options." In *Developing Countries and the Global Trading System, vol. 2, Country Studies from a Ford Foundation Project*, ed. J. Whalley. London: Macmillan Press.

Chenery, H. B. 1960. "Patterns of Industrial Growth." *American Economic Review* 50, no. 4: 624–54.

Clarete, R. 1984. "The Cost and Consequences of Trade Distortions in a Small Open Economy: A General Equilibrium Model of the Philippines." Ph.D. dissertation, Economics Department, University of Hawaii.

———. 1989. "The Recent Philippine Trade Liberalization: Can the Multilateral Trade System Sustain It?" In *Developing Countries and the Global Trading System, vol. 2, Country Studies from a Ford Foundation Project*, ed. J. Whalley. London: Macmillan Press.

Clarete, R., and J. Roumasset. 1983. "An Analysis of the Economic Policies Affecting the Philippine Coconut Industry." Working Paper, Philippine Institute for Development Studies, Makati, Philippines.

Clarete, R., and J. Whalley. 1988a. "Pitfalls in Evaluating Labor Adjustment Costs from Trade Shocks: Illustrations for the U.S. Economy Using an Applied General Equilibrium Model with Transaction Costs." Mimeo, University of Western Ontario, London, Ontario.

———. 1988b. "Interactions between Trade Policies and Domestic Distortions in a Small Open Developing Country." *Journal of International Economics* 24: 345–58.

———. 1989. "Trade-restricting Effects of Exchange Rate Regimes: Implications for Developed-Developing Country Trade Negotiations." In *Developing Countries and the Global Trading System, vol. 1, Thematic Studies from a Ford Foundation Project*, ed. J. Whalley. London: Macmillan Press.

Cohen, B. I. 1977. "The Stagnation of Indian Exports 1951–61." In *Some Problems of India's Economic Policy*, ed. C. D. Wadhva. New Delhi: Tata McGraw-Hill Publishing Company. 590–604.

Corbo, V., and J. de Melo. 1987. "Lessons from the Southern Cone Policy Reforms." *World Bank Research Observer* 2, no. 2: 111–41.

Culbertson, W. 1988. "Empirical Regularities in Black Markets for Currency." Paper presented at the Harvard Institute for International Development Workshop on Parallel Markets, November 10–12, 1988, Cambridge, Massachusetts.

Destler, I. M. 1986. *American Trade Politics: System under Stress*. Washington, D.C.: Institute for International Economics.

Dewulf, L. 1974. "Fiscal Incidence Studies in Developing Countries: Survey and Critique." *IMF Staff Papers* 22 (March): 611–31.

Edwards, S. 1984. "The Order of Liberalization of the Balance of Payments: Should the Current Account Be Opened Up First?" Washington, D.C.: World Bank.

Eglin, R. 1987. "Surveillance of Balance-of-Payments Measures in the GATT." *World Economy* March: 1–26.

GATT. 1986. *The Text of the General Agreement*. Geneva.

Glen, J. 1988. "Black Markets for Foreign Currency." Paper presented at the Harvard Institute for International Development Workshop on Parallel Markets, November 10–12, 1988, Cambridge, Massachusetts.

Goswami, O. 1988. "Taxes, Fines, and Bribes: A Model of Tax Evasion and Black Money in India." Paper presented at the Harvard Institute for International Development Workshop on Parallel Markets, November 10–12, 1988, Cambridge, Massachusetts.

Greenaway, D. 1981. "Taxes on International Transactions and Economic Development." In *The Political Economy of Taxation*, ed. A. T. Peacock and F. Forte. Oxford: Basil Blackwell 131–47.

Guo, C. D. 1987. "China." In *Dealing with the North*, ed. J. Whalley. Research Monograph, Centre for the Study of International Economic Relations, University of Western Ontario, London, Ontario.

————. 1989. "The Developing World and the Multifiber Arrangement." In *Developing Countries and the Global Trading System, vol. 2, Country Studies from a Ford Foundation Project*, ed. J. Whalley. London: Macmillan Press.

Harris, J. 1988. "Parallel Markets for Foreign Exchange in Uganda." Paper presented at the Harvard Institute for International Development Workshop on Parallel Markets, November 10–12, 1988, Cambridge, Massachusetts.

Harris, J. R., and M. P. Todaro. 1970. "Migration, Unemployment, and Development: A Two-Sector Analysis." *American Economic Review* 60 (March): 126–42.

Helleiner, G. K., ed. 1986. *Africa and the International Monetary Fund*. Washington D.C.: International Monetary Fund.

Hong, W.-T. 1979. *Trade, Distortions, and Employment Growth in Korea*. Seoul: Korea Development Institute.

Imam, M. H., and J. Whalley. 1985. "Incidence Analysis of a Sector-specific Minimum Wage in a Two-Sector Harris-Todaro Model." *Quarterly Journal of Economics* (February): 207–24.

Kim, K. S., and L. E. Westphal. 1977. "Industrial Policy and Development in Korea." International Bank for Reconstruction and Development, Staff Working Paper no. 263, Washington, D.C.

Krueger, A. O. 1974. "The Political Economy of the Rent-seeking Society." *American Economic Review* 69, no. 3: 291–303.

Lee, C. H., and S. Naya. 1988. "Trade in East Asian Development with Comparative Reference to Southeast Asian Experiences." *Economic Development and Cultural Change*. 36, no. 3, Supplement (April): 123–52.

Leith, J. C. 1974. *Foreign Trade Regimes and Economic Development: Ghana*. New York: Columbia University Press for the National Bureau of Economic Research.

Lewis, W. A. 1954. "Economic Development with Unlimited Supplies of Labor." *Manchester School* 22: 139–91.

McKinnon, R. I. 1973. *Money and Capital in Economic Development*. Washington, D.C.: Brookings Institution.

Mohammed, S., and J. Whalley. 1984. "Rent-Seeking in India: Welfare Costs and Policy Implications." *Kyklos* 37: 387–413.

———. 1985. "Controls and the Intersectoral Terms of Trade: The Indian Case." *Economic Journal* (September).

Musgrave, R. A. 1959. *The Theory of Public Finance*. New York: McGraw-Hill.

Myint, H. 1958. "The Classical Theory of International Trade and the Under-developed Countries." *Economic Journal* (June): 317–37.

Myrdal, G. 1957. *Economic Theory and Underdeveloped Regions*. London: Duckworth.

Nguyen, T., and J. Whalley. 1989. "Coexistence of Equilibria on Black and White Markets: An Applied General Equilibrium Approach." Mimeo, University of Western Ontario, London, Ontario.

Oyejide, T. A. 1989. "Primary Commodities in the International Trading System." In *Developing Countries and the Global Trading System, vol. 1, Thematic Studies from a Ford Foundation Project*, ed. J. Whalley. London: Macmillan Press.

Pinto, B. 1988. "Black Markets for Foreign Exchange, Real Exchange Rates, and Inflation: Overnight vs. Gradual Reform in Sub-Saharan Africa." Paper presented at the Harvard Institute for International Development Workshop on Parallel Markets, November 10–12, 1988, Cambridge, Massachusetts.

Prebisch, R. 1962. "The Economic Development of Latin America and Its Principal Problems." *Economic Bulletin for Latin America*, 7: 1–22.

Roessler, F. 1988. "The Relationship between the World Trade Order and the International Monetary System." In *The New GATT Round of Multilateral Trade Negotiations: Legal and Economic Problems*, ed. M. Hilf and E.-U. Petersmann (forthcoming).

Shaw, E. S. 1973. *Financial Deepening in Economic Development*. Oxford: Oxford University Press.

Shoup, C. S. 1966. "Taxes and Economic Development." *Finanzarchiv* 25 (November): 385–97.

Todaro, M. P. 1985. *Economic Development in the Third World*, 3rd ed. New York: Longman.

Wadhva, C. D. 1977 "India's Export Performance and Policy: 1951–74 and Planning for the Future up to 1981." In *Some Problems of India's Economic Policy*, ed. C. D. Wadhva. New Delhi: Tata McGraw-Hill Publishing Company, 590–604.

Whalley, J. ed. 1987. *Dealing with the North*. Research Monograph, Centre for the Study of International Economic Relations, University of Western Ontario, London, Ontario.

———. 1988a. *The Small among the Big, vol. 2, Country Studies from a Ford Foundation Project on Developing Countries and the Global Trading System*. Research Monograph, Centre for the Study of International Economic Relations, University of Western Ontario, London, Ontario.

————. 1988b. *Rules, Power, and Credibility, vol. 1, Thematic Studies from a Ford Foundation Project on Developing Countries and the Global Trading System.* Research Monograph, Centre for the Study of International Economic Relations, University of Western Ontario, London, Ontario.

————. 1989a. *The Uruguay Round and Beyond, Final Report: The Final Report from the Ford Foundation Project on Developing Countries and the Global Trading System.* London: Macmillan Press.

————. 1989b. *Developing Countries and the Global Trading System, vol. 1, Thematic Studies from a Ford Foundation Supported Project.* London: Macmillan Press.

————. 1989c. *Developing Countries and the Global Trading System, vol. 2, Country Studies from a Ford Foundation Supported Project.* London: Macmillan Press.

————. 1989. "Recent Trade Liberalization in the Developing World: What Is Behind It, and Where Is It Headed?" Paper presented at a conference on global protectionism held at Lehigh University, Bethlehem, Pennsylvania, May 22–23, 1989.

Williamson, J. 1983. *IMF Conditionality.* Washington, D.C.: Institute for International Economics.

Wolf, M. 1986. "Timing and Sequencing of Trade Liberalization in Developing Countries." *Asian Development Review* 4, no. 2: 124.

World Bank. 1989. *Adjustment Lending an Evaluation of Ten Years of Experience.* Washington D.C.

Young, S. 1987. "Trade Policies of the Republic of Korea." In *Dealing With the North,* ed. J. Whalley. Research Monograph, Centre for the Study of International Economic Relations, University of Western Ontario, London, Ontario.

4. Wayne R. Thirsk, Financial Institutions and Their Quasi Taxes—A Little Bit of Craziness

Notes

1. In some countries financial institutions may be required to hold a certain percentage of low-yielding government bonds in their portfolios. More commonly, however, governments seek to reduce their borrowing costs by making the interest on their liabilities tax exempt.

2. To see this point more clearly, let L, R, and D denote, respectively, interest-earning loans, required reserves, and bank deposits. If r represents the interest rate paid on loans and i is the deposit rate, zero profit competitive equilibrium, ignoring intermediation costs, requires $iD = rL$ or $i = (L/D)r$. If p is the required ratio of reserves to deposits, $p = R/D$, and since $L + R = D$ from the bank's balance sheet, $L/D = (1 - p)$; so the equilibrium condition can be rewritten as $i = (1 - p)r$. Clearly, for a given value of r, a larger reserve ratio p is consistent with a lower value for the deposit rate.

3.   Chamley 1987 has argued that the implicit subsidy to interest on government debt is in fact paid by the implicit tax on deposits. Therefore, to the inflation tax revenue that arises from taxing the monetary base should be added an amount equal to the value of public debt times the difference between a normal real rate of return on investment and the real rate of return actually paid.

4.   My favorite example is the employment security law passed by Brazil in the 1950s. Under that law employees with a continuous record of employment of ten years or more with a single employment could not be fired. In light of the unintended incentive to fire long-term employees before their tenth year of employment, the regulation is alleged to have contributed to greater, not less, job insecurity in that country.

5.   In an unindexed tax system real effective interest rates are sensitive to the inflation rate, as Hanson and Neal (1986) have shown.

6.   At a macrolevel foreign exchange controls are needed if a country is to maintain real domestic interest rates that diverge significantly from real interest rates in the rest of the world.

7.   The real estate analogue to relending is the practice of "flipping" properties if their value is more than what was paid for them.

8.   For the sake of simplicity reserve requirements against deposits are ignored in Figure 4.1 so that all deposits are transformed into loans.

9.   Strictly speaking, personal income taxes on interest income in many countries also create a wedge similar to AF in Figure 4.1, a wedge whose size is extremely sensitive to the rate of inflation in an unindexed tax system.

10.   In a competitive environment financial firms would be expected to engage in nonprice competition for deposits through greater advertising, more branches, and payments in kind to new depositors.

11.   A more important source of finance for the ICT is the forced lending to it by insurance companies and the commercial banks. The latter are required to hold 1 percent of their reserves in the form of low-yielding ICT notes. This requirement, of course, acts as an implicit tax on depositors of commercial banks.

12.   This is perhaps the principal result of the Harberger model, that a tax on a factor in one sector results in a burden that is shared by that factor no matter where it is employed. Here a quasi tax on loans in the formal sector depresses lending rates in both sectors.

13.   If banks are unable to profit from risky high-return loans, they would be expected to concentrate on making low-return, short-term (and less risky) loans, a strategy that conforms with the practice of inefficient rationing.

14.   In both Korea and Taiwan investment increased along with savings since the rate of return on investment remained higher than the augmented real interest rate on loans.

15.   Chamley 1988 also documents the failed liberalization experiment of the Philippines after 1980. The attempt at liberalization was thwarted by a high

inflation rate and the taxation of financial institutions through a high reserve requirement and a tax on all bank receipts.

16. If quasi taxes and the consequent rationing of loans encourage greater economic concentration and the exercise of monopoly power, a liberalization that reverses this tendency could potentially improve both efficiency and equity through the creation of more competitive market structures.

17. Ngee and Whalley 1989 challenge the conventional wisdom of taxing banks. In their view banks and other intermediaries supply an intermediate input rather than a final product.

References

Adler, R. W. 1965. "The Organized Financial Markets of Colombia." Ph.D. thesis, University of Oregon, Eugene, Oregon.

Bird, Richard M. 1984. *Intergovernmental Finance in Colombia*. International Tax Program, Law School of Harvard University, Cambridge, Mass.

Brown, G.T. 1973. *Korean Pricing Policies and Economic Development in the 1960's*. Baltimore: Johns Hopkins University Press.

Chamley, Christophe. 1987. "Taxation and Financial Institutions, Part I: A Normative View." Mimeo, World Bank, Washington, D.C.

Chamley, Christophe, and Q. Hussain. 1988. "The Removal of Taxes on Financial Assets in Thailand, Indonesia, and the Phillipines: A Quantitative Evaluation." Mimeo, World Bank, Washington, D.C.

Fry, M. 1988. *Money, Interest, and Banking in Economic Development*. Baltimore: Johns Hopkins University Press.

Hanson, J. A., and C. R. Neal. 1986. *Interest Rate Policies in Selected Developing Countries, 1970–82*, Industry and Finance Series, volume 14, Washington, D.C.: World Bank.

Harberger, A. C. 1962. "The Incidence of the Corporation Income Tax." *Journal of Political Economy* 70 (June).

McKinnon, R. I. 1973. *Money and Capital in Economic Development*. Washington, D.C.: Brookings Institution.

Ngee, Choon Chia, and John Whalley. 1989. "Should Banks Be Taxed?" mimeo, University of Western Ontario, London, Ontario.

Ranis, Gustav. 1977. "Economic Development and Financial Institutions." In *Economic Progress, Private Values, and Public Policy: Essays in Honour of William Fellner*, ed. Bela Balassa and Richard R. Nelson. Amsterdam: North-Holland.

Roemer, M. 1986. "Simple Analytics of Segmented Markets: What Case for Liberalization?" *World Development* 14, no. 3.

Van Wijnbergen, S. 1983. "Interest Rate Management in LDC's." *Journal of Monetary Economics* 12.

Virmani, Arvind. 1982. *The Nature of Credit Markets in Developing Countries: A Framework for Policy Analysis*. World Bank Staff Working Papers no. 524, Washington, D.C.

————. 1984. *Evaluation of Credit Policy, Credit Allocation in Bangladesh.* World
    Bank Staff Working Papers no. 672, Washington, D.C.
World Bank. 1989. *World Development Report 1989.* Washington, D.C.

5.   Malcolm Gillis, Tacit Taxes and Sub Rosa Subsidies through State-owned Enterprises

The author is grateful for comments received on earlier drafts from several
economists, including Bill Ascher, Allen Kelley, and Anne Krueger at Duke, Richard
Bird (Toronto), and Johannes Linn (World Bank).

Notes

1.   The term "state-owned enterprises" means different things to different
       people. This paper uses the following criteria developed earlier by the
       author (Gillis 1980b) to determine whether an enterprise qualifies as a state-
       owned firm:

       (a) that the government is the principal stockholder in the enterprise, or
       otherwise has the ability or the potential to exercise control over the broad
       policies followed by the enterprise, and to appoint and remove enterprise
       management. The government, however, does not necessarily control day-
       to-day operations of the firm.

       In most cases, the state is the *only* stockholder in the enterprise, so that
       the distinction between "public" or "state" and "private" ownership is quite
       clear. But, in other cases, the government may have entered into a joint
       venture with private capitalists. As long as the government share is 51% or
       more, such a joint venture is clearly an example of a state enterprise. But
       majority ownership should not be viewed as essential. In some cases, the
       state may effectively control an enterprise with only a minority share of its
       equity, depending on the distribution of ownership of the other shares, and
       on any concordats established between the government and the private
       partner(s) at the time of creation of the enterprise.
       (b) that the enterprise is engaged in the production of goods and/or services
       for sale to the public, or to other private or public enterprises.
       (c) that, as a matter of policy, the revenues of the enterprise are supposed to
       bear some relation to its costs. For a state enterprise whose charter calls for
       maximization of profits (as with the nearly 100 *Persero* state enterprises in
       Indonesia, or most government-owned hotels and airlines in several coun-
       tries) this criterion is clearly satisfied. But it may also be satisfied by state
       enterprises for which profit maximization is *not* the prime stated objective,
       but which rather are expected to pursue profitability subject to constraints
       implicit or explicit in "social" functions assigned the enterprise by the state.

2.   In addition, domestic consumption of refined petroleum products was

further subsidized by the absence of road user charges collected on gasoline and diesel fuel. Taking this implicit subsidy into account, Bolivia's subsidy was about $8.80 per barrel, or 43 percent of the economic cost of the fuels (McLure 1981).

3.   I am indebted to Anne Krueger for this information regarding fertilizer subsidies in Turkey.

4.   As late as 1986 natural gas supplied to Indonesian SOEs producing fertilizer was priced at $1.00 per million Btu. This compares to a price charged other industrial users of $3.00 per million Btu, and an export value for LNG of $4.80 per million Btu.

5.   Information provided by Anne Krueger.

6.   Heavy implicit subsidies on high-speed diesel oil used in power generation in Indonesia are discussed in Gillis 1980a and World Bank 1981. Implicit subsidies to power generation declined sharply from 1983 to 1986, not because of government policy decisions but because of the sharp drop in oil prices in those years.

7.   For an explanation of the relationship among the liquid asset ratio, budget deficits, and monetary expansion, see Gillis et al. 1987, pp. 356–58.

8.   When liquid assets are, say, 30 percent of GDP, this indicates that the public is generally willing to hold money balances roughly equivalent to 3.3 months of income. A state enterprise sector deficit of 8 percent would itself increase the stock of money by one *more* month of income, or by an amount more than the public would be willing to hold. The excess tends to spill over into higher prices sooner or later.

9.   In Indonesia, for example, the kerosene subsidy protected annually, at most, only about 20,000 hectares of land vulnerable to erosion. Seen as an erosion control program, the kerosene subsidy cost about US$77,000 per hectare protected in 1980. Given that the most expensive replanting program cost only US$500 per hectare, the kerosene subsidy appeared to be grossly unsuited for protecting the environment (Gillis 1988).

10.   In some countries where SOEs are not exempt from income taxes on enterprises, state-owned firms have provided as much as two-thirds of total corporate tax collections (Indonesia) and often pay sizable dividends to the government as well.

References

Anderson, Walter. 1970. "The Cocoa Marketing Board." Unpublished. Accra, Ghana, Development Advisory Service, Harvard University.

Ansu, Yow. 1984. "Comments." In *World Economic Growth*, ed. A. C. Harberger. San Francisco: ICS Press.

Berry, Brian J. 1979. "Urban Water Supply in Indonesia." Unpublished, Harvard Institute for International Development, Indonesia Project, Jakarta.

Bird, Richard M. 1983. *The Allocation of Taxing Powers in Papua New Guinea*. Port Moresby: Institute of National Affairs.

———. 1984. *Intergovernmental Finance in Colombia*. Cambridge: International Tax Program.

Bird, Richard M., and Susan Horton, eds. 1989. *Government Policy and the Poor in Developing Countries*. Toronto: University of Toronto Press.

Bird, Richard M., and Barbara D. Miller. 1989. "Taxation, Pricing, and the Poor." In *Government Policy and the Poor in Developing Countries*, ed. Richard M. Bird and Susan Horton. Toronto: University of Toronto Press.

de Kuijper, Mia, and David Erickson. 1979. "Taxes and Subsidies on Petroleum Products in Pakistan." Unpublished, Karachi Institute of Development Economics.

Floyd, Robert. 1977. "Some Aspects of Income Taxation of State-owned Enterprises." Washington, D.C.: IMF, DM/7716.

Gillis, Malcolm. 1969. "The Timber Marketing Board." Unpublished, Accra, Ghana, Development Advisory Services.

———. 1977. "Efficiency in State-owned Enterprises." Discussion Paper 27, Harvard Institute for International Development, April, Cambridge, Mass.

———. 1980a. "Energy Demand in Indonesia." Development Discussion Paper 92, Harvard Institute for International Development.

———. 1980b. "The Role of State-owned Enterprises in Economic Development." *Social Research* 47, no. 2.

———. 1982. "Allocative and X-Efficiency in State-owned Mining Enterprises." *Journal of Comparative Economics*.

———. 1984. "Episodes in Indonesian Economic Growth." In *World Economic Growth*, ed. A. C. Harberger San Francisco: ICS Press.

———. 1985. "Micro- and Macroeconomics of Tax Reform." *Journal of Development Economics* 19: 221–54.

———. 1988. "Indonesia: Public Policies, Resource Management, and the Tropical Forest." In *Public Policies and the Misuse of Forest Resources*, by Robert Repetto and Malcolm Gillis. New York: Cambridge University Press.

———. 1989. "Tax Reform: Lessons from Postwar Experience in Developing Countries." In *Tax Reform in Developing Countries*, ed. Malcolm Gillis. Durham, N.C.: Duke University Press.

Gillis, Malcolm, and Charles E. McLure Jr. 1978. "Taxation and Income Distribution: The Colombian Tax Reform of 1974." *Journal of Development Economics* 5: 233–50.

———. 1981. "Standards of Conduct for Public Enterprise." In *Fiscal Reform in Bolivia*, by Richard Musgrave et al. Cambridge: International Tax Program.

Gillis, Malcolm, and David Dapice. 1979. "Energy Policy in Indonesia." Unpublished, Harvard Institute for International Development.

———. 1988. "Indonesia." In *The Open Economy*, ed. Rudiger Dornbusch and Leslie Helmers. New York: Oxford University Press.

Gillis, Malcolm, and Ignatius Peprah. 1981. "State-owned Enterprises in Developing Countries." *Wharton Magazine* (Winter).

Gillis, Malcolm, Glenn Jenkins, and Donald Lessard. 1982. "Public Enterprise Finance: Toward a Synthesis." In *Public Enterprises in Less Developed Countries*, ed. Leroy Jones. New York: Cambridge University Press.

Gillis, Malcolm, et al. 1987. *Economics of Development*. New York: Norton.

Heraty, M. J. 1980. "Public Transport in Kingston, Jamaica, and Its Relation to Low Income Households." Crowthorn, Berkshire, Overseas Unit, Transport and Road Research Laboratory. Cited in *Government Policy and the Poor in Developing Countries*, ed. Richard M. Bird and Susan Horton. Toronto: University of Toronto Press, 1989.

Horton, Susan. 1989. "Food Subsidies and the Poor: A Case Study of Tanzania." In *Government Policy and the Poor in Developing Countries*, ed. Richard M. Bird and Susan Horton. Toronto: University of Toronto Press.

Jenkins, Glenn. 1985. "Income Taxation and State-owned Enterprise." Unpublished, Harvard Institute for International Development.

Lele, Uma. 1984. "Tanzania: Phoenix or Icarus?" In *World Economic Growth*, ed. A. C. Harberger. San Francisco: ICS Press.

Linn, Johannes, and Deborah Wetzel. 1989. "Public Finance, Trade, and Development." World Bank Working Paper no. 181, Washington, D.C.

McLure, Charles E., Jr. 1981. "Taxation of Domestic Consumption of Petroleum." In *Fiscal Reform in Bolivia*, by Richard Musgrave et al. Cambridge: International Tax Program.

————. 1988. "Fiscal Policy and Equity in Developing Countries." In *Policy Reform and Equity: Extending the Benefits of Development*, ed. Elliot Berg. San Francisco: ICS Press.

McLure, Charles E., Jr., and Wayne R. Thirsk. 1978. "The Inequity of Taxing Iniquity: A Plan for Reduced Sumptuary Taxes in Developing Countries." *Economic Development and Cultural Change* 26: 487–503.

Musgrave, Richard, et al. 1981. *Fiscal Reform in Bolivia*. Cambridge: International Tax Program.

Repetto, Robert. 1986. *Skimming the Water: Rent Seeking in Public Irrigation Systems*. Washington, D.C.: World Resources Institute.

Repetto, Robert, and Malcolm Gillis. 1988. *Public Policies and the Misuse of Forest Resources*. New York: Cambridge University Press.

Roemer, Michael. 1984. "Ghana: Missed Opportunities." *World Economic Growth*, ed. A. C. Harberger. San Francisco: ICS Press.

Short, R. P. 1983. "The Role of Public Enterprises: An International Statistical Comparison." Washington, D.C.: International Monetary Fund, DM 83/84.

Shoup, Carl. 1989. "The Tax Mission to Japan, 1949–50." In *Tax Reform in Developing Countries*, ed. Malcolm Gillis. Durham, N.C.: Duke University Press.

Summers, Larry. 1979. "Demand Equations for Indonesian Oil." Unpublished, Harvard Institute for International Development.

Tait, Alan. 1977. "The Fiscal Policy Objectives of Nonfinancial Enterprises." Washington, D.C.: International Monetary Fund Working Paper FAD/77/s.

Timmer, Peter, and Walter Falcon. 1984. *Food Policy in Developing Countries*. Baltimore: Johns Hopkins University Press.

Urrutia, Miguel. 1980. "Urban Transport Policy in Indonesia." Unpublished, Harvard Institute for International Development.

World Bank. 1981. *Indonesia Issues and Options in the Energy Sector*. Washington, D.C.: World Bank.

————. 1986. *World Development Report 1986*. New York: Oxford University Press.

————. 1987. *Indonesia: Strategy for Economic Recovery*. Washington, D.C.: World Bank.

————. 1988. *World Development Report 1988*. New York: Oxford University Press.

Contributors

Richard M. Bird, professor of economics at the University of Toronto, writes extensively on fiscal policy issues. His contributions to academic journals reflect the range of both industrial and developing countries in which he has consulted. His books include *Intergovernmental Finance in Colombia: Final Report of the Mission on Intergovernmental Finance*, *Federal Finance in Comparative Perspective*, and a just-published volume that he coedited and contributed to, *Government Policy and the Poor in Developing Countries*.

Maxwell J. Fry, professor of economics at the University of California at Irvine, has devoted most of the past two decades to research on monetary and financial aspects of economic development. This work has resulted in over 100 articles and ten books. His most recent book, *Money, Interest, and Banking in Economic Development* (Baltimore: Johns Hopkins University Press, 1988), is now being translated into Chinese and Spanish. He has been called upon as a consultant to central banks and ministries of finance in several developing countries and by such international agencies as the International Monetary Fund and the World Bank.

Malcolm Gillis is professor of public policy and of economics, and, since 1986, dean of the Graduate School and vice-provost for academic affairs at

Duke University. His extensive research and advisory activities have taken him to numerous countries in Asia, Africa, and Latin America. The framework for an entirely new tax system in Indonesia, in operation since 1984, was provided by a team organized and directed by Gillis. He is the author of over fifty articles on public finance, natural resources, and economic development, and his writings also include *Fiscal Reform for Colombia* (with Richard Musgrave) and coauthorship of the widely used textbook *Economics of Development*.

Charles E. McLure, Jr., formerly assistant secretary of the Treasury for tax policy, is now a senior fellow at the Hoover Institution of Stanford University. He is a prolific writer and consultant on tax policy; his recent book-length study on the taxation of income from business and capital in Colombia is being published by Duke University Press. McLure's treatment of "quasi taxes" in "Fiscal Policy and Equity in Developing Countries"—his contribution to the first seminar volume in the present series (Elliot Berg, ed., *Policy Reform and Equity: Extending the Benefits of Development*, San Francisco: ICS Press, 1988)—was a definite catalyst for the extended consideration of the present seminar volume.

Jesus Seade serves as Mexican ambassador to GATT and has taught at Warwick University and Colegio de Mexico as well as working in the public economics and Brazilian divisions of the World Bank. He has also published widely in academic journals on public economics, industrial organization, and welfare.

Joel Slemrod is associate professor of economics and associate professor of business economics and public policy at the University of Michigan. He is also director of the Office of Tax Policy Research, which is devoted to the interdisciplinary study of tax policy issues. His current research is largely focused on the role of administration and enforcement in the design of tax systems.

Wayne R. Thirsk is professor of economics at the University of Waterloo, Canada. His interests lie in the areas of development and public finance. He has worked previously on development issues in Jamaica, Colombia, and Ecuador and is coordinating a project on tax reform in developing countries for the World Bank.

Dan Usher is professor of economics at Queen's University in Kingston, Canada. He is the author of *The Measurement of Economic Growth*, *The*

Price Mechanism and the Meaning of Economic Growth, The Economic Prerequisite to Democracy, and numerous articles on various aspects of public finance and economic theory.

John Whalley is the William G. Davis Professor of International Trade at the University of Western Ontario, where he is also the director of the Centre for the Study of International Economic Relations. Known for both his work on general equilibrium modeling and policy-based research in international trade and public finance, Whalley coordinated a Ford Foundation research project on Developing Countries and the Trading System. He is also a research associate of the National Bureau of Economic Research in both its taxation and international studies programs.

Participants

Robert Asselin, PRE/I/AID

Janet Ballantyne, PPC/CDIE/AID

Alan Batchelder, PPC/EA/AID

Richard M. Bird, University of Toronto

Warren Brookes, Syndicated columnist, *Detroit News*

Wayne Brough, AFR/DP/AID

C. Stuart Callison, PPC/PDPR/AID

David Carr, ANE/DP/AID

Christophe Chamley, World Bank

John Chang, PPC/EA/AID

John A. C. Conybeare, University of Iowa

Edward Costello, PPC/EA/AID

L. Gray Cowan, PPC/PDPR/RPD/AID

Clive Crook, *The Economist*, London

Raghawendra Dwivedy, APR/DP/AID

Jim Fox, LAC/DP/AID

Robert Friedline, PRE/DP/AID

Maxwell J. Fry, University of Birmingham

Sandra Frydman, PRE/PD/AID

Antonio Gayoso, S&T/HR/AID

Malcolm Gillis, Duke University

David Hagen, ANE/PSD/AID

Donald Harrison, AFR/DP/PAR/AID

Robert Higgs, Seattle University

Rita Hilton, S&T/RD/AID

Jerry Jenkins, Sequoia Institute

Ken Kornher, S&T/RD/AID

George Laudato, DAA/PPC/AID

Dwight Lee, University of Georgia

Cliff Lewis, DAA/PPC/AID

Johannes Linn, World Bank

Don Masters, ANE/PD/AID

Don McClelland, PPC/PDPR/RPD/AID

Michael McKee, Quick, Finan and Associates

Charles E. McLure, Hoover Institution

Bruce Odell, ANE/PD/AID

Alvin Rabushka, Hoover Institution

Gordon Rausser, A/AID

Neal Rider, PPC/EA/AID
Fred Ruggles, A/AID
Meredith Scovill, ANE/DP/AID
Jesus Seade, Ambassador, Government of Mexico, GATT
Sandy Shapleigh, ANE/SA/AID
Joel Slemrod, University of Michigan
Wayne R. Thirsk, University of Waterloo
Doug Trussell, AA/PRE/SA/AID
Michael Unger, PRE/DP/AID
Dan Usher, Queens University
Jan van der Veen, PPC/PDPR/RPD/AID
Warren Weinstein, AFR/MDI/AID
John Whalley, University of Western Ontario
Neal S. Zank, PPC/PDPR/RPD/AID

This book is a product of one of the seminars in a series addressing critical issues of foreign development and its assistance. The series, entitled

INCLUDING THE EXCLUDED
Extending the Benefits of Development

is conducted by Sequoia Institute, with the sponsorship of the Agency for International Development. Contributions of the following academic advisers to the Sequoia seminar series have distinguished the series and its publications:

Robert H. Bates
  Political Economy Center
  Duke University

Brigitte Berger
  Department of Sociology
  Boston University

Peter Berger
  Director
  Institute for the Study of
    Economic Culture
  Boston University

Richard M. Bird
  Department of Economics
  University of Toronto

L. E. Birdzell, Jr.
  Coauthor
  How the West Grew Rich

Philip L. Brock
  Department of Economics
  University of Washington

William O. Chittick
  Director
  Center for Global
    Policy Studies
  University of Georgia

Hernando de Soto
  President
  Institute for Liberty
    and Democracy
  Lima, Peru

Robert Higgs
  Department of Economics
  Seattle University

Douglass C. North
  Director
  The Center in
    Political Economy
  Washington University

Elinor Ostrom
  Codirector
  Workshop in Political
    Theory & Policy Analysis
  Indiana University

Han S. Park
  Director
  Development Policy Studies
  Sequoia Institute

John P. Powelson
  Department of Economics
  University of Colorado

Lawrence H. White
  Department of Economics
  University of Georgia